THE JADE STEPS

The Empire of the Incas

Lords of Cuzco

A Rain of Darts: The Mexica Aztecs

Two Earths, Two Heavens: A Comparison of Inca and Aztec Cultures

The Fifth Sun

The Phoenix of the Western World:
Quetzalcoatl and the Sky Religion

The Juniper Palace (poetry)

No Chance Encounter (poetry)

Gian Carlo (story of a Siamese cat)

THE JADE STEPS
A RITUAL LIFE OF THE AZTECS

Burr Cartwright Brundage

Foreword by Arthur J. O. Anderson
Illustrations by Neverne Covington

University of Utah Press
Salt Lake City

Library of Congress Cataloging-in-Publication Data

Brundage, Burr Cartwright, 1912–
    The jade steps.

    Bibliography: p.
    Includes index.
    1. Aztecs—Religion and mythology.   2. Indians
of Mexico—Religion and mythology.   I. Title.
F1219.76.R45B77   1985   299'.78   85-13358
ISBN 0-87480-247-4

About the illustrator: Neverne Covington is a free-lance
illustrator who also teaches art in Tampa and Saint
Petersburg, Florida. Her work has appeared in *American
Illustration*.

DEDICATED TO
DORIS HEYDEN,
ESTEEMED COLLEAGUE

Contents

Foreword

Few of us specialists in the field of pre-Conquest Middle America are at the same time poets, masters of many languages, and experts in fields of knowledge other than our own. Our limitations may be unfortunate—our expression precise enough but unimaginative, unliterary; our understanding of foreign experts and original sources dependent upon others' translations; our interpretations limited in perspective.

No such limitations apply to Burr Cartwright Brundage, who with *The Jade Steps* completes the fourth in his series of books devoted to the Aztecs. Author of two well-received books of poems (*The Juniper Palace* and *No Chance Encounter*), and of a charming tribute to one of the Siamese cats in his life (*Gian Carlo*); expert in Egyptology, in ancient Egyptian writing (with a University of Chicago doctorate), and in various other languages of the past and present; practised in ancient Near East history; instructor of French in his youth, successful diplomat in the United States Department of State in his maturity; professor of history in his later years; and author of striking and deeply pondered interpretations of the civilizations of the Incas and the Aztecs, he is a man whose many accomplishments, literary, erudite, artistic, and practical, would have made him comfortable and productive in any epoch from the Renaissance to the present. The fact that because of his success in promoting the interests of the United States in South Polar affairs there today is a mountain on the Antarctic Continent named after him, attests to his manysidedness.

Speaking, in *The Juniper Palace*,
> *of Man daedalean, architect supreme,*
> *contriver, warrior*

—who might as well be Aztec—he asks:
> *Who will unriddle him and* find his meaning?

As a man of many parts, not alone as the poet that he can be, he has in this book again tackled the unriddling which is of interest to us, that of one aspect or another of the Aztec—or, more exactly, the civilization that produced the Aztec man—a field fraught with difficulties and uncertainties and interpreted in many divergent ways. For not only are we of a civilization so different from that of the Aztecs that it is hard for us to evaluate or even to understand what we know about it, but we are half a millennium removed from it in our sources, whether they be native records, the chronicles of Spanish eyewitnesses, or archaeological remains. It may take a scholar with a poet's insight to synthesize what the sometimes restricted experts have with much labor and precision succeeded in analyzing.

Nothing in the civilization of the Aztecs is more difficult for us to understand than their religion, beautiful in its way and at the same time ugly, repulsive, and contradictory to our sensibilities. It may be, of course, that the Aztecs considered it no more brutal, odious, or inhuman than the natural environment that they lived in. But nothing in their civilization was more important to the Aztecs than their religion: it pervaded every moment, every action, of their lives. Perhaps one can apply to it this book's final statement, concerning cult: "it is a second, and a separate, form of living."

Although not everyone may agree with all of the author's conclusions, they are well thought out, they are logical, and they make compelling reading.

It is rumored that *The Jade Steps* may be Burr Brundage's last book. This must not be. It would be a pity if one with so many voices were not heard from again.

ARTHUR JAMES OUTRAM ANDERSON

Preface

In this book Aztec worship will be broken down into several categories, beginning with images and temples and ending with burial. Not all of these items in the ritual life of the Aztecs can be thoroughly scrutinized, but the salient points at least are here. And of all these items the essential one is the calendar. Without some knowledge of the sequence of their festivals, the reader will be unable to properly judge the sometimes bizarre and often sanguinary character of the Aztecs. A complete roster of their feasts has therefore been placed in two appendices at the end of the book. The reader is advised to consult them in order to savor the incredible variety in the Aztec ritual year.

I have employed here the terms *god* and *man* (as in all my previous works) in a generic sense. The roles of priestesses and cult women were of importance as can be seen from even a cursory scanning of the cults. It would not do to demean the female in a culture that portrayed the mother goddess as powerfully as did the Aztec.

The designations of the people referred to in this book may need clarification. The Nahuas were the peoples (including the Toltecs and most probably the Teotihuacanos) who spoke one of the idioms of Nahuatl; the Aztecs were therefore Nahuas. Aztec is the designation of those Nahuas who inherited the traditions of both the Chichimecs of the steppe country and the city-dwelling Toltecs. The various groups of Aztecs are each known by the name of their major urban center—thus the Mexica (emphasized here in this work) were those Aztecs whose capital was Mexico (today, Mexico City). Mexico was divided into two moieties: the Tlatilulca, who inhabited the island called Tlatilulco, and the Tenochca, who inhabited the island just to the south called Tenochtitlan. Both islands joined were considered as one city and therefore can be designated as Mexico.

I wish to express here my gratitude to Bancomer, S.A., Mexico City, for their generosity in providing me with a copy of *El Templo Mayor*. This splendid and up-to-date publication has been of great value, particularly in regard to the matter of chapter 3.

I am also indebted to Cecelia F. Klein for providing me with an advance copy of the paper ("The Ideology of Autosacrifice at the Templo Mayor") that she presented at the Dumbarton Oaks symposium in October 1983.

Helpful as always, Doris Heyden continued to provide me with publications and personal evaluations on the Coyolxauhqui Stone and related matters. Her expertise in Mexican studies was matched by her kindness in acceding to all of my requests for information.

Finally I wish to thank Esther Pasztory for graciously reading the entire manuscript. Her encouraging remarks on the same were much appreciated.

And also at the top were circular stones, very large, called techcatl, *upon which they slew victims in order to pay honor to their gods. And the blood of those who died indeed reached the base; so did it flow off. All were like this in each of the temples.*

And this temple of Huitzilopochtli and Tlaloc faced there toward the setting sun. And its stairway was very wide; it was reaching there to the top. There was ascending there. And of all the temples that there were, all were like this. Very straight were the stairways.

Sahagún, bk. 2, Appendix on the Mexican temples

Is there weeping on the jade stairs,
And on the shores of blood?

From a song in the Chichimec style
Garibay. *Poesía Náhuatl* 3:48.

The preceding quotations refer to the concept that a warrior destroyed in battle or on the sacrificial block as a captive performed thereby his duty toward the gods. In either case he fed them with his flesh and blood. The battleground is here figuratively referred to as "on the shores of the divine liquid," a metaphor for either the ocean or for blood. Sacrifice is alluded to by referring to the captive's final ascent up the pyramid steps to his death at the top. The steps of Aztec pyramids were stained with years of blood—whatever the rains did not wash away. They were therefore poetically alluded to as the "jade" or "precious" stairs.

1

Aztec Cult and Ritual Renewals

PREVIEW OF THE ARGUMENT OF THE BOOK

The Aztecs were a people who rode the whirlwind while knowing at the same time that they did not control the storm. Their religion was one of Sturm and Drang, heavily orchestrated and laced together in a powerful sequence of cultic events. In this array of rituals the supernaturals were much in evidence, each one dramatically represented, all of them endlessly coming and going. A depiction of such a monstrous logic makes for difficult writing.

Though the Aztec gods were restless and omnifarious, they moved about like sleepwalkers, not purposefully. Though visible, they had only the most meager connections with mortals. They were a breed apart. This is the key to the Aztec's religious world. When the gods walk without cessation among you, never out of sight and never out of mind, then the daily imperatives of your existence can take on strange meanings—for which the gods need not be responsible. The knowledge that the gods could be always physically contiguous to you was perhaps more intensely realized among the Aztecs than in the case of other preliterate peoples. Yet this nearness was not a reassuring proximity. The full logic runs as follows in this book.

First, the divine had to be crystallized out of its omnipresence and its lack of definition to something more tolerable and more measurable. On the tabula rasa of time the Aztecs, like their predecessor cultures, joined two grandiose structures, the calendar and the almanac (chapter 1) in the hope of containing the supernatural; and along with that they pointed to the language of fire as being the true language of cult and of renewals in particular. The effort to manage images was also a prominent part of the Aztec cult, its most theatrical success being the compression of the god into a surrogate human being, the *ixiptla* (chapter 2). Some of this reduction of course involved localization in idols and temples and the creation of a geography and a time frame in which the gods and demons could play out their roles (chapter 3). But because of the dangerous localities and taboos within which cult had to function, only trained specialists—priests in other words—could be allowed to codify the limitations that the supernaturals placed on the Aztecs, and only they could handle the various sacred objects that society used in its approach to the divine (chapter 4). The logic became even more powerful, however, when it proposed that conflict was basic to any statement about the relations between the human and the divine. Aspects and postures of antagonism thus appeared in ritually dramatized forms (chapter 5), in all of which confrontations man was necessarily the loser and death was inevitable. The logic then moved on to place the possibility of society's renewal over against the facts of individual mortality and the threat of annihilation, coming to a half conclusion that reprieve from mortality possibly might be gained through blood sacrifice (chapter 6). Out of this unresolved tension arose a series of stabilizing rites, normal to any society, by means of which the Aztecs affirmed themselves and the efficacy of their institutions. For the Aztecs the logic ended hesitantly in an attempt to further assert something about the individual through the forms of burial (chapter 7), but no convincing soteriology ensued. In other words, the cultic logic reached a point but not a resolution.

To a great extent the preceding logic underpins religious life as it is lived everywhere on the globe, but the actual forms in which the Aztec logic clothed itself are remarkable.

SOME GENERAL REMARKS ON AZTEC CULT

In life man moves to his destiny in a series of primary activities, such as seeking food or mates, rearing the young, avoiding excessive heat and cold, and so forth. These are primary in the sense that any failure on his part to implement them soon results in death, death either to the individual or the group.

There is another level of activity that we may refer to as secondary because failure to perform the activity is not punished by death. Failure in it leads rather to the disorientation of the group and the unpinning of its value systems. This is cult.

Though the requirements for the correct performance of cult are not as stern as those connected with man's primary activities, they are unnerving to us because of their spiritual import. Any spiritual activity involves dramatic, urgent, and sometimes tragic confrontation with the supernatural. In the spiritual world there is no such thing as a satisfying ending or a successful completion of activity, as there are in the cases of harvesting, or the bringing home of game, or the birth of a child. In the spiritual realm man creates cult as a kind of holding operation in the face of his ignorance. By means of cult he extracts a certain amount of understanding with which to clarify the dark or twisted wills of gods or spirits. The primary activities I noted previously demand only that they be perfectly repeated. Cult as a secondary activity operates in an always unreliable context, a situation of constant change. Thus, there results the need to probe further, to discover new geography in the dark land of unseen forces. Cult tries to become ever more explicit, as if that would force the gods themselves to emerge into the light. Cult is restless; it responds rapidly and uneasily to perceived inconsistencies in the divine wills; it even anticipates them. In the preliterate world, cult seldom contracts or simplifies—rather it is additive, automatically expanding whenever the group is more than customarily aware of the divine world. In other instances, ritual may remain as before but is radically reinterpreted. This potential for growth and change can never be wholly controlled, even by explicit dogmas, so the total cultic life of a people often becomes murky—even to them. In such a case turbid intellectual currents can close in, destroying the unity of the group.

We must note however that although cult performances may become more detailed and baroque as time goes on, the awe within the human breast that propels all human beings towards religion remains, as ever, blind, vast, and amorphous. Man's uncertainties place his conceptual life at the hazard. This spiritual insecurity cries out, demanding that the supernaturals become visible, and concomitantly pours out of itself a gush of increasingly concrete edifices, idols, and images. But no sooner are these made than they are subject to change, for the spiritual power that initiates cult produces few sureties where one can permanently rest. It has only shifting visions. Thus, if we are to understand the religious mind of a people and probe its necessities, we must first take note of the variety and spread of their cults.

After a period of gestation, of addition and change, it is necessary for cult to be fully institutionalized. This is accomplished in numerous ways, but a common form of organization is a calendar with a priesthood to maintain it. The opening chapter of this book therefore begins with an introduction to the Aztec methods of dividing time and a survey of the fire religion that permeates much of the cult and that is necessarily concerned with the subject of time. Although our sources do not always agree on all the details of the cults or on the sequence of ritual acts, the general outline that they offer is clear enough, so we may feel some confidence in our appraisal.

The richness of Aztec cult is remarkable. Every festival was assigned to one of the two schedules, either that of the solar calendar or that of the almanac. From these two schedules a torrent of intermingled religious images flowed out through Aztec life at all levels of society. Aztec cities were drowned in gods. No day dawned that was not a holiday marked by processions and sacrifices. No night closed in without vigils. And as dawn came, ferocious services were still being offered to the god in the flaring light of braziers. Something very like a cult mania afflicted the Aztecs.

All cult is predicated on man's original endowment of spiritual energy, which itself is a mirror image of his human awareness. He is pushed to invent cults that will take stock of the invisible realities he knows to be about him, and just as naturally these cults turn out to be tentative and imperfect. Because they are imperfect, they are constantly being discarded or reworked, or even fought over, as I have already pointed out. Nevertheless, the spiritual energy of the group will always produce rituals in an unending supply. Even in the preceding unstable sense, Aztec cult is exceptional.

I must admit here that when the reader is finished with a description of Aztec cult he or she may feel bemused rather than informed. If so, this is attributable to the fact that so much of Aztec cult was an accretion from the past, wherefore the whole appears to be a potpourri. In addition, the brevity of the Aztecs' historical experience provided them little time in which to consolidate their religions. So the reader may get the impression that Aztec cult is overstuffed and unarticulated. I shall endeavor to show that this is not the whole truth, and that in reality Aztec religion is made up of a fairly homogeneous mass of cults.

First, I note that the cults I will be describing tend to congregate around one of two poles: god or man. We can call these ritual conglomerations, respectively, "deity cults" and "reinforcement cults." The deity cults are outward directed and in general tend to exalt the god specified. They preserve a relatively pure and disinterested type of worship. *Because the god is great and because he is there we worship him* is the attitude. The cults of Tezcatlipoca, of Itzpapalotl, or the Cihuateteo are examples. The reinforcement cults, from society's point of view, are inwardly directed. They do not so much worship a god as they reiterate and define his or her special relevance to some part of human culture, whether it is hunting, agriculture, war, or some such. The cults of Tlaloc, Cihuacoatl, or Mixcoatl come to mind here. The deity who patronizes such a cult becomes almost an abstraction—in some cases he or she is merely a personalization of a certain institution or human vitality. This second type of cult is utilitarian; for the Aztecs it served to strengthen their confidence in the elements of their culture. The movable cults of the almanac tend to be of this second type. The cults of the solar calendar are a mixed lot.

When taken all together, the reinforcement cults can be thought of as folk religion, where the real center of worship is not the god, but the ruler, the tribe, the war band, the guild, or the family. In this religion of the folk, man is thought of as a younger brother or at least as a pensioner of the gods, a being in whom the gods should rightly have a protective interest. To that extent the state can deify itself, the lineage extol itself, the merchant perform his miracles of enrichment, and the warrior claim heaven. Our reason for distinguishing the preceding two categories of Aztec cult is merely to keep the reader aware of the responsiveness of the Aztec to multiple aspects of the divine, whether as the "wholly other," or as a source of human life and a validation of its many orders.

One item of possible confusion should be mentioned here, and that is the relationship of the cults to the festivals. In any study of the Aztecs they should not be confused. A cult or elements of it may appear in more than one of the eighteen Aztec months; in fact it may float through the year surfacing in several of the festivals. As an example of this, we can cite initiatory rites for the young that appear in the months of Izcalli, Panquetzaliztli, and elsewhere. Two or more cults can join in one presentation as is the case in the worship of the earth mother Cihuacoatl that includes victims sacrificed to her as well as the sacrifice of victims in the eternal hearth—this marking where a religion of fire has intruded into an earth religion. This tendency to the dispersal and repetition of cults is owing to a long history of Mesoamerican religions previous to the Aztecs, all differing in detail but fundamentally all saying the same thing.

This jungle of cults sheltered many dark places of the Aztec spirit. It is difficult for us to push our way through the miasmas of anxiety that stretched out alongside the calendar road of every Aztec year. Insecurity was everywhere, whether it pertained to the food supply, to the threat of disease, to the omnipresence of sacrifice, or to an individual's hidden sins. In such an atmosphere cults bloomed, fruited, and then withered. The imagination of the neurasthenic priest was powerfully stimulated by the already existing plethora of cults, and his piety often became in consequence a ferocity.

As for Aztec society as a whole, we have also to note the differing religious tensions or mind sets of its component classes. When faced with the supernatural, the knight (*teuctli*) in the Aztec state responded in fascination, the priest (*tlamacazqui*) in intellectual submission, and the commoner (*macehualli*) in fear. These three attitudes—and there were others—produced different cult responses and called up different gods as patrons. The knight or warrior felt that although Tonatiuh, the sun god, could not be crudely coerced, he could certainly be pleased. The knight looked on the face of the sun and as if mesmerized served him the foods that he loved and required. The priest, rooted in routine, thought of meticulous discipline as the summa of his profession. He knew that he possessed a special awareness of the supernatural and a knowledge about it given to him by Quetzalcoatl. The commoner sought only to avoid the giant supernaturals whenever he could, hiding in the littleness and comfort of his many spirits—his normal affinity for the earth mother Cihuacoatl was displayed in cult fragments and figurines. Nothing of this will surprise the reader, and it is being mentioned here to further prepare him or her for the complexity to follow.

THE ROLE OF FIRE IN AZTEC RELIGION

In the Aztec world, cults had a tendency to clot into larger aggregations that we may refer to as religions.[1] One of these is the fire religion, one so central in the Aztec calendar that we offer here a discussion of it to serve as an underpinning for what follows.

The fire religion is very old in Mesoamerica. As an iconographically recognizable god, fire goes back at least to Teotihuacan and very probably to Cuicuilco. At the former site I believe that he was connected in some way with the Pyramid of the Sun. That imposing monument probably housed the sun god at its summit, whereas his élan vital or substance, namely the fire god, lived within.

Excavation has recently revealed a long corridor cave under the pyramid terminating in a sanctum sanctorum, once a natural antrum.[2] Along the corridor are rock barriers partially projecting down from the roof, perhaps eighteen in number. Great quantities of ash and charcoal cover the floors, whereas sherds of a special ceramic not found elsewhere are strewn about. This could well be a simulacrum of the underworld where the fire god lived. In the early days the cave also was the scene of rituals utilizing running water, for drain covers have been found there. The holiness of such a site needs no emphasizing.

There can be no doubt that this pyramid of Teotihuacan was consciously built over the cave to contain and to further sanctify it. The rites performed there so many centuries ago almost surely showed the sun god escorted into the infernal regions to die there and to be revived in new fire, ascending thence in triumph to the peak of the world mountain where he flared out in glory. We shall see later that every fifty-two years the Aztecs ritualized the revivification of the dead sun from new fire. The Pyramid of the Sun in Teotihuacan is in fact the site specified in Aztec myth where the god Nanahuatl incinerated himself to rise as the first sun, but in the myth the primacy of fire in the earth was deleted. As mentioned previously, recent excavation has disclosed that ritual fires were indeed lighted deep in the earth at this site.

Although the fire religion in Aztec days was shared equally by priests and people, each had their own rites, though both agreed that the hearth was central. The fire god here could be called "Yellow Face" (Ixcozauhqui) or simply "Flame" (Cuezaltzin), perhaps his most primitive avatar. But if the god was generally Yellow Face to the people in their homes, to the priests he was more often the Turquoise Lord (Xiuhteuctli), an anthropomorphic god whose regalia could be described and whose mythology was known.[3]

The fire religion, in other words, could take on either familial or cosmic aspects. Though individual and state were equally at home with the god, his demands upon them were in both cases different.

We are reaching far back in time when we consider the familial aspects of the fire religion. A child's connection with the family fire began early. There is a moving passage in one of the sources that illustrates this graphically.[4] At the birth of a child, the family laid a new fire in the hearth and kept it constantly replenished for the first four days of the child's life. No one was allowed to take a brand from this fire—it had to remain intact. For those four days the child *was in fact* the fire itself or a double, a *nahualli*, of it. The fire was the child's integrity and to remove embers from the hearth at that time would be to lessen the child by that much as a person. So at the end of that sacred four-day period, the child separated himself from his true father, the fire, and became human. At this point cult did not need a matching cosmogonic myth; origins were clearly indicated by the fire.

The primacy of fire was acknowledged at every hearthside; before any meal could begin, a crumb of bread or several drops of *octli* ("pulque") were offered to Yellow Face.[5] As a proprietary force in the home, fire could be the Revered Old One, Hueuetzin; as an ancestral guardian he was lovingly called *Tota* or "Our Father." This domiciliary spirit of fire had an animal familiar, the dog, who acted in connection with fire almost as a nahualli or alter ego acted toward its god—in fact in the *tonalpohualli* (almanac) the day One Dog was the priestly recognition of this connection. When Mesoamerican priests decided to change the fire spirit into a deity, he was named *Huehueteotl*, the "Old God." We do not know whether in the predawn darkness it was to him or to Yellow Face that the woman of every household offered her pinch of incense or her crumb of bread.[6] Most of the popular folklore of Aztec focal worship has been lost to us, obscured by or contaminated with the public rites of Turquoise Lord, Xiuhteuctli, the fire god of the state.

The reason why the state considered fire and the god of fire to be central was that the cults of all the other gods depended on his presence. In front of certain temple shrines, at the top of the frontal steps, two great clay braziers pierced with holes flickered continuously night and day. In front of Tzonmolco, the temple of Turquoise Lord himself, rows of braziers lit up the night in an avenue of fire leading to the steps of the god.[7] The city of Tenochtitlan also had a hearth of its own, almost in the nature of an eternal flame, and this became another of the god's avatars. Like all the god's fires, this was fed only with a preferred type of aromatic wood stockpiled in the temple yard. It was death for any of the attendant priests to allow this fire to go out.

The city hearth was called the "Fire Navel" (*Tlexictli*).[8] It was a stone enclosure open in front, and it stood at the very doorsill of the Earth Mother's house, the Tlillan. This proximity is explained by the fact that the fire god was known to live in the deep underworld; he can, in fact, be accounted a chthonic being. On occasions such as the Greater Feast of the Dead, victims could be hurled alive into this bonfire as precious offerings to the god. It was thus a hearth in every sense as holy as those in private homes, only it served a whole people.

When considered as a formalized religion, fire worship was confined to four celebrations: Izcalli (which I shall describe at length in this chapter), the Greater Feast of the Dead, the thirteenth movable feast (One Dog), and finally the New Fire ceremony every fifty-second year. I have already pointed to its necessary presence, however, in every other cult of importance. At such times, it was no doubt fire as a force, rather than fire as the deity, that was understood, yet it effectively cemented the whole cultic life of the Aztecs into a loose religious continuum. The fires that flared up in the cities, sparkling throughout the night, were in that sense egalitarian.[9]

But if Yellow Face was the hearth fire, the fire god in his full form as Turquoise Lord was also the deity of time and space. To our minds this is a strange non sequitur, yet it flows directly from the Aztec view of the hearth as placed at the meeting point of five directions. The concept of the hearth as a radial point around which the family gathers is certainly a parochial way of thinking, yet when one uses it as a directional pivot it immediately becomes cosmic. Thus in the Izcalli festival we will see four avatars of the god—each representing a cardinal compass point—appear as *ixiptlas* who are then sacrificed.[10] Fire as a central point creates an automatic four-sided or four-cornered spatial grid within which all possible directions are contained. The line passing vertically through the fire gives the fifth direction.

New fire was drilled every Izcalli festival in the fire temple of Tzonmolco and from there was distributed to such householders as desired it. It was probably from such a cultic recurrence as this that the priests finally extrapolated their view of fire as an ontology of time. We shall also see how every fourth celebration of the Izcalli specified that time at that point was particularly sacred, and the fire derived from it therefore more desirable. This presence of the count of four, here applied to time, also applies to space, for there were only four directions emanating horizontally from fire, and each was therefore an avatar of the Turquoise Lord. These spirits of locus, because of their derivation from the god, could be thought of also as spirits of time. One of the Turquoise Lord's common names was Nauhyotecatl ("He of Fourness") where the division of space into four directions is being referred to, but he could just as well be called Nauhyohuehue, the "Old Man of Fourness," where undoubtedly a temporal flavor also entered, whether four years were thought of, the four year bearers, or the four aeons preceding our own.[11]

But it is in the tonalpohualli where we discover fire's most intimate cross-reference to time. We have indicated before that the god's day sign in the tonalpohualli was "dog" and that therefore the day One Dog plus the twelve succeeding days formed a cluster of thirteen whose luck or fortune were in part reflections of the god Xiuhteuctli. If we count to the fourth day of this packet of thirteen, we find that it was Four Reed.[12] This therefore—because it was numbered four—was a day that must have conformed to the sacred structure of time and, not unexpectedly, when we turn to our sources we find that, indeed, this was the special feast of the fire god and was the day when the new fire was drilled and distributed. As a birth date, the name "Four Reed" is given both to the god and to his nahualli the Fire Dragon, whose heraldic image he carries on his back. The Turquoise Lord thus had several descriptive names and at least two date names, as we might expect from such a venerable deity.

FIRE ELEMENTS IN THE CULT OF THE SUN

Our discussion of the religion of fire has so far concentrated on fire itself as the deity worshipped. But we will note in the Xiuhtlalpilli festival to be described at the end of the chapter that *fire* shifts roles with the *sun*, so that the observer has to see fire and sun as homologues. Fire was essentially of the earth, but when it did climb up into the sky it became the sun. Nevertheless, the cults of these two supernaturals were generally distinct. Only in the great sacrifice made in the Xiuhtlalpilli festival do our sources encourage the understanding that fire was indeed sun and sun fire. Let us see how the solar cult was structured.

The Mexica Aztecs had at least six avatars of Tonatiuh, the sun god in the day sky. The sum of all their rituals can be called the "day sun cult." The six were Huitzilopochtli (the sun in his specifically Mexican tutelary form), Xipe (a solar god found in many places in Mesoamerica), Xochipilli (the joyous sun of the morning venerated by the palace people), Macuilxochitl (a variant of the preceding who patronized song, games, and dance), Piltzinteuctli (the young sun being created in the underworld and emerging as the maize plant), and finally Xiuhpilli who is much like Xochipilli but about whom little is known.

What the diurnal sun cult insists on is the overriding vitality of the sun. Tonatiuh, whose name means "He Goes Forth Blazing," is before all else a hero or "brave" (*tiacauh*) and an adventurer or "goer" (*yaqui*). It is not difficult for us to imagine that in some early time predatory warrior groups took over a solar cult, remodeling both the sun's mythology and his rites to conform to their ideals. Before its fall, the venerable city of Teotihuacan had drawn up at least some of the outlines of the cult. The Toltecs later embellished it and passed it down to the Aztecs who carried it to its ultimate. The little we know about the Chichimec religion, which fed into the Toltec world, confirms that they were hunter-braves worshiping the sun as their father.[13]

The sun cult was thus a complex affair. Mexican rulers and priests in the expanding urban context of the fourteenth and fifteenth centuries had used Tonatiuh as the model upon which they had formed Huitzilopochtli, their city mascot, thus grafting the tribal onto the cosmic. In the cult of Huitzilopochtli it is the narrow interest of a tribal god—who was naturally a tiacauh—that is stressed, whereas the features of a new creation, which is an almost inevitable spinoff of the myth, was virtually ignored. The men of the new city of Tenochtitlan were wholly oriented to a life of war and so failed to see their god as other than a warrior. The priests had adjusted to this fact when they invented or reworked the Panquetzaliztli festival, but they were unwilling or unable to move on to make a larger claim and reveal their god also as a universal creator.

Huitzilopochtli remained underneath a minimal god who was

only by a little removed from the sun. This is evident from the myth of the gigantomachy. In that myth, Huitzilopochtli uses as his most lethal weapon a bolt of fire referred to in the sources as the *Xiuhcoatl*, or "Turquoise Snake." At the base of the god's temple in Tenochtitlan was uncovered a marvelous sculptured image in stone of this thunderbolt; the whole was painted red and yellow and was identified as Four Reed, namely fire.[14] Nothing could more clearly explicate the coefficiency of sun and fire in Aztec thought.

Focusing even more on heroics was the Tonatiuh worshipped in the almanac. Here, under his avatar as Four Movement, he is narrowed even more to become the peculiar fetish of the warrior lodges, the Eagle and the Jaguar knights. He is not even strictly Mexican anymore, for the knightly orders were actually international in their brotherhood, existing in perhaps a majority of the cities of central Mesoamerica. In these rites the sun has nothing whatever to do with the people, the priests, or even the rulers (except insofar as the rulers were themselves knights). In Tenochtitlan Tonatiuh's shrine was set aside for the warriors.

Tonatiuh was greeted in his rising every day with censing and appropriate words of welcome.[15] This cult of the risen sun took place in the Cuauhcalli ("House of Eagles"), the meeting house of the knightly orders where the great warriors foregathered for discussions, cannibal meals, and worship.[16] Whereas the priests in their appeals to the sun spoke for the city and all who were in it, the warriors in the House of Eagles, when they addressed their commander god, spoke only for themselves.

The cult of the sun as Xipe is very old. In the festival called the "Flaying of Men," he will be seen as a multifaceted god whose patronage extended from war, to the spring verdure, to blood rites, and to general abundance for all the people. A universality not found in the other sun cults is noticeable in his rituals. All levels of Aztec society were involved in his baroque celebrations. His rites reenact the myth of creation in a far more sophisticated manner than was the case in the Panquetzaliztli. I will consider both festivals later.

The rites of Xochipilli and Macuilxochitl were strictly elitist in character. We know little about them beyond the fact that the courtiers and the others in the palace, in their worship of those two closely related avatars of the sun, saw them as patrons of their prerogatives and pleasures.[17] They were important gods, and the observance of their rites was the badge of nobility.

Piltzinteuctli appears to have been, in the main, a mythic figure who is the sun as progenitor—whence his name "Lord of Children."[18] It is not certain where he appears in cult—if indeed he appears there at all. The role of Xiuhpilli is equally unclear.[19]

Thus there was a rich variety in the cult of the daytime sun. It was like a ritual rocket that had burst into many fragments. The sun appears in the Panquetzaliztli festival ("Erection of Banners") as a tribal validator; in the Flaying of Men festival (Tlacaxipehualiztli) he appears as a principal of near-cosmic proportions, universal and renovative. In the first movable feast he appears as the genius of war and, more narrowly still, as the fetish of the elite warrior lodges. These divagations are evidence of a long cultic background behind Aztec sun worship, yet the many formulations appear to have increasingly reflected the interests of the nobles. The cult of fire had a broader base.

THE DANCE

If fire was the centerpiece of Aztec cult, dance was its supreme theatrical embellishment—consequently a word must be said about it here. Although it is impossible to reconstruct any of the dances from the meager descriptions left to us, it can still be said without fear of contradiction that it was the Aztec's most splendid art, one woven into the very fabric of his society.

Dance had been brought to men by Quetzalcoatl, the god of culture.[20] There was a dance for every mood and every ceremonial occurrence.[21] Each important god had his own exclusive repertoire.[22] So seriously was the art taken that any small error made by a dancer, caller, or drummer on the occasion of a great feast might, under certain circumstances, be punished by death.[23] The discipline, agility, and grace required in the art were widely believed to be a necessary training for the exertions of war—newly installed rulers were accordingly cautioned to pay especial attention to it. So important was the dance in Tenochtitlan that the Cuicacalli ("House of Song") was attached to the palace. Groups could be found there constantly rehearsing or dancing for their own pleasure.[24]

The common Nahuatl word for dance was *netotiliztli*. This included dancing in private homes, at weddings, knighting ceremonies, and clan gatherings. The cult dance, however, was known as *macehualiztli* and implied a far greater solemnity. This latter category of dancing brought pleasure to the gods and was therefore of necessity a matter of cult; it also had the advantage of bringing merit upon the dancers and the society at large.

The *tlatoani* (ruler) had much to say about the forms and occasions of the dances. Dance directors, drummers, choreographers, and composers were attached to the palace and altogether formed a numerous professional group.[25] They assembled daily in a part of the palace called the "House of Mixcoatl" where were stored costumes and instruments used in every style of dance, and there they waited to hear what the ruler's pleasure was in regard to projected performances.[26] All of these experts were under the control of a high official called the "custodian" (*tlapixcatzin*), and all were supported by the palace.[27] They were consulted well in advance of the time when an old dance might have to be redone, or when it was appropriate to insert a totally new dance. In the case of those dances customarily performed as a part of the great state festivals, there were naturally few changes to be made, and most of the work consisted of simple rehearsals. However, in the various netotiliztlis performed in the calendar cults and in the palace worship of the gods of pleasure, the novel, the extravagant, and the exotic were sometimes uppermost. Orders in fact for new dances frequently went out from the tlatoani's chambers. Veritable cotillions were invented for some of the lighter cults as well as for the celebrations of victories, births, marriages, hunts, cosmic histories, and the like.[28]

The dance form was usually understood as concomitantly being sung—the whole ensemble included dance, costumes, percussion and wind instruments, and singing. Song composers (*cuicapixques*) were attached to both the larger temples and to the palace. In the temple circles they were the hymnodists lauding the gods and singing of their deeds. In the palace they created lays of past kings and praises of the present ruler.[29] Such canticles as these latter were incorporated into newly invented dances for large and small groups of nobles or professional dancers who rehearsed them assiduously beforehand. Singing was also performed by women in the cults of the goddesses. To honor the goddess of salt, women of all ages wearing flowers in their hair danced and sang:

And they went singing; they cried out loudly; they sang in a very high treble. As the mockingbird takes it, so was their song. Like bells were their voices.[30]

In all cases, these essentially secular dances were drawn inevitably into the realm of cult by being placed under the patronage of the god of pleasure, Macuilxochitl ("Five Flower"), the deity worshipped by the palace people. The two-toned wooden drum (the *teponaztli*), struck with rubber-ended drumsticks and used in all the more pretentious dances, was treated as a god.[31] Of the other sort of drum, the *huehuetl*, its stretched hide face was beaten only by the drummer's hands. We learn that it was

> the means of awakening the city, and a source of joy to Tloque Nahuaque [Tezcatlipoca]; a means by which he is requested, a means by which his word is sought . . . and it is a means of remembrance, a means by which warfare is cast, is bored as with a fire-drill, is instigated.[32]

The fact that there were so many dance forms means that we cannot even roughly describe the average dance.[33] For the more showy ones a reed mat was spread out in the middle of an open patio and the two drums, alto and bass, were positioned on it. Besides the two drummers there were also two callers who intoned the opening couplets of each portion of the dance, to be answered by the dancers with short phrases. If the dance was conceived of in linear fashion, two dance leaders led off the respective files side by side with the dancers twirling to face each other, posturing, and stamping their feet. If it was a ring dance, it could be made up of several concentric circles, with the nobles in the center close to the drums and the youngest warriors in the outer rings—all of them circling and interweaving at set rates in such a way that on every radius out from the center the dancers never lost the ones closer in. This meant that the rings turned at different rates, the inner ring with the magnates moving in ponderous dignity, the outer rings leaping and racing.[34]

We are told that the costuming was brilliant.[35] A nobleman would don all of the finery and insignia allowed to him, in this fashion displaying his prowess in war or in statecraft. Thus the most resplendent rings were the innermost ones. The young warriors in the outer wheels made up for the lack of feathers, capture insignia, and other devices by the flashing of their limbs and the lightness of their steps, but everywhere precision was absolute. The earliest Spaniards, who witnessed only the remnants of these superb spectacles, were still spellbound by the precision manifested by the dancers of whom there could be as many as 2,000 or more circling at once.

The dancer's whole body was used, heads dipped, arms were crooked, joined or flung up, hips swayed, and feet were lifted or slipped sideways, all in differentiated patterns, all in perfect unison. On truly extraordinary occasions a dance might have as many as 4,000 dancers,[36] but in every case the timing of gestures and foot movements was accurate to the tiniest fraction of a second. A lifetime of training made that possible. There is no way of telling whether syncopation was used in these dances, but the high degree of sophistication that we know to have been characteristic of them leads us to believe that the beat could be highly complex and variable. Probably some of the cult dances could be seen as ballets, with a complete story told in several movements.

The dances were arranged in stages, and an entire festive dance could go on for as long as eight hours, with groups withdrawing and reentering periodically for reasons of hunger or fatigue. At times whole choruses could be withdrawn and simultaneously replaced. Most dances ended with sundown, but others went on until midnight. The usual dance began in a rather somber adagio rhythm, but as the movements succeeded one another, the voices and drumming heightened in tone while the movements became more urgent and staccato.[37] Comic relief was added at times by outlandishly garbed buffoons weaving in and out of the files or somersaulting in toward the center.

The variety of dances was indeed impressive.[38] Many were taken from peoples subdued in former wars who had been forced to turn over certain ones of their national dances as a part of the tribute imposed on them. Some of the dances came from the Huaxtecs, some from farther along the coast of Anahuac. The dances were taken over in all of their detail; exact replicas of the costumes were made, and professional dancers were meticulously trained in the correct gestures, music, and steps of the dance. There were dances about the origins of the Chichimecs, the people of the bow and arrow, dances of the Otomí, and derisive dances of peoples classed as barbarians. There were women's dances, as well as mixed dancing of warriors and harlots (*ahuianis*).[39] There were rain dances, traveler's dances, and maypole dances of girls who circled with colored ribbons. There were comic dances, dances on stilts, dances of vice and debauchery, dances by torchlight, victory dances, even dances of cripples. Here is a description of the effect made by the hand-waving dance performed at the Ochpaniztli festival.

> And in this manner was the hand-waving: they went in various rows as has been said; they moved like flowers. They indeed went in glory. They kept circling the temple.[40]

Each dance was a virtuoso performance. The youths of the city, both boys and girls, were trained by priests in the proper performance of both song and dance. Assembled in their *calpulli* divisions, they would be escorted at the close of day to the Cuicacalli for arduous training sessions.[41] Practically everyone in the city was thus able to contribute his or her skill to the staging of these dancing spectacles when called upon to do so.

Although dancing permeated all of the Aztec cults, there was one period in the almanac set aside by the ruler and the nobles solely for their own delight. Well before the day One Flower, which was especially marked for dancing, the tlatoani had announced what dances would be featured for that day and the twelve succeeding days that it controlled.[42] Poles entwined with flowers were set up just outside the palace portals, and the first groups of celebrants always emerged out of that floral gate. Shrill whistles began the dance, then singing, and finally the drums came in.

> The horizontal drum was beaten, trumpets were played, conch shells and reed pipes were blown. There was song. The horizontal drums lay croaking; they lay growling; it was as if they lay droning; and gourd rattles were rattled.[43]

If all the calendrical signs were right, these dances might go on for as long as forty days. It was a time beloved of the palace folk, an occasion for an extended display by them of the symbols of their rank and prowess as well as of the elegance of their dancing.[44] To mark the end of the set of festive days the two flowering poles in front of the palace were taken down to be burned, and the last of the dancers wound their way back into the palace.

It is evident to us that these flower dances were secular in their intent, being staged primarily to enhance the prestige of the ruler and his close supporters. Nevertheless the set had been converted into cult by assigning it to a day in the tonalpohualli that was the birthday of the youthful sun, Xochipilli, or "Flower Prince." We will see it transformed every eighth year into the colorful Atamalcualiztli festival ("Eating of Water-Tamales"). A society that constantly invented new dances and new costumes for its members and absorbed foreign choric styles is a society clearly aware of an esthetic of living. When at the same time that society has chosen a cult-oriented existence, the esthetic cannot be autonomous but must become a part of cult.

Suffused throughout the cultic life of the Aztecs are the two elements—fire and dance. They are the cement bonding together many of the religious practices of these people. We have seen the part played by fire in Aztec life and thought. Fire was an element used to charm the supernaturals, and its use in cult thereby became almost a morality, pointing to a condition of warmth and light that could exist in a dark universe. Dance bound man to the gods in an esthetic of color, rhythm, and beauty, and lightened for the gods the dimensions of darkness. Fire deified, dance humanized.

THE STRUCTURE OF THE AZTEC CALENDAR

A ritual calendar gives to a people an approximate locus in the supernatural world in spite of their changing relations with the divine. The calendar that the Aztecs used is simply one witness to the fascination with which man tries to orient his spiritual life. Yet the Aztecs did not invent the calendar that they possessed. It was simply the latest edition of a remarkable solar chronometer passed down to them over the centuries from earliest Mesoamerica, and we must see it as the enduring skeleton over which their constantly evolving ritual could drape itself.[45]

The calendar itself was called *ilhuitlapohualli*, which in Nahuatl means "the count of festival days." It was built on the vigesimal system; each of its eighteen components or months was of twenty days duration. These added up to 360 days which thereby became their calendar year. Each of these 360 days was an *ilhuitl*, or "day." The flavor of the word, however, was far richer than our word "day," which connotes nothing more than a single alternation of one period of daylight followed by one of nighttime. An ilhuitl was all of that, of course, but to the Aztecs it was even more a periodic ritual commemoration, a day made sacred by the ritual performances assigned to it; the two could not be separated. Our phrase "festival day" more nearly approximates the meaning of ilhuitl. The ilhuitl was not a measurable day in our sense of the word so much as it was a period set aside for a ritual performance. By this definition, therefore, the calendar was to the Aztecs the muster roll of all of their important rites organized in an unalterable sequence.

The five days necessary to complete the sum of days in the correct solar year were called by the Aztecs *nemontemi*, a package of unnamed days totally without rites, and one therefore presenting a discontinuity in the normal unrolling of the sacred. The literal meaning of the word is something like "it is completed without results," pointing to the nullity that was the nature of such an evil clutch of days. To the priests the five days were, of course, mathematically necessary in counting the days of the solar year and in seeing that the full coursing of the sun, namely 365 days, was accounted for. But to the Aztec individual, the nemontemi represented that which he could least well understand—the cancellation for five days of all familiar supernatural beings; whence came, therefore, the essential grotesqueness of those five days. A child born on one of those days was asssured of a short and miserable life; he or she was a person with no true name and no birthday to point to.[46]

I have mentioned that the calendar was built up of eighteen bundles of twenty-day periods that we can refer to as "months." These months came down from a distant past and must have changed their names and cult references many times as they passed through different cultures. However, among the various Aztec cities there was a standard list of month names (with some variations) in which the sequence was fixed. Although several minor cults might be celebrated in a month, there was always one special cult that distinguished it from all the others. This cult revolved around one of the great deities, usually found in company with certain of his avatars and associated supernaturals. But in no case is the name of a month the name of a god. It would thus appear that the Aztec month was conceived of as essentially a cult cadre rather than as the commemoration of any one god. This is of importance as it suggests to us that the objective of an

Aztec cult may be paramount over the presence of its divine patron; that it is the god who is forced into the mold of a cult rather than the god imposing on the cult his own peculiar requirements. Be that as it may, the calendar was the single most significant cultural determinant in all Aztec life. The Aztecs assigned the inception of the calendar to that legendary year when they made their egress from Aztlan, the distant homeland.[47]

The number eighteen had no symbolic meaning to the Aztecs, whereas twenty in their vigesimal system of counting was a completed set. The necessity of making up the correct number of days in the solar year forced the early Mesoamericans to accept the fact that there would be only eighteen months. To achieve the symmetry of "twenty," the Aztecs (more probably some one of their predecessor cultures) chose two of the months, the fourteenth and the twentieth, to split, so that four cults and not two were observed in them. Thus the meaningless number eighteen was bypassed, and a full and proper score achieved.

Twenty festivals became canonical in the eighteen months. These twenty major festivals generally occurred (or culminated) on the tenth or the last day of the month. There was also a tendency to present the months in pairs, referring to them as "the lesser" and "the greater," eight of them being so designated. The names given to the months are not of much help in our understanding of the calendar, and the translations of several remain doubtful. Inasmuch as they represent centuries of ritual accumulation and change, it is probably impossible to ascribe to the final Aztec calendar any single meaning; we have already seen, however, that it does have a logic.

THE ALMANAC DESCRIBED

There was another pattern of organization for Aztec cults, one unique to the cultures of Mesoamerica, having been designed by the Zapotecs at least as early as the sixth century B.C. This was the tonalpohualli that in a sense stands over against the ilhuitlapohualli or calendar that we have just considered. As a casual comparison of the two words shows, each was a "count" (*pohualli*) of days, but the days in each case were differently conceived. We have seen that the ilhuitl was an annual festival day, sacred in the sense that it was connected with some god or divine entity. The *tonalli*, on the other hand, was the day conceived as an augury, sacred in the sense that it was primarily connected, not with a supernatural, but with a destiny or fate.[48] Every day in the year (except for the five nemontemi) was subsumed under both counts at once. If considered under the former, it belonged purely in the public domain and was always known to be in a set place in the sequence of 365 days. If considered under the latter count, it belonged in the domain of omens—in fact it was an omen —and had no set place in the solar year. There were 260 days in the tonalpohualli, and if one positioned its first day to correspond to the first day of the calendar, then after fifty-two revolutions (i.e., fifty-two solar years) the two initial days would again correspond, and the cycle would begin anew.

The tonalpohualli was internally constructed of twenty day signs, or glyphs, plus the numbers one through thirteen. These two sets, both signs and numbers, completed their permutations in 260 days. That number of days therefore defined the duration of the complete tonalpohualli.

Inasmuch as the twenty signs were sacred entities, each one had to be appropriately honored. This was done at the beginning of each tonalpohualli week of thirteen days when the sign in question had the number one as a coefficient. In this week each sign carried with it, in a package, the twelve signs that followed in their immutable order numbering two through thirteen. All of the days of this package were dominated or influenced by the initial day sign. Thus, throughout the tonalpohualli of 260 days, each one of the twenty day signs was honored once. Birthdays, whether of gods or humans, were celebrated not in the solar calendar but in the tonalpohualli, namely on one's day sign when it came up carrying the number one.[49] Thus a person's birthday could occur twice in one solar year, though he or she celebrated it only once.

Of equal if not more significance was the way in which the tonalpohualli impinged upon the life of the individual, hemming him in with signs, auguries, and expectations. The day sign of his birth was fundamental, as was the closely connected date of his name giving. In consultation with the priests on the matter of his marriage, a man's parents chose for him a lucky sign among the twenty available. Marriage thus became a rite plotted into the tonalpohualli.

Each of the twenty day signs was symbolic of a destiny or fortune attached to an enterprise, a birth or some other event or situation taking place on the day of said sign.

Every person felt obliged to revere his individual day sign and scrupulously observe it when it came around; otherwise it could turn against him—this was especially true of signs that indicated good and bad luck simultaneously. The ilhuitl upon which a person had been born was of little account to him; its only relevance was to the position of the sun in the sky during the year and to the timing of the public festivals.

The tonalpohualli was thus an almanac and not a calendar. Additionally, it had a different pantheon from that of the calendar. Pursuant to priestly interests any one of the 260 tonallis might itself become a full-fledged godling or divine presence demanding worship. It could do this either because it was the birth date of some god, or because it was a date that had a cosmic significance in myth. The tonalli day thus often acted as if it were an avatar or alter ego of a supernatural, and it was generally inseparable from that god or cosmic association, though it was never a full equivalent. For instance, Four Movement (Nauholin) was a day in the tonalpohualli associated with the sun god. Nauholin thus acted as an obligatory festival day; yet it had also become, over the centuries, a divine entity or spirit on its own, connected with the sun in his journeyings through the underworld.

The Aztecs canonized at least fourteen of these tonallis to play the previously mentioned roles.[50] The festivities that accompanied them show them to have been important but less elaborate than the calendar cults. When it happened that one of the fourteen tonalli cults happened to coincide with one of the set pieces of the calendar, both were simultaneously observed, though the ruler might announce beforehand certain accommodations.[51] In some years, depending on the urgencies of the times, the movable feasts of the tonalpohualli might actually displace the calendar feasts, though they did not cancel them. Thus the two festival systems, calendar and almanac, were frequently on collision courses, but the endless zeal of the Aztecs in the medium of cult generally found room for both. Certainly the movable feasts were never obliterated.

Of Sahagún's list of the fourteen tonalpohualli feasts, three of them (the third, eighth, and twelveth) were days of terror, for they marked the descent from the skies of the female demons known as the "goddesses," or the "princesses," bringers of diseases and monstrous deformities to children. Their shrines stood at all important crossroads. The remainder of the fourteen feasts were consecrated to certain of the major gods perceived in their tonalli-epiphanies, or avatars. These gods, known by their tonalli names, often acted as patrons to certain guilds or social orders, differing to that extent from the gods of the calendric pantheon who were of significance to all the people. The full list of feasts is found in the back of the book.

The seeming randomness in this list of tonalli feasts should not blind us to one of its outstanding features—the total lack of celebrations in the almanac honoring agricultural or hunting gods. The sectors of Aztec society operating this system of tonalli cults were mainly nobles on the one hand and merchants and artisans on the other. Commoners as a class are not much in evidence as celebrants. The tonalpohualli cults are thus in the main elitist, whereas those of the calendar more generally concern the entire populace.

The Aztecs had thus produced two sets of gods; the pantheon, which belongs essentially to the calendar and is closely connected with mythology, and the tonalli deities, who are avatars or special aspects of the calendar gods and have only faint appearances in myth, if any. Not all of these latter tonalli spirits acquired full godhead or distinctiveness. Those that did included Four Movement (Nauholin), Two Rabbit (Ometochtli), One Reed (Ce Acatl), and Two Reed (Omacatl).

It is interesting to consider the fact that Aztec cult created deities out of itself. The detailed story of how this happened is not known to us, but it must have begun with the manufacture of an almanac by priests and the imposition of a meaning onto that new and artificial list of days. The naming of each day in double terms (both sign and number) produced the assignment of various fortunes to each. Then, at some point, the older gods of the pantheon were each assigned birth dates in the tonalpohualli. This inevitably led to the secondary deifications we have been considering here, where the day-sign deity was known to be an aspect of some god of the pantheon, but one more rigidly defined and circumscribed—in other words an avatar.

These avatars would never have appeared had it not been for the invention of the tonalpohualli. By inventing the almanac the priest-hood produced an intellectual construction to help them explain the universe. This in turn dictated the appearance of a second generation of gods, for whose worship new cults then emerged. By that time there had crystallized out of Mesoamerican society an elite class supported by the priests, and it was this corporation of upper classes that seized the opportunity to harness these second-generation gods to their own world view.

THE IZCALLI FESTIVAL

Completed parcels of time occurred for the Aztecs every four, eight, and fifty-two years. Each one of these cycles was marked by a special renewal cultus. The festival celebrating the completion of the four-year period was a special augmentation of the important *Izcalli*, which was the name of the eighteenth calendar month. In this rite, the people themselves were renewed. The festival marking the end of the eighth year was an augmentation of the Tepeilhuitl, the thirteenth month; in it the staple corn was rejuvenated. The festival celebrating the completion of a fifty-two-year cycle, or Aztec century, was a unique renewal in fire of the whole cosmos, a vast, priest-oriented ritual drama, in its staging and rich symbolism seldom equaled in any of the religions of the past.

For the Izcalli our scenario is set in Tenochtitlan, the city that the Mexican Aztecs founded in the midst of Lake Tezcoco. The time will be their year's end, the last one of the eighteen months of the calendar, and specifically that one given over to the Turquoise Lord, who was both fire god and master of the year.

Aztec myth had it that a fire festival was the first one to be created by the gods, which act thus set it at the inception of time even before day and night began.[52] The month chosen for it corresponds to our middle winter, spanning parts of January and February. It was named *Izcalli*, meaning "a shoot" or "a sprout," which is certainly an apt symbol for the renewal of time. But as understood by the Aztecs, time ran in four-year bundles, and so it was the fourth celebration of the Izcalli that was especially significant, and this is the one we are reviewing.

Because time was comprehended in four-year quanta or packets, and because the fire god was the god of the year, this was a festival central to the whole calendar. Therefore, though the Izcalli normally was free of human sacrifices, in the celebration every fourth year the practice was observed in order to lend luster to the event.[53]

One of the effects of this fire festival was to confer renewal on all who participated, and so it could also be called *pilquixtia* ("becoming young again.")[54] It had reference to man and his culture only— the renewal of nature and of nature's stages of dearth or abundance were left to be celebrated in other months. Thus, when the Izcalli is understood in the basic sense of renewal, it becomes clear that it was no more the end of the year than it was the beginning. In reality it was interstitial, and this accounts for the confusion in the Spanish sources as to whether it was the first or the last month of the year.

The cult began with the making and installation of a special image of the fire god that was named *Milintoc*.[55] A permanent image of the fire god was kept, of course, in Tzonmolco, his temple, but this quadrennial Milintoc was different; it was built on an armature of curved slats of wood, was provided with a yellow wig, a feathered cape, and a mask of mosaic turquoise. The idol was light enough to be moved about at will. Once it was completed, the priests seated it upon a jaguar skin, the symbol of sovereignty, and then all those present waited and watched into the night. The braziers that customarily burned at the top of the god's temple terrace were allowed to die out; until midnight all was silence.

A priest then knelt before a fireboard and began to rapidly twirl a drill stick between his palms.[56] Theoretically at midnight the crucial spark was elicited. The priest gently blew up the tinder and then, with the utmost care, transferred the glowing fragment to a great brazier filled with the rare wood beloved of the fire god. A sigh went through the priests crowded in front of Milintoc, and at the moment when the first flame flickered up, the great conch-shell trumpets broke into a hoarse uproar heard all over the darkened city. The old had ended and the new had begun.

All night the flames were fed until what had been a pinprick of light in the night became a series of flaring beacons announcing the presence of the new fire god who was at the same time the oldest god in the pantheon. This theophany of his would last until three Izcallis had passed and a fourth had come around. Then another visible manifestation of deity would take place.

For some days previously the population had been preparing for the day now dawning. Youths had scoured the hillsides for small game and had seined the lake for fish, all taken alive.[57] The women spent their time preparing the special stuffed tamales dipped in crab sauce that were eaten only at that time.

It is of interest that the young were the first group to present their offerings to the temple. In the grayness of early dawn the boys formed in files before the priests at the Tzonmolco and presented their catch: rattlesnakes, crayfish, scorpions, frogs, fish, and birds of all kinds. While they were dancing in front of the temple the priests accepted the writhing, clicking, and squawking animals and cast them into the new fire. The smaller items disappeared in the flames almost instantly, but the larger items—snakes, rabbits, and so forth, were allowed to roast a minute and then were hooked out for later consumption by the priesthood. Some adults brought the sanctified tamales to offer to the god in his temple, but others offered them to him in their own homes, for the god lived in every hearth in the land as well.

We already know that fire was universally acknowledged to be the great progenitor. Because he was the lord of paternity, his rites within the privacy of every family inevitably also concerned the ancestors. Therefore, after first offering to the hearth fire, the heads of families turned to the ancestors, who could be present as jars and cups set up around the hearth.[58] They were the honored uncles, aunts, grandparents, and distant forebears, each one garlanded for the festivities and filled to the brim with *octli* for their pleasure. Those of the family who had died within the previous four years could be simulated as pine knots, each identified, richly wrapped, and seated on mats. At the end of the banquet these close family members would be placed in the fire to be there consumed. Every household, rich or poor, that day ate the stuffed tamales required for the occasion; no other food was allowed. Tamales were eaten as hot as possible, and one sat close to the fire to invite burning, this being an acknowledgment of the presence of the father. Later the old men—we remember that the god was called the "Old God"—went to the Tzonmolco to drink octli and sing songs. The day, which had begun with dawn and the young, ended with sunset and the aged.

So much for the private ceremonies. Now came a sterner and

more formal passage in the cult. As this fourth year of the Izcalli began, three types of human sacrifices were being offered to the fire god on this day of his renaissance. The first were his four ixiptlas, that is to say, living men chosen to be vicarious images of him for that occasion. The fifth and central ixiptla was the god in all his completeness—Xiuhteuctli.[59] He had been chosen some days previously, adorned in the regalia of the god, and provided with a harlot to cater to all his desires. The ixiptlas were each painted the color of one of the four directions of the world and arrayed appropriately.[60] This was in recognition of the fact I have already noted, that while the hearth fire was the only true direction in the world, namely the center, there still radiated outward from the hearth the four cardinal directions, each one a necessary avatar of the god.

The second category of sacrificial victims was drawn from the pool of war captives. These were kept by the state acting as agent for the captors who were the real donors. They were looked upon as sacrifices preliminary to the more important third type, the "bathed ones," who were men and women purchased by affluent merchants and artisans at the slave market at Azcapotzalco, beautifully dressed, coddled and fattened for some weeks previously.[61] Of both sexes, they were dressed much as the deity was, and so we can see them, though in a less rigorous sense, as also ixiptlas of his.

These focal sacrifices took place in the precinct of the god's temple.[62] Previous to the day of sacrifice all of the five ixiptlas as well as the others were escorted under guard and forced to ascend the temple steps in single file. At the top they circled the stone upon which they were shortly to die (the techcatl), and then came down to be returned to the various city wards where they were being kept. All that night they were forced to remain awake during which time their top hair was cut off and patches of down, signifying a heroic end, were pasted onto their scalps.

As day was dawning, the victims were rounded up and marched off again to the fire god's temple. All of that morning they were expected to dance and sing on the apron in front of the temple, in celebration of their approaching end. They sang, says one source, until their voices cracked and died into hoarse shouts. The slaughter began at noon with the ruler officiating as the god's high priest. The first to go were the war captives who were considered here to play the role of predecessors and supporters. Then came the five ixiptlas, and finally the many slaves purchased by the merchants. That closed the offertory.

Because of the significance of the occasion—namely that fire, the All-Father, had been renewed—the ruler and his great men at that time visited the god's temple, clad in an array peculiar to this cult, the most significant item of which was a paper pendant hung about their necks, painted blue and cut out to represent the dog monster Xolotl. In Aztec thought, fire and dogs were connected. Additionally, each nobleman wore a yellow wig falling down to his waist, in imitation of the long golden hair of the fire god. The ruler wore the turquoise diadem that he and the god of fire customarily assumed—the symbol of sovereignty. Together then and in a rapid line, led by the ruler, all the magnates descended from the temple into the spacious enclosure upon which it faced and began the Dance of the Great Ones, an energetic circling dance that went around the temple four times, ending up with a symbolic return to the palace.[63] But the Dance of the Great Ones did more than display the nobles as being invested with the same domestic authority in their spheres as that possessed by the Turquoise Lord in the world at large. In the procession led by the ruler, priests were also included, each representing one of the major gods of the pantheon, including the gods of all the conquered peoples. The choreography of the dance was thus designed to link the nobles with all the gods in a way not allowed to commoners. We can conclude that this dance was an elite addendum to the more popular forms of the cult, and quite obviously one directed to the maintenance of the royal prerogative and its supporters. It was probably at some point in these rites when they brought out and worshipped an image of the ruler that had been made for this occasion only.[64] The lordship wielded by the god of fire was the very model of the lordship exercised by the current tlatoani.

The sequence of rites with which the fourth Izcalli closed was of extraordinary importance. It had to do with the way by which the social group maintained itself and co-opted new members. It was called the *pillahuanaliztli*, or "the drinking of the young folks."[65] Its implications were twofold; it served as an initiation of the young into the tribe as well as a rejuvenation of those who were adults. It was thus at least in part a new year's celebration.

Parents of children who had not been initiated in the pillahuanaliztli of four years previously had in the interim been actively seeking godparents for their children.[66] With gifts and polite approaches
they had attempted to induce high-ranking men and women not
related to them to accept such responsibilities. Now, on a certain
midnight during the Izcalli, the accepting godparents went to the
homes of their new charges, awakened the children and took them off
on their backs to a special priestly dwelling where they had their ears
pierced with pointed bones. The very young were then passed
through the fire by priests, thus slightly singeing them in a true baptism of flame—in which fashion the little ones were thought of as
taken under the Old God's protection and inducted into the tribe.

The godparents then returned the children to their homes where
yellow feathers were pasted on their heads to visually announce their
affiliation to the fire god. All that night the parents and godparents
sat up in vigil. This ended at the first sign of light in the east when
the banqueting promptly began. The very young children and infants
were carried about the family courtyards on the backs of the godparents while the old men of the family sang for them. Children too
large for this were led about by the hand and made to hop and dance
with the adults. When evening came, the celebration was moved to
more public areas outside.

Octli was now introduced and a bacchanal ensued. Everyone was
expected to drink and become drunk. Even the babes in arms and
those just baptized were given sops soaked in octli; the slightly older
children became drunk along with the adults.

> With ruddy faces, crying out, short of breath, with glazed eyes, all
> mingled with one another; there were disputes; all circled and milled
> about. Becoming more intense, all crowded and pressed together, el-
> bowing each other. All took one another by the hands; they were be-
> mused.[67]

So ended the Izcalli festival and with it the last (or perhaps the
first) month of the year.

The other nineteen cults of the Aztec year in some ways were far
more bizarre than this one. But this one was central; in their mythical
thinking the Aztecs could go no further back in time than the fire
god. It is true that food and rule, war and weather were constants in

their lives and received appropriate representation in cult, but in those cases the patron gods were capricious at best in answering the human need. The fire god, however, came always when he was called. Warmth and comfort he never failed to extend. He was stern and could be cruel, but he was never tyrannical. Though he was an ultimate lord, he was infinitely divisible. He was equally present in his eternal fire in the city's center, in the commoner's hut, and in the palace. For all beings he stood in loco parentis, so it is no wonder that the festival which celebrated the punctation of time—the simultaneous eclipse and birth of the year—should be a fire festival.

All of the rites of the Izcalli festival were consistently locked into a pattern. The month was a carefully constructed whole. It was made up of the renewal of fire, offerings by individuals as well as by the state, the display of the perquisites of rule, and finally the reconsolidation of society in an initiation rite and festival of goodwill.

THE ATAMALCUALIZTLI FESTIVAL

The rationale behind the Atamalcualiztli festival[68] assigned to the staple maize a psychic life of eight years.[69] During these eight years the corn had been decapitated, buffeted, ground between stones, pricked with salt, and burned with chili until—overwhelmed by such insults—it died. The need to apologize to the corn, to cajole it, and to rejuvenate it was of prime importance for all men, whether nobles, priests, or commoners. The festival drew on one of the central passages in Aztec mythology: the descent of one of the Aztec "mothers" (Xochiquetzal) into the earth, and the birth there of her son, the next year's corn (Cinteotl).

We are fortunate in having the words of the hymn that was sung at that time as an accompaniment to the ritual action.[70] The rites had begun with the fasting of all the people for eight days beginning, where possible, with the day Seven Reed (which was the birth date of Quetzalcoatl in Cholula) and ending on the date One Flower, the birth date of Cinteotl, the maize god.[71] The dates are significant for they compress between them the divine action that was the matter of the ritual.

From the hymn we can gather that the following was mimed or somehow symbolized during the eight holy days. Tonan, the goddess of fecundity (who is specified to be Xochiquetzal), appears as the hymn begins. The time is said to be before dawn, which is another way of designating the scene of action as the underworld. Mention is made of the "flowering tree" in Tamoanchan that the goddess desecrated, thus giving rise to her expulsion into the underworld. There can be no doubt that the whole scenario is placed in the underworld for it is identified as the place where "the old Xolotl" is playing his crucial game of *tlachtli* in the enchanted ball court. In myth Xolotl is the psychopomp, the evening star, and the eternal enemy, whereas his adversary in the ball game is the stripling sun Piltzintli (equally the young corn) who is valiantly struggling to be born. Victory in the game will allow him to rise over the land, initiating both the new day and the new corn.

Now appears Quetzalcoatl, the sinister lord of Cholula. He is seen here as an underworld figure, a form of Xolotl—in fact his brother—who has seized the goddess, thrown her over his back, and has then raced down into the underearth with her. The hymn does not tell us that he copulates with Xochiquetzal in the darkness, but he must be understood to have impregnated her, for she subsequently bears her son on the day One Flower, thereby giving him his name.[72] This is of course Cinteotl, the god of corn.

It is obvious that the myth was duplicated, for the maize, in the form of the young sun, either reappears as a result of the winning of a ball game, or he is produced by an underworld hierogamy. Quetzalcoatl (and/or his twin Xolotl) acts as the enemy aggressor in both versions. The teleology suggested in both versions is the same—the renewal of the young hero who is either the rising sun or the first shoot of corn appearing above the ground.

Although the hymn is indispensable to a study of the Atamalcualiztli festival, there also exists a pictorial source giving us details of the ritual seemingly at variance with the preceding.[73] In this post-Conquest representation we see the temple of Tlaloc (the Epcoatl) being circled by a procession of all the gods and by people who are dressed as birds.[74] Tlaloc's temple is glossed as a mountain (shown right beside it). In front of this central shrine is a pool or receptacle of water filled with snakes and aquatic animals. Men whom we know to be from Mazatlan are seen capering around the water, each chewing a snake and each intent on consuming it alive. This rain dance needs no elaboration.

The picture further spells out the Aztec plea for agricultural abundance in the persons of three women and a priest who are offering bowls of food, undoubtedly cornbread (tamales). Again, the fact that this is the month of Tepeilhuitl is certified by the presence of several squat figures of mountains, moulded out of a thick corn mush, effigies that were diagnostic for that month. And finally Xochiquetzal—for this is her month that is being celebrated—is shown out in front of the pyramid temple, depicted as beautifully dressed and weaving her lovely textiles on a back-strap loom under the blossoming tree of Tamoanchan. Here she is the armorial figure, absolutely central; all the other gods, each in their own regalia, are shown processing around the whole temple area with her alone seated. Paradise is depicted as here and now, and once again sin is absent from the world. The thronging deities round about Xochiquetzal proclaim a cosmic state of innocence re-achieved.

What is not touched upon in the picture is the theme of the hymn, namely the rape of the goddess into the underworld and her delivery there of her son Cinteotl. We have her here rather as the "great mother" immaculate and untouched by darkness.

Other written sources help us to unravel the meaning of this cult that the Aztecs celebrated every eighth coming of the month of Tepeilhuitl.[75] We are told that this synod of all the gods every eight years occurred in an atmosphere of prophecy. This part of the festival was known as *ixnextihua* ("good fortune is sought"), for it was hoped that each one of the gods would offer his or her individual blessing to the world in the coming eight years. During the eight days of fasting, which included two days of dancing, the folk ceremonially cleansed themselves, pleaded with the gods, and watched them attentively.

Naturally a saturnalia followed the seven days during which time the people had eaten only tasteless bread cakes. The license that then reigned was a final manifestation of popular confidence in the gods before the onset of the cold season. Yet it could not be forgotten that the dead season was at hand. Although it was true that Cinteotl had been persuaded into renewed life, the Atamalcualiztli was still in the last analysis a farewell to flowers and the end of the growing season. The "mother" who was being honored was about to sink underground as the myth foretold. Her son lived again only as the seed corn kept against the next sowing. She herself returned to darkness.

The Atamalcualiztli festival was placed in the month of Tepeil-huitl because of the compatibility of the two deities honored in its rituals—Tlaloc and Xochiquetzal. This compatibility becomes clear when we remember that Tlaloc, who brings the rain, is in reality a special god of the earth, namely the earth congealed into mountains from whose peaks streamed forth the storms. In inclusive terms the earth was more accurately the "mother," Xochiquetzal, matchless in her grandeur. The hymn does not even mention Tlaloc.

We can perhaps understand why this festival did not belong wholly either in the almanac or in the calendar. It was ambiguous, poised between the whimsies of nature (Tlaloc), and its eternal verities (Xochiquetzal).

THE XIUHTLALPILLI FESTIVAL

The Izcalli festival talked about men and women, the Atamal-cualiztli talked about corn, and the Xiuhtlalpilli talked about time in all of its cosmic implications. This latter festival was the supreme cultic example of the fire religion and was held every fifty-second year. Basically it was a lustral celebration. In it the priests surpassed themselves, creating a ritual of such power and drama as to be classed as spectacular.

The reason for the ritual in the first place was to mark the re-newal of time as it moved along within the fifth or present aeon. If four was the basic bundle of years, fifty-two was the ultimate and finally completed bundle, itself composed of four bundles (*tlalpillis*) or sets of thirteen. Both four and thirteen were foundation numbers of sacred significance. Time and our world, according to Aztec thought, would come to an end only at the completion of a fifty-two-year bundle (*xiuhtlalpilli*), or lustrum. Such a dire possibility obvi-ously called for the shielding intervention of cult. And the cult action that had evolved over the years to delay that annihilation was the re-enactment of the myth of the world's beginnings. This forms the skeleton of the festival.

Briefly the myth ran as follows.[76] All was nothingness and dark-ness after the collapse at the end of the fourth aeon, at which time the gods decided upon a universal recreation. Finding that they could not manage it in a collegial fashion, they called for a volunteer from their ranks to sacrifice himself. One of the lesser gods, a being racked with various blemishes and deformities, responded and heroically cast himself into a great fire that was burning in the darkness. His diseased body was consumed, purified, and then rejuvenated to become a new sun, the present and last one in a series of five. But this sun refused to rise above the horizon to bring forth the light unless the entire assembly of gods was sacrificed to him, their hearts and blood to become his food and drink. Under the presidency of the priest-god Quetzalcoatl (and/or his twin the monster-god Xolotl), this was done, and the Fifth Sun rose. Some of the elements of this myth are to be found also in the festivals of the Flaying of Men and the Panquetzaliztli, but the essential ones are developed most dramatically here. When in 1507 it was adjudged time to perform the great lustral renovation, the Mexican authorities decided to insert the cult into the month of Panquetzaliztli inasmuch as that month also had behind it a version of the origination myth and was therefore an appropriate time.[77]

On a hill called *Huixachtlan* just outside of Culhuacan, which was a city on the south shores of the lake and successor to the prestige of Tula, there stood a temple of the dawn.[78] The priests explained that at the beginning of time the sacred fire sticks (*mamalhuaztli*) had fallen down from the sky and had come to rest on an eminence sacred to Mixcoatl. This hill was almost surely Huixachtlan. From those fire sticks the first fire of the Fifth Sun was evoked. Mythology goes on to gloss this as the drilling of the first fire by the god Mixcoatl. This famous shrine was resurfaced and expanded for the 1507 ceremony by Moteuczoma II.[79] Nothing of it remains today.

Four days before the end of the lustrum all fires in the Basin of Mexico were extinguished, and for that period people could eat only uncooked food. Lacking fire, those days were therefore unholy, and in every sense they were similar to the nemontemi. Kitchen and field utensils were discarded, the domestic hearth in every home was broken up, while idols, the lares and penates, were thrown into rivers and other waters—all this leaving an awesome void in the spiritual lives of the people. It was a frightening and foreboding time.

Just after sunset on the last night the high priests of all the gods, dressed in their most elaborate attire, marched in a single file out of Tenochtitlan and down the southern causeway. At their head moved the high priest of Quetzalcoatl, who was the inventor and patron of the tonalpohualli and the first priest. In the procession were additionally the four avatars of the Turquoise Lord, one for each of the directions. This concourse of gods arrived at the hilltop shrine just before midnight.

Some time before, Moteuczoma II had given orders to the priesthood to screen all the captives taken in past wars and to set aside any in whose name the word *xihuitl* (year) occurred, as he considered this would be a fortunate sign. Such a captive was indeed found, and it was he who now lay stretched out and pinned down in front of the many gods. Observations were taken of the skies and the constellation of the Pleiades was breathlessly followed as it rose toward the zenith. If it crossed that line, the rebirth of time had been determined, and the sun would rise again. In Mesoamerican star lore the Pleiades played a crucial role that is just now coming into focus.[80] Whereas the Greeks saw them as the seven daughters of Atlas, the Mesoamericans undoubtedly saw them as fire in the sky—the stellar cluster to the naked eye appearing to be a small wad of glowing tinder with its embedded sparks, ready to burst into flame. Thus, on this night of nights, when all else hung in the balance, the slow climb of the constellation into the sky was followed with apprehension. And when it had at last reached its highest station and prepared to cross the zenith, that would be the signal that the cosmic fire had been rekindled and that the greatest fire of all, the sun, would soon emerge.

So in the dim starlight a priest knelt down and drilled fire from a mamalhuaztli placed on the victim's breast. That was the moment of suspense. When the tiny spark that the priest had elicited had been fanned into flame, it was carefully transferred to a pile of sacred wood gathered for the occasion and before long a great blaze sprang heavenward. The victim was now sacrificed; his heart was torn out, offered to the sun in the underworld, and then thrown into the fire. Contrary then to the usual procedures of sacrifice, but conforming strictly to the myth of Nanahuatl, the corpse was cast into the flames to be there incinerated.[81] At dawn he would reappear on the eastern horizon watched by all the gods assembled. Another fifty-two years had been granted to mankind! An idol of this most important victim, who was an ixiptla of the god Nanahuatl, would be molded of amaranth dough and offered in small crumbs to the people of the Basin, so that they might partake in person of the great event.

Throughout the great Basin of Mexico, which was filled with Aztec cities and adjoining communities, people had held vigil during the night, gazing in the direction of Culhuacan. When the first pinprick of light appeared, these people exploded in joy for they were assured of the renovation of time and of their own continuation. All individuals drew blood from their ears and flicked it toward the distant diamond of light to help it grow. This was the *xiuhtzitzquilo* ("the years are taken up again").

Each city in the Basin and even some from beyond the mountains had sent their swiftest runners to take advantage of the event.[82] The runner from Mexico-Tenochtitlan carried off the first flaring pine torch to touch to the waiting wood pile in that city's hearth. The braziers of Huitzilopochtli and Tlaloc on the central temple platform were the first to be lit from this brand that was called the *tlepilli* ("the son of the fire"). From here it was distributed downward in an order of preference as day was breaking, first to Huitzilopochtli's *calmecac*, then to the other temples and calmecacs, then to the various *telpochcalli*s, and finally to the individual householders who came to the local temples to carry away the burning brands. Food could now be prepared and the hardships of cold and darkness eased.

Had the effectiveness of this ceremony weakened, or had the priest not been able to drill fire at midnight, the sun would have never risen again, and demons would have swept down out of the black skies to devour all of mankind. Time as well as light would have been extinguished.

The ceremony continued on this first day of the new cycle with the sacrifice of four hundred victims who in their numbers commemorated the great victory of the sun over his stellar enemies, the four hundred Huitznahua.

When the calendrical year drew to its end, the fait accompli of the New Fire ceremony was sealed with a curious burial.[83] This came at the end of the Aztec year in the month patronized by the Earth Mother in her avatar as "Old Woman." In some one of the city temples (probably the fire god's shrine) all during the lustrum priests had kept careful count of each year's passing by putting aside in a special depository a length of reed or cane—one for each year. It was thus for them a simple matter to foretell the approach of the end of a fifty-two-year period. At the moment when a fifty-third cane might have been added to the number, all fifty-two were tied in a bundle and ritually entombed in a special square-sided altar marked with skull and crossbones. On at least one occasion that we know of, the reed bundle was carved in stone, dated Two Reed, and interred. The sun (in this case his avatar Huitzilopochtli) had been born and had died in the same named year, namely Two Reed. His life was thus the full measure of a lustrum of fifty-two years. If thought of in this way the sun was a manifestation of fire as the Lord of Years.

2

Definitions and Reduction
of the Divine

I have said that the Aztecs suffered from a cult mania. Evidence supporting this statement is everywhere, in the fantastic reduplication of their fasts, vigils, penances, food imperatives, and especially in the plethora of blood sacrifices and deity impersonations. An organized flow of religious acts and images guided the lives of all Aztecs. Wherever they looked in their culture, the Aztecs saw the vast bible of cult opened to them, in which they could discover all that might be known about the supernatural. But the public participation in this cult was only the surface manifestation of a deep and powerful religious flood. Individuals also could be caught in the currents of piety and swept along.[1] In the cult of Huitzilopochtli, for instance, individuals might feel obligated to perform certain onerous duties for the god in preparation for his annual feast.[2] Thus, for a year in advance of the Panquetzaliztli festival, such persons might even have finally contributed their entire wealth, leaving them at the end reduced to poverty—from which disaster there might be no remedy other than to flee from their homes or rush off to war to seek death. Individuals might also vow to offer a feast for a certain god and for two or more years work to acquire the wherewithal. If, as the time of the promised feast drew near, the individual had not acquired enough wealth to please the god, he might have to sell himself into slavery and with the proceeds complete the banqueting of the god before his own final ruin. Such examples of the power of Aztec cult are not unknown.

Some of this Aztec fascination with cult, however, can be seen as a craving for theater. Many of the monthly festivals were traditional masquerades; others were very complex histrionic passages. Wherever cult is found in the world, it always, to some extent, partakes of theater, but among the Aztecs we are aware of a heightening of dramatic effects. If one should wish to advance a reason for such intensity, one might perhaps find it in the Aztecs' sense of doom. A people whose manipulation of numbers produced a vision of the end of all things after five aeons, while specifying that it could come only at the interstitial point between two sets of fifty-two years—such a people lives cheek by jowl with many dark demons.

The Aztecs seem to have felt an almost neurotic need to perform as if they were on a stage, and this produced in their cults highly vivid effects. A theatrical and perverted sense of reality as experienced in cult competed on even terms among the Aztecs with the realities of their everyday living. Witness, for example, a typical midnight sacrifice. Here the stage (i.e., the pyramid top), high overhead, is set among the stars, and the actors are visible only in the flaring light of two immense braziers flanking them. What the spectator below can see is only a swift huddle of figures and the flash of a knife, and then the sudden appearance of a bleeding corpse tumbling and thudding down out of the darkness toward them. Grotesque as it may seem, this was a calculated art form, whose virtue it was to underline the awful meaning of that death.

One can carry on the metaphor and say that no society ever re-enacted "god time" as compulsively as did the Aztecs. Even in their more society-oriented rites, such as the baptism of a child, the consecration of a warrior or a hunter, the ritual taking of narcotics, or some guild celebration, a god was always on parade. In such situations the deity, in the person of his or her *ixiptla*, was slaughtered to enhance the dramatic effect. In other words, the locus of the staged event was projected back to the time of the gods, the "dreaming time," in which antique framework of reality all things were writ large. If to the Aztecs all the world was a stage whereon the actors were the gods and spirits, then they, the Aztecs, must have seen themselves as scene changers.

MASKS

To many preliterate peoples the world of appearances—mountains and grasslands, births and deaths, hunger and feasting—seems to fit like a mask over the armature of another world. This world within was the home of supernatural beings, gods, spirits, and forces, a swirling numinous mass that occasionally poured out of the world of

the surreal through vent holes, either with violence or with long sigh-
ings of doom, to face man with the true terms of his existence. So also
did it appear to the Aztecs.

Teotl is the Nahuatl word most commonly used to mean
"god."[3] It carried nuances of something rare, precious, and greatly to
be desired, or, contrarily, something extreme, outrageous, and therefore perilous. Not only were the common gods called teotl, but so
also were destiny signs, spirits of disease and deformity, and other beings approaching the demonic.[4] Teotl thus defined a very ambivalent
realm of the supernatural behind appearances. It was that world
which had to be reduced and then shaped into cultic patterns, images, and gestures so that men could converse with it. To thus harness
the spirits, the Aztecs selected two of the more common ways of reduction: masks and anthropomorphism. The two operated quite differently.

The use of masks is commonplace in cult the world over. In
Mesoamerica, masks have a long history and contributed greatly to
the development and proliferation of cults throughout the area. The
linguistic feature that the word for face in Nahuatl (*xayacatl*) is the
same as the word for mask, is also a worldwide occurrence, as witness
our own term "false face." The implication of this is always sinister,
for it involves the ambiguity of not knowing which of two items presented is the real—and therefore the dependable—one. To wear a
mask is to disguise the real you, but it does not hide the fact that
there is a disguise and therefore a deceit. This curious ambivalence of
screening the real while at the same time attesting to it by the artifice
of an unreal substitute has many uses in different cultures. Here in
Aztec life, where the mask was used at all, the inner reality had mi-
grated outward to attach itself to the mask. Thus, the god who dons
the mask is no longer the whole reality of a specific god but in a sense
has been vaporized into a mere carrier of that or other masks. As a
named god, he is sometimes reduced to the implications of the mask
alone and his powers have by that been straitly limited.

We may illustrate it in this fashion. An earth god, whom we call
Tlaloc, places on his face two round eye pieces or "goggles" and a
large mouth mask with fangs. These give him the power to hurl lightning, to withhold water stored in the mountains, or to scatter rain
over the land. Elements of this mask, however, may be appropriated

by other gods, and when they do so they assume all of the powers that reside in the mask itself. There thus exists a supernatural mask pool where fragments of abstract power are stored in the form of known masks and bits of masks.[5] Not every god can dip into this and seize any mask that suits his whim. There are limits to the plasticity of the masks. Nevertheless, although the number of gods does not vary, the number of supernaturals casting the thunderbolt and bringing rain will fluctuate as certain ones put on or slough off the Tlaloc mask. Thus, until the mask truly deifies him, the god is a numen, electric but still poorly defined.

This is one way of explaining a puzzling feature in Aztec culture whereby their gods have the property of flowing into other gods, seeming to take on their signs and personalities, only to flow back again. The concept of the mask pool describes the ways whereby the gods are related in Aztec religion. The fact that the whole mask or a part of that mask allows a specific power to be wielded is a statement of the fact that the numen wearing it has been successfully reduced and restricted to that meaning.

In the preceding paragraphs I have discussed the meaning of the mask in the structure of the Aztec pantheon, but I have not really described its use in Aztec cult. By the term "mask" I intend here to include all the elements involved in the practice of verisimilitude, face and body painting, customary dress, hair style, weapons, mace, and so forth. Customarily it was the god's high priest who wore or bore such items in the various ceremonies. Accoutered as the deity, he did not, however, become an alter ego of the god—as did the ixiptla —he remained in the eyes of his peers only a man wearing a mask. (This will be discussed at greater length in the succeeding section. Here I merely wish to point out that the cult practice of putting on the mask might or might not be followed by the wearer's death on the sacrificial block.) If the god's mask was given to the high priest then the mask was thought of as a sign of the priestly office—it did not automatically transform him into the god indicated (as for instance did the kachina masks of American Indians of the Southwest).[6] If, however, the mask were given to an ixiptla, a slave who had been consecrated and cleansed, or a captive taken in war, then the mask did indeed have that miraculous power. It was all that was needed to transform the human being into the deity. Certain confusing situations in cult arose because of this ambiguity. It often happened that an ixiptla brought to the block was sacrificed by the high priest in person—and both could wear the same mask!

THE IXIPTLA

The other method of god reduction, as stated, is anthropomorphism. Around the globe, in preliterate times and even today, mortals have clad themselves in the habiliments of the gods and have then been taken to be such. This is simply a roundabout way of saying that gods are portrayed as humans. The Aztec case is outstanding, however, because of the extremely graphic way in which this was done. They inserted into their rituals the ixiptla, a man or woman who was accepted as the true but residual person of the deity. The ixiptla is one of the most impressive cult inventions of all time.

The word *ixiptla* means "an image, a likeness," or sometimes a "stand-in" or "deputy."[7] To keep to a clear line in this argument, however, I am going to restrict the word to specify that person chosen to be a known god and to act out his role in cult. This person was always specially designated in terms of his provenience, being either purchased in the slave market or captured in war. He was never a priest, and his tenure of office always ended with a sacrificial death. The life of a priest was expected to go on until his own natural demise. The priest was a servant of the god, but the ixiptla was the god himself.

The ixiptla was a man, woman, or child who was ritually cleansed and then, for a stated period, was dressed in the regalia of the deity and forced to move about or otherwise appear among the people, playing the role of the deity and receiving worship. On any understanding, such an institution would have brought "god time" well into the ambient of "human time." We know that here the fusing of god time and human time automatically created a sacred society where a mortal for a period could become the god, and where the role he played was circumscribed only by his death. Aztec society never ceased to be a world where men were butlers and hostelers, helots and clients, and finally food for the gods—all that was part of the rationale behind the ixiptla. The ixiptla was indeed a vicar of the god and therefore divine, but nevertheless at the same time he was also merely one of the god's meals. The effect may have been to reinvigorate the deity, but the reinvigoration was only temporary, and had to be repeated, that is, it took place in "human time." This two-edged concept remained undeveloped in the Aztec mind for as long as their society lasted. The ritual role of the ixiptla continued to be ambivalent. The fusion of god time and human time was always incomplete.

The ixiptla differed from carved or otherwise contrived idols in the sense that he was an even more reduced form of the god. He was the god as acculturated and brought down from the levels of the "wholly other" to a level that was intelligible. He enjoyed movement and participated in mythology, the essence of which is always narrative. Idols could not do that. The insertion of ixiptlas into cult was, in short, a response to an extreme need to grasp the divine by detailed description and reiteration and thus to reduce it to a quality acceptable to all.

But the ixiptla was the divine seen as a god, not as a demon. Aztec cult generally kept the two separated. The demonic could not be reduced—at least not in the same way—because it was necessarily conceived of as the totally venomous, the ultimate in the anarchic. For instance, the demonic Tzitzimitl, death oriented and carnivorous, a being that lived in the night sky and relished catastrophe, did not have and indeed could not have an ixiptla—for one thing, cult did not provide much in the way of a pedestal for the Tzitzimitl to stand on. A demon, however much dreaded, could not ordinarily be worshipped as a god, for a demon could not be propitiated.[8] An Aztec god could relent and show at least a primitive kind of mercy, a change of mind or purpose. A demon was adamantine and could not be swayed. Every god had some connection with man's social order—at least a minimal connection—but demons owned no law, and though they were undoubtedly supernaturals they ruled no parts of nature. Therefore, they had no cults important enough to insert into a calendar based on nature. They were, however, found in the almanac.

The restriction of the use of ixiptlas to the cults of the gods therefore tells us much about the way the gods were viewed. The ixiptla was an ordering device, that is to say his presence in a god's festival or in the time period leading up to it enabled worshippers to focus their religious energies. At the same time the ixiptla radically reduced the opportunities for ecstatic behavior. The reduction of godhead to a clear visual packet in general satisfied the curiosity and expectations of the Aztec worshipper. Mysticism and possession as religious modes of action were thereby precluded. The priests must have realized that the inclusion of an ixiptla in cult lessened for them their own responsibility, and averted for them the danger of having to stand *in loco dei*. And the ixiptla was of course always destroyed at the culmination of his festival. He was thus seen as a divine figure who had to be consummated so that the god in his essence could remain intact.

We have seen that almost all the gods could have ixiptlas.[9] In fact, we have reason to believe that all the gods in the Aztec pantheon were killed in the person of their ixiptlas at least once in every calendar year. Even Mictlanteuctli, Lord of the Land of the Dead, could suffer sacrificial death in the person of his ixiptla.[10] To us, this last seems irrational—we would assume that before all others the god of the dead was immune to death and could not be touched by it. A few gods, however, who existed only in myth or popular wisdom—and not in cult—had no ixiptlas. They were the high gods like Tonacateuctli and his consort, deities who over the long centuries had been pushed back into offices of misty authority, or gods like Tloque Nahuaque who were more on the order of philosophical abstractions.[11]

On a cursory count I have been able to list fifty-seven differently named gods whose ixiptlas were annually sacrificed in Tenochtitlan. There were undoubtedly more. This rough muster includes all of the major gods, a few of their avatars, and some gods barely known in the sources. My count of fifty-seven does not include deities who died in groups of ixiptlas, like the Cihuateteo, the Centzonhuitznahua, the four fire gods (directionally colored), children sacrificed as Tlaloque in the early part of the agricultural year, or the gatherings, in pantheonic assembly, of all the gods together—it would be impossible to estimate the numbers in those inclusive groups. Most of the fifty-seven named gods who could appear as ixiptlas played out their cultic roles for anywhere from twenty to forty days; a few had more extended roles, whereas three of them (the ixiptlas of Titlacahuan, Huitzilopochtli, and Nappateuctli) served a whole calendar year before they were destroyed.[12]

So throughout the year there passed before Aztec eyes a ceaseless procession of gods portrayed as humans, each set off by his special regalia and all marked by the bloody end that was their destiny. Few peoples in human history can have so crowded the divine canvas and so orchestrated its themes into one vast and consistent drama—the inversion of life and death.

TOXCATL AND THE IXIPTLA OF TEZCATLIPOCA

As examples of ixiptlas, I shall outline the roles of four of them as they appear in cult, those of Titlacahuan, of Xilonen, of Toci, and finally of the children sacrificed in the cult of Tlaloc. As parts of cults they will be mentioned in appendix A. Here I want to separate them out for purposes of analysis. The theatrical aura surrounding each will be self-evident.

Inasmuch as Tezcatlipoca was the leading god of the Aztec pantheon, his ixiptla was uniquely conceived. Specifically this ixiptla played the role of that avatar of Tezcatlipoca known as *Titlacahuan*, "He Whose Slaves We Are."[13] He died on the last day of the month of Toxcatl, which was the tenth day of his festival, and at that same time another candidate for the divine office was selected so that there should be no single moment out of the entire calendar year when the god did not physically walk among his people.[14] This constant and suffocating presence spoke much about the Aztecs' appreciation of the scope of the divine.

The ixiptla was chosen to be as nearly without blemish as possible[15]—for the god himself was known to be perfect in youth and vigor. Whenever possible, he was selected from among war captives from Tlaxcala or Huexotzinco, Aztec cities whose warriors were acknowledged to be the bravest of the brave.[16] At the beginning of his annual tenure, he was adorned as the god and assigned a retinue of eight young male companions as well as four veteran warriors who acted as guards; they attended him day and night both to amuse him and to prevent his escape.[17]

Came the month of his celebration and the public veneration accorded to him rose to peaks unusual even for the Aztecs. The reason for this fervor was that, more than any other god, Tezcatlipoca could affect the individual directly. For that month only, the curtain closing the entrance of the god's shrine was drawn aside so that all could behold him. And to this spot came also all the greater and lesser nobles to do obeisance, not to the black obsidian statue of the god, but to the ixiptla himself. And when he walked abroad, they, on occasion, accompanied him.

He seems to have gone about through the city streets only from midnight to dawn, for the dead of night was his preferred environment.[18] Whenever he emerged from his quarters on the summit of the pyramid surrounded by his retinue, he first saluted each of the four directions with shrillings on his flute—this to notify the inhabitants of all parts of the world that he, their master and the arbiter of their fates, was coming among them. On his ankles and arms he wore bells that jangled and flickered in the torchlight. Wherever the thin whistling of his flute and the rattle of his dancing was heard, women with small children come to their doors holding out their little ones and begging health and good fortune for them. As for their warrior husbands, they were more likely to request courage in battle or many captives. To the contrary, sinners and criminals everywhere huddled down in anguish at the flute's cry, for it told them they had been discovered in their most secret parts. As dawn came, the young ixiptla was escorted back to the temple and disappeared within.

As his month Toxcatl began, he was given four public women each one of whom stood for a goddess, prominent among whom was Xochiquetzal, the goddess of love.[19] With these he could now perform the sexual exercises for which Tezcatlipoca was renowned. Then, five days before the ixiptla was to meet his end, the ruler of Tenochtitlan ceremoniously acknowledged the god's sovereignty by divesting himself of his insignia of rule and turning it over to him. After that the ruler retired incommunicado within his palace, thus delivering the city over to its legitimate lord Tezcatlipoca. During these last days the ixiptla, accompanied by his women, danced and sang and was banqueted at various places in the city.

On the last day of the festival custom was breached, for on that day *only* the ixiptla himself was sacrificed. At the festivals of other gods it was usual to perform multiple sacrifices, for the greater the number of hearts offered, the greater the merit. The Toxcatl reversed this by putting the ixiptla in center stage—no others were killed that day.[20] Thus was the god's singularity emphasized. In a splendid finale, the ixiptla, accompanied by his four wives, was then taken in a state canoe from Tenochtitlan to the south shore of Lake Tezcoco. Once they were all disembarked, his wives left him and he moved on, surrounded by escorts, priests, and other participants, to a very ancient shrine of his at a place called Tlapitzahuayan. Here he slowly ascended the fronting staircase while ostentatiously breaking the flutes upon which he had played during the year. On reaching the summit he was swiftly dispatched and his opened body—again contrary to custom—was not tumbled down the steps but was instead reverently carried. At the bottom the body was decapitated and dismembered, and that night his flesh was served up in a solemn collation to all the great lords of Mexico. On this occasion the newly chosen ixiptla of Titlacahuan also partook of the flesh, thus highlighting the uninterrupted presence of the god. During the year the ixiptla's skull adorned a special pole just outside his temple.[21]

Every fourth year the Toxcatl was expanded to mark the god's power to cancel the effects of crime, treachery, or neglect of the gods. In this celebration, the Toxcatl became a plenary remission of sins. To celebrate the divine clemency, many others died along with the ixiptla to provide him with cannibal meals in the world beyond.[22]

I have described the preceding in some detail so as to bring out its remarkable sense of playacting. The whole month—indeed the whole year—was designed to permit the intermingling of a varied dramatis personae, gods, votaries, ruler, nobles, and even sinners. The subject matter of the drama was that of place holding and the contingent nature of office. Only the god is forever, and only he legitimately rules. The Mexican *tlatoani* sits vicariously on the god's royal mat, but he must humbly divest himself of the rule during the last five days of the festival in recognition of Tezcatlipoca's superior claim. Not only are the god's prerogatives thus depicted, but his career from virginal youth to perfect adult and warrior is displayed. And beyond all this there is added to the drama, on every fourth replay, the god's exercise of full glory, the power to erase sin and offer, if not his pardon, at least his forgetfulness. When seen in this theatrical context the ixiptla's death becomes a purely divine consummation, a true deus ex machina, for though he dies on the sacrificial block, he does not die but lives on in the person of the new ixiptla. The man dies; the god lives. An authentic miracle play has been enacted, presenting the ways of one of the Aztec gods to men.

IXIPTLAS OF THE GREAT MOTHER

Equally striking was the Aztec use of the office of the ixiptla in the great harvest festival of Ochpaniztli that fell roughly in our month of September. In this month, not one but four ixiptlas of the

Great Mother were in evidence, each representing her in one of her significant aspects.[23] These four faces of the Magna Mater were Cihuateotl ("*the* Goddess"), Atlantonan ("Our Mother of Atlan"), Chicomecoatl ("Seven Snake"), and Toci ("Grandmother"). The first was the latrian form of that bevy of sinister female spirits called the "goddesses" (*Cihuateteo*). The second was the Magna Mater as she patronized certain diseases and maimings and who was additionally connected with water. The third was the Aztec Ceres, the provider of fruits and grains from the earth, particularly maize. The last was a grandly inclusive goddess, the mother of the gods, a war goddess, a corn goddess, maker of earthquakes, and patroness of sweatbaths and curing. What distinguished Toci was her derivation from the coastal area of the Gulf of Mexico (in particular that part inhabited by the Huaxtecs), though she came to the Mexicans via Culhuacan. Like Cybele in Rome, she was an import.

Four aspects of the Great Mother thus dominated the Ochpaniztli festival through her ixiptlas, making the month a concentrated statement of the deity's irritability as well as her bounty. No male god, displayed in four separate persons, dominated any of the eighteen months in such a fashion. Whereas the ixiptla of Titlacahuan expressed the sovereignty of Tezcatlipoca, it was a simple emphasis made evident by isolating a single ixiptla for the whole year. In the Ochpaniztli rites the Magna Mater could not be condensed in that way—the tale of her attributes was too long.

The rites of Ochpaniztli were arranged so that on three consecutive days, the fourteenth, fifteenth, and sixteenth of September, the ixiptlas of the last three deities mentioned before, and in that order, were sacrificed. The last two were the important ones, and each brought to its culmination a cult that had been carried on over several consecutive days. Thus, for part of the time, the two ixiptlas, a girl in the case of Chicomecoatl and an older woman in the case of Toci, were to be seen wandering about the city simultaneously, without however interfering with each other. Their respective activities can now be described. At what point in the ceremonies the ixiptla of Cihuateotl was sacrificed is not known.

A young slave girl, a virgin, was purchased to represent Chicomecoatl, whereas Toci was represented by a matron of forty years or over (the age differential speaks for itself). Both had to be ritually washed before they could legitimately be given their goddess's name and invested with her regalia.

For Chicomecoatl, a seven-day period of rigorous public fasting and penance preceded her sacrifice.[24] During this time the young ixiptla was forced to go from one nobleman's residence to another's, dancing and singing, and being housed at night in the goddess's temple. Finally, on the terminal night a litter piled with fruits, chili peppers, squashes, and ears of corn was brought to the temple and set down in front of her. A priest struck off a part of her unbound hair and also the lovely green quetzal feather that she wore in her headband—this to symbolize the reaping of the ears of corn—and he offered them to the goddess's statue. The ixiptla was then helped into the litter and placed in a standing position, her wrists being tied to two upright bars on either side of the litter to prevent her from pitching off.

The litter, surrounded by men carrying torches, then processed slowly about the ceremonial area. As dawn was appearing she was taken to the temple of Huitzilopochtli where she was forced to ascend the stairs and enter the holy of holies. Here she remained briefly incommunicado, the intent no doubt being to suggest a sacred coupling. With the full advent of daylight she was returned to her own temple, where there had been heaped up in the cella a mound of all the fruits, gourds, and grains grown by the Aztecs. She was made to stand on this extravaganza spilling over from Chicomecoatl's cornucopia while one by one the nobles came in to do her obeisance and to offer to her the scabs from ears and legs lacerated in her honor. With this the public fasting ended, and banquets could now begin in a splendid harvest home celebrated all over the city. After a final censing, the ixiptla was decapitated on top of the pile of fruits, her blood being spattered about the inner room and over the harvest. She was then flayed, and a priest wearing the skin presented himself to the public and led the dance that ensued. As a final symbol, the girl was eaten.

In the Aztec myth, the sacred mating, which we have guessed at before as being reenacted in this cult, ended in the birth of a son (Cinteotl) who was the spirit of maize; the father was the sun in his avatar here as Huitzilopochtli. This affiliation was mimed in a curious subsidiary ritual. Part of the thigh of the former ixiptla's skin was separately removed, holes were cut in it, and it was worn as a mask by a priest who played the part of "Frost," the enemy and alter ego of Cinteotl. This derivative but reversed ixiptla, now accompanied by a warrior escort, left at great speed, canoeing and running, for the heights of Mount Iztaccihuatl on the east side of the Basin. Along those heights ran the boundary that separated the Basin Aztecs from their inveterate enemies beyond—the Aztecs of Tlaxcala and Huexotzinco. At a designated place, the Cinteotl group attempted to place the mask on a wooden frame prepared in advance for it—thus was Frost escorted to the land of the enemy and left there to perpetrate his evils on them. The antagonists might be waiting, however, to prevent the contamination, and the escorting warriors were sometimes killed in the skirmish that ensued.

While the ixiptla of Chicomecoatl was performing her festive and tragic role, the other, who represented Toci, was also playing out her part, oftentimes in the same temple environs.[25] She had been chosen, washed, and named forty days before her festival, though for the first twenty of these she was kept in a cage. When she was finally revealed to the public in all her regalia, her activities could then properly begin. Like the other she, too, was prodded to dance and sing, simulating joy in all possible ways. Seven days before her death the rites became much more specific. The older midwives and female curers in the city were now enlisted as her escort, constantly surounding her and performing mock battles for her amusement. Any signs on her part of despair or melancholy were thought to be unfavorable omens and were countered where possible by more merriment. Most of her time was taken up in woman's work; she was forced to wash, card, and spin cotton and with the thread weave some rudimentary woman's apparel. Finally, in the marketplace she squatted down on the ground and pretended to be engaged in vending the items to passersby.

The night preceding her death the midwives dressed her with care, all the while assuring her that she was being prepared for sexual relations with the ruler, an inestimable honor. Then, in the blackness just preceding dawn and in absolute silence, she was escorted from her temple at Atempan to Huitzilopochtli's shrine. Here, at the first light she was seized, hoisted face up on the back of one of the stronger priests, and there had her throat cut, her blood completely drenching the carrier. She was then decapitated and flayed with great speed and the still-dripping skin donned by the aforesaid priest. As a derived emanation of the goddess Toci, he was now joined by an escort of priests waving bloody brooms and representing Huaxtec Indians, a people of the Gulf Coast who were probably her first devotees. Standing at the top of the temple steps the skin wearer now seized the sacrificial knife and proceeded to dispatch four victims by tearing out their hearts. The skin wearer lastly put himself at the head of a retinue and charged into a party of nobles who had been attending the rites equipped with shields and weapons. A mock fight ensued with the nobles fleeing in the end, after having first spit at the skin wearer while pelting him with flowers. That ended the warlike part of the cult, and the nobles dispersed.

Surrounded by priests and by his (her) Huaxtecs, the skin wearer at the last went to Tocititlan, an elevated timber scaffold on the lake's edge on the south side of the city. At the very top was a roofed platform and seated therein was a straw statue of the goddess. Here the rites terminated. A sacrificial victim was forced to climb the dizzying height up to the platform, and on reaching the top was received with a blow on the head that toppled him off into space. The blood of this broken victim was collected below in a bowl and offered to the skin wearer who, dipping his hand in the still hot liquid, greedily sucked it from his fingers with loud croaks and groans that were supposed to imitate the sounds of an earthquake, the ultimate manifestation of the Magna Mater. The cult ended with the skin wearer laboriously ascending the trellis logs and placing his skin on the straw image of Toci at the top. As he and his escort descended, they removed all the crosspieces of the shrine to prevent any further ascents for the coming year.

THE CHILD IXIPTLA

In the cult of Tlaloc, we have a different and very ancient type of ixiptla. These were children aged approximately three to seven years.[26] They first appear during the sixteenth month and continue through the first four months of the new year. The seven consecutive months indicated previously were all in one way or another concerned with the rain god Tlaloc and two other associated dieties, Chalchiuhtlicue, goddess of running and standing waters, and Quetzalcoatl in his aspect as god of the wind that brought the storm clouds.

The juvenile ixiptlas were understood to be Tlaloque, who were dwarflike replicas of the rain god Tlaloc, resident in mountains and springs. Tlaloc himself was the conceptualization of the storm king as unitary, namely a single Jovian presence. As the personification of a series of localities connected with rain, lakes, springs, mountains, and clouds, however, he fragmented into a thousand different Tlaloque, each named for a given peak or body of water. The Tlaloque were thus localizations of the fructifying power of water, and their ixiptlas were generally not adults but small children. There were probably several reasons for this unique compulsion to incunabula in the cult of Tlaloc; the most obvious one is the similarity between the as-yet unformed human person and the sprouting corn. The juvenile ixiptlas, once sacrificed, were presumed to enter the mountain whose name they bore and to dwell there in an angelic existence as one of the *teteopohualtin* ("those accounted gods").[27]

Children destined to become ixiptlas were impounded in various of the *calpulli*, or wards, of the city. During unusual or protracted periods of drought, the pool of potential victims would naturally be depleted, and extraordinary efforts would be made to secure more children. They came from three sources. Most commonly they were from slave mothers and were purchased in the markets,[28] though they could also come from free parents who sold them to the priests or to the calpulli as an act of merit. In certain dire situations when starvation had become widespread and the very existence of the state was threatened, the ixiptlas would come from highly placed or noble families.[29] The preferred ixiptla was always a child without obvious blemish, with a dark complexion, a double cowlick and, where it could be known, a fortunate birth date.[30]

For the ceremonies, sprigs of green quetzal feathers were stuck in the children's hair, fluted paper wings attached to their backs, and liquid rubber spattered in their faces.[31] They were carried to their deaths on the backs of priests or conducted in canopied litters to the sound of flutes. Accompanying them was always a large crowd of people wailing and weeping—sympathetic imitations of the sounds and sights of the rain. In the festival of the fourth month the nobles themselves carried the litter that for that celebration contained a small boy. The cortège set out from Tezcoco before dawn, moving up the rough trails and through the forest to the great central shrine of Tlaloc near the summit of the mountain. The child was there sacrificed, and his blood used to anoint Tlaloc's idol. In the same ritual, children destined for other nearby peaks were sometimes walled up in caves under the crags and abandoned.[32] The lords then retraced their steps down the mountain so that they could be present at a closely associated ceremony in the lake. In this rite the victim was a little girl who as an ixiptla was a water spirit representing the goddess Chalchiuhtlicue.[33] With great solemnity she had been brought down to the landing on the east side of Tenochtitlan where numerous canoes were waiting to escort her to her place of death. When the flotilla had arrived at a shallow part of the lake known as *Pantitlan*, the child's throat was cut with a duck spear and her blood spattered into the lake. The rites culminated when her body was flung overboard with the lords casting additional treasured objects into the lake to accompany her.

This definition of the ixiptlas of Tlaloc as generally children did not militate, however, against the use of adults to play the role of ixiptlas in that cult. The two customs did not contradict each other, for in a sense they meant different things. The adult sacrifice was orthodox and could be employed in any ceremony wherein the state made offerings. The child sacrifice was a more compelling reference to a very ancient popular belief in little people, puckish spirits who frequented wild places, who were malicious or beneficent as the whim took them, and who were always connected with rain.[34]

QUESTIONS RAISED BY THE IXIPTLA

The preceding examples of incarnation in Aztec cult should suffice. Perhaps the best way to understand the role of the ixiptla is to compare it with the role of the idol, for both represented the god. The crucial thing about the ixiptla is that he dies. The statue is a receiver of services and worship; it is purely passive. The ixiptla is a donor; he lives and ultimately donates his life to the god. The idol can donate nothing, and cannot die.

It must have occurred to many scholars to ask, "Why kill the ixiptla?" After all, sacrifice and god impersonation are two different things, and the latter by no means implies or necessitates the former. If the ixiptla were indeed the true ego of the deity, then no insult, certainly no death, could be properly offered to him. On the other hand, if he were only a likeness or a simulation of the god then one can understand his final destruction. One must conclude that in this area the Aztecs were conscious of dealing with an ambivalent situation. They knew when they were in the presence of the "wholly other," and they knew that the only correct response to it was through a death—for men everywhere death always translates into "the other." With death as a way out of their cultic dilemma then, the Aztecs' next problem—how to embody that death—was easy of solution. A numen, a god, or a spirit, was almost always tied to one of the seasons (and therefore to the circling calendar), so the response to the divine presence had to be repeatable—wherefore the ixiptla who was annually killed.

The reasoning behind this pouring of divinity into human forms is still unclear. Is the thinking behind it that the god is killed as a sacrifice to himself, or the assumption that like demands like? This seems to me to be illogical. Or is it a case of pure theater where the need for supreme visual content equates with human sacrifice—the ultimate possible coup? I do not feel that it would serve any purpose to try to prove one of these against the other. In any confrontation with the surreal, men do not ratiocinate—they act. And the action by necessity has to be a theatrical invention of the highest intensity It cannot belong to the daily routine. Only in an arbitrary cultic act can the divine be adequately met and to some extent dealt with. Whereas the idol spoke mutely about the "otherness" of the god, the ixiptla hinted at the god's kinship with men. The two things that clearly distinguish men from the beasts are language and the drive toward play-acting. Cult is merely the earliest example of this latter in preliterate societies, and what we today call *theater* is simply a late distillation from that.

A final point arises in conjunction with our exploration of the reduction process used in Aztec cult, and this is the use of a threefold level in god representation. The god, of course, defines himself by simply *being* himself; men then utilize myth to speak about that essential godhead. But below this, other levels of description via cult are possible. The first level we have already considered, the lifeless idol—it exists in order that humans may know where a god is when they need to make their petitions. The statue is a locus, a "place where." Below it comes the ixiptla, whose comings and goings and dyings have just been considered. The ixiptla is the injection of the

god, as an actor, into cult. The lowest level of reduction is seen in the
skin wearer who removes the ambivalence surrounding the ixiptla and
defines the death that he had died as now translated into life. The
skin wearer does not die in cult; as the god he simply melts back into
cult.

When the deity is taken through the three steps I have isolated
here, it may be said that he has sufficiently accounted for himself to
the people. From the realm of the "other," via the religious cult, he
has emerged into man's daily life, and he has then returned to the
"other." Such a full cycle—of entry and return—could not be made
by man. Only the divine is capable of it. Aztec cult pointed to this
ability of the divine.

THE DOUGH IMAGE

Eating the god is also a common way by which men in all ages
have reduced the divine to their dimensions. The Christian communion meal is simply the best known of such rituals. God eating should
never be confused with the cannibal meal where the person devoured
was a man and not a god.

The Aztecs killed their gods more often and more systematically
than any other people known to history. Indeed, several gods might
die in a single Aztec ritual. It could almost be said that god killing
was the nub of Aztec cult. And eating the god afterward was a frequent consequence.

Among the Aztecs, eating the god (*teocualo*) was performed in
two ways, eating the statue or eating the god's ixiptla—both being
likenesses. The statue employed in the first method was, needless to
say, not the well-known wooden or stone idol, but a new one fashioned for the occasion out of a dough generally made from amaranth
seed flour that was then mixed with a syrup made from the juice of
the maguey.[35] In every case the dough was moulded into a thick paste
and then pressed over an armature of sticks. Cereals other than amaranth could be added. The goddess Chicomecoatl was represented in
her festival as a dough image made of corn meal and eaten at the ter-
mination of the ceremonies. An image of Huitzilopochtli was
moulded out of amaranth dough and kept a whole year, at the end of
which it was ritually seized by warriors, as if it had been an enemy
captured in war, and then was broken up to be partaken of by all the

males in the city.[36] Besides this, the bones of Huitzilopochtli (who in myth was described as a skeleton) were modeled in cakes and then eaten by all his people. The participants of this communion meal could be called *teopia* ("those who keep the god"), the reference being to the incorporation of the spirit of the city into its special guardians, the men of war.

The most interesting of the dough images, however, were undoubtedly the *xoxouhqui tepictoton* ("the small green ones"), another name for the Tlaloque as they were revered not by the state but by individuals.[37] Should a person have experienced some great danger in the highlands or have been afflicted by a disease sent by one of the evil airs off the mountains, in gratitude for salvation or cure he could identify the particular mountain or mountains responsible and then venerate them during the ceremonies of the thirteenth or the sixteenth month—such thank offerings are common all over the world.[38] Knowing the Tlalocs who were involved, the individual in his home would then pat up masses of amaranth dough into squat forms, inserting squash seeds or corn kernels to represent the eyes and teeth. This crude image might also recall a kinsman who had been struck by lightning or had died of dropsy or drowning—all of them endings that marked their victim as one beloved by the Tlaloque and claimed by them. If the spirit in question, however, had been one of the dragon winds that howled around the peaks of the mountain and brought fierce cold and wasting diseases, then the dough was moulded around a twisted root or bough and given a serpent's head. These images were the *ehecatotontin* ("the little winds") and could also be considered as Tlaloque.[39] For a whole night the family would stay up feasting and singing to amuse the mountain spirits in question, and then as dawn came they would slay them with a woman's weaving stick, first, however, extracting a small heart in imitation of a sacrificing priest's actions, and finally toward dawn, lopping off the image's head.

MOUNTAIN AND TREE IN CULT

Mountain worship and the closely associated worship of trees were pervasive in Aztec cult, far more so than has been generally believed. When the Aztecs thought about place, they tended to wrap it up in the context of "mountain." They did not, however, view a mountain as merely an item of the topography—we know this because in their language mountains were classified as animate entities. Their term for "town," for instance, was *atl tepetl*, which literally means "water and mountain." The two resources essential to a community were thereby specified to be potable water and the products of the mountain, namely timber, firewood, stone, game, maguey, fruits, and so forth. In other words, the Aztecs used the concept of "mountain," not as we use the terms "earth," "land," or "ground," for which they already had a designation (*tlalli*), but as referring to a whole environment, a homeland. Thus the word *tepetl* ("mountain") possessed a flavor of usufruct. One could be at home on the mountain because every mountain was named, individualized, and sometimes mythologized. Tlalli was too depersonalized, too huge a concept to connote a man's community. In brief, the Aztecs saw the mountain as a providential personality.

Mountain, tree, and water cults were all parts of the greater Tlaloc cult. I have already adverted to the dough images of the mountains and to the images of the wind and rain storms that issued from them. The worship of the Tlaloque was concentrated in the two months of Tepeilhuitl and Atemoztli, but at need it appeared anywhere in the calendar. Like most preliterate peoples who were familiar with the awesome closed environment and silence of the mountainside, the Aztecs were quick to reduce the sylvan numen to the form of a tree, preferably a great tree leaning over a spring or watercourse.

Trees of every kind were given consideration, from the giant *ahuehuetl* that in ritual was carried, intact and trussed up, into the city, to the erection of slender green poles, or to fir boughs thrust into the ground or placed on low shrines. Taken all together, trees brought in from the forests formed an extensive symbolic language dealing with verdure, growth, and social solidarity.[40] A stripped pole (*cuenmantli*) was very specifically assigned to the rain cult by having paper flags, spotted with liquid rubber, affixed. When thus set up, the pole with its banner stood for the same promise of rain and future abundance as could be found in the child sacrifices of the Tlaloc cult; in fact the children who were carried in procession on their way to slaughter were called "human banners" suggesting the interchangeability of the two.[41]

The great tree, however, when cut down and brought into the

city, could stand for the tribal spirit, and thus was somewhat apart from the Tlaloc cult. In the fourth month (Hueytozoztli), which was the month when the new maize was up and when children born in the preceding year were given names, a tall tree was selected on the Hill of the Star, a sacred site just outside of Culhuacan.[42] It was cut and lowered with great care so as not to break any of the branches or score the bark, after which, carefully bound and escorted with jubilation over the southern causeway, it was brought into the heart of Mexico-Tenochtitlan. This tree was Tota, Our Father. It was erected in the center of a square of four other smaller trees, all of them artificially planted and all tied together with cords of twisted grass. Thus, Tota simulated the center as occupied by the god while still projecting his dominance over the four directions of the world. But in the end, the tree was absorbed back into the Tlaloc cult by being taken, again bound up to prevent injury, into the shallows of the lake where it was erected for a second time. Towering above the canoes clustered about it in the waist-deep waters, the tree presided over the sacrifice of that small girl child who had been chosen to represent the Lady of the Lake.

More specifically tribal was the celebration of that part of the Mexican people who were of Otomí descent and who claimed the god Otonteuctli ("Lord of the Otomí") as their mascot and magnifier. This cult was spread over two of the months, the ninth and tenth. Whereas the Tota tree had been preserved with all its boughs leafy and intact, the *xocotl* tree of this ceremony was hewn to present a trimmed and artificial appearance, though the plume at the top was left to simulate a warrior's topknot. Thus lopped, the xocotl tree counterfeited a corpse and stood for the tribal dead. For twenty days the huge log was left to lay in its deathly state just outside the city, the people wailing around it and performing penitential acts of bloodletting. Finally, the tree was dressed in the paper adornments of Otonteuctli and thereby came alive again. The vast bulk, often over one hundred feet tall, was erected to become the center of elaborate rites celebrating the Tepaneca ancestors and ending in a communion meal wherein the god was eaten. The widespread volador festival still performed in a few places in Mexico is a vestige of this cult.

Though the veneration of trees was widespread among the Aztecs, it did not produce for them such a central symbol as did the cross for the Christians, possibly because the idea of blood sacrifice was not as intimately tied to the tree as it was to the cross. Children did die as "human banners," and these banners were indeed tied to green saplings, but the connection is secondary. And when the tree was seen to be the body of the folk, as was the case with both Tota and the xocotl, death and resurrection was specified only for the latter, and even here the latter stood, not as "the other," but as an abstraction of an entire people. Thus, the xocotl was fundamentally a talisman employed in self-perpetuation.

PARADISE IN CULT

The sources give another instance of the Aztecs' reduction of the divine, this one a complicated tableau performed in the twelfth and thirteenth months (the Pachtli months) depicting an aphrodisiac paradise, and centering around Xochiquetzal, the goddess of love. Myth had it that this goddess had been the first being to commit sin, for it had been she who had plucked the flowers (or alternately had eaten the fruit) of the forbidden tree.[43] But cult was not necessarily a reenactment of myth, and the rituals connected with the goddess show her here—not as a fallen deity—but as a gracious and perfect mistress seated in joy in paradise. The emphasis is important.

Throughout all ages with which I am familiar, men have ritually described and told stories about a paradise in some never-never land, infinitely desirable. These creations are among the most moving demonstrations of man's urge to reduce the divine to the level of his invention, lest he be overwhelmed by its "otherness." If man inhabits a vale of tears, then the divine must in contrast inhabit a land of beauty and contentment. By thus imposing on the "wholly other" the concept of men and women engaged in pleasure, the divine can be partially comprehended, and—more to the point—can be envied. And what more obvious reductionary method than to produce a paradise of bright beings, all absorbed in colors, in luxurious fragrances, in feasting and sexual excitements—and then into this narrowed space to fit the deity! In any paradise invented by men, the gods living there are really hostages existing in an aura of golden indecision and relaxation—surely a low common denominator for any set of gods, however much a desideratum for humans!

The paradise in question here was Tamoanchan. The festival was staged as an appendage to the twelfth month.[44] In this month the Aztecs celebrated the return of all the gods who had departed en masse after the harvest home that had ended the agricultural year. This had been cultically reenacted over a four-day period beginning with the advent of the youngest god, Tezcatlipoca, and ending with that of the oldest ones, the fire god and his congener, the god of travelers and merchants. With the Aztecs now convinced that the heavens had not abandoned them, a carnival ensued. It is interesting that it was not the all-powerful Tezcatlipoca who was chosen to sit at the center of this splendid celebration, as one might have thought, but rather Xochiquetzal. Flowers were peculiar to this goddess and one of her titles was the "Virgin." She was the goddess of love, of pregnant women, of all womanly skills, and, being an avatar of the Magna Mater, she was of course the goddess of verdancy.

The celebration began with the investiture of a young girl as her ixiptla. Immediately after the death of this ixiptla, and the flaying of her body, a priest assumed her skin and entered upon the role of the mistress of Elysium. A sylvan bower, laced with flowers, had been erected in front of the temple of the goddess, and now within it, the derived ixiptla sat in state while feigning to spin and weave. At some point in the scenario the whole pantheon of the gods, newly returned from their exile, appeared in the persons of their high priests, all elegantly and appropriately clad. Flowering trees had been set up just outside the goddess's bower, and in these trees boys dressed as birds and butterflies climbed about among the branches, while the gods milled about below, pretending to shoot them with blowguns, smoking cigars, and offering each other bouquets.

It was also a day of disguises, especially for the master craftsmen who appeared as animals of all kinds, each one identified, however, by the tools or other paraphernalia of his or her trade. Much dancing followed. Jugglers, mountebanks, and comics appeared out of nowhere, and the whole city gave up its tensions and sorrows to exist—if only for a moment—in paradise. For that brief time the people, in company with their gods and under the presidency of her who was love itself, expressed their joy with flowers, drunkenness, and sexual license.

It is of interest that every eighth year this cult was greatly expanded to become the Atamalcualiztli festival of which we have already taken notice.[45] On that occasion also the goddess sat in felicity under the flowering world tree, wove her lovely fabrics, and watched the gods dancing about her.

At first sight this appears to have been a typical carnival, but while it was all of that for the Aztecs, it was also something more—it was another way to reduce the divine. There in front of their eyes, moving merrily about among them, like any of their noble neighbors, were the gods. Such a fellowship, in such a casual situation, could not help but humanize the gods, removing them by that much from the "wholly other." It was not only that they could be approached more easily in this festival; it was also that they could be felt to be more comfortable, that they were something less than the "wholly other," and were therefore less terrible.

The subject of paradise, displayed in cult as a mode of divine reduction, exemplifies the Aztec use of the pantheon. The Aztecs were obsessed with arranging gatherings of all the gods, synods of the divine world as it were. In the fifty-two-year New Fire ceremony, it is the totality of the gods who await the dire possibility that time will, at that ceremony, fail to renew itself. Again the whole pantheon appears in the eight-year Atamalcualiztli, just mentioned, in a celebration of renewal. And together, as we have also just seen, they appear in a Pachtli month in order to be understood as validating the human cultural achievement. Additionally, they appear in a most vivid unity in the Flaying of Men, all walking as one, their legs bound together. And we have just seen them in their twelfth month returning en masse from some unspecified absence. The actual number of the gods in these gatherings is not of great importance. Our sources show them as groups of from four to nine, sometimes as thirteen, and by implication as twenty. There was no agreement on the full count of the gods. The fact that they appeared in concert (so different from their singular performances in myth) is what we should take note of. This does not mean that the gods were thus of one genus and one mind.[46] A category is the ultimate in reduction, for there the many become one, and "the one" is better able to bear human judgments than the many.

TWO

3

Nodal Points of Meeting

THE AZTEC IDOL

We have seen in the preceding chapter how the Aztecs reduced the supernatural world to manageable proportions. We need now to know the points and places chosen by them for their confrontations with the divine. As we might expect, idols were the most highly charged points of contact.

All over the world and for thousands of years men have handled fetishes and bowed before idols. To my knowledge, no people ever exceeded the Aztecs in the profligacy with which they shaped images and endowed objects and parts of nature, such as stones, bits of wood, springs, and the like with either godhead or mana. These talismans and images proliferated in a torrential stream. Idols spawned new idols or attached themselves to older idols.

This profusion is a remarkable thing about the Aztec holy images. It points to the attraction that the palpable and the immanent together had for the Aztecs. Nevertheless, this characteristic alone does not itself explain the profusion.

The iconographic profusion—it would seem to me—was in historic terms a result of the Aztecs' obsessive need for defenses against a world of enemies. The history of the Mexica Aztecs is that of a tough but depleted and despised people who inherited from their first mentor, the Toltec city of Azcapotzalco, a tradition of aggressive statism, and the fears that normally accompany such emergent imperialism needed reassurance. Their overwrought piety also hinted that their true enemies were the gods, particularly those of foreign peoples. Such nonaligned gods had to be understood as concrete images; otherwise they might escape detection.

As far as we can tell, the number of indigenous Aztec gods was not excessive. The Mexica invaders, for instance, originally possessed as authentically theirs, only a goddess Mecitli and her son or consort

Huitzilopochtli (a form of Tezcatlipoca). By the time of the Spanish entry there were many more, the number reflecting the far-flung activities of Aztec merchants and warriors as well as the Aztec desire to participate in a larger pan-Mesoamerican religion, as was the case, for instance, with their worship of Tlazolteotl, Xipe, the Four Hundred Rabbits, and others.

It was fear then that impelled them to seek out the gods and throw a net of specificity over them. What is more significant is the Aztecs' lack of a sense of pantheistic oneness in nature. They were a people acutely aware of the world as differentiated and therefore reducible to many discrete images. We could characterize them as religiously anomistic—unaware of any universal code or of any single will.

In the early period of their Chichimec wandering, the Aztecs had an object that indicated deity in more general terms than did an idol. It was in fact a taboo marker. This was a reed, an arrow, or a slender staff to which was attached a bit of white bark paper.[1] Thrust into the ground, or into a ball of wadded grass if it were an arrow, this banner always indicated the near presence of the divine. It may also have acted as a kind of a prayer stick, importuning the goodwill of the deity or spirit of a place. Itself, it was not a god but rather the sign of a god, and it announced his or her immanence. Later, these banners are found in pairs at the tops of temple pyramids, fluttering on both sides of the shrine entrance.

An ordinary idol was understood by the Aztecs to be a *tlachichihualli*, literally "a counterfeit," a thing fashioned by men and appropriately adorned. It could be a stone god, *teteotl*, or a wooden statue, *cuauhximolli*, though there was a more general term, *tecuacuilli*, that could mean either. Another category, *colotli*, apparently meaning something curved or bent in its construction, was no doubt reserved for that class of idols formed over an armature of wood or reeds.[2] The figurines used in household cults were the *tepitoton* ("the very small ones"), and they could be of any sort, including even crude yarn images.[3] A very ancient idol—perhaps descended from the female figurine of Preclassic times—was the *nenetl* ("doll"); in some of their forms these dolls were the *tlazolteteo*, a pluralization of the name of the great Earth Mother.[4] In essence, they were the lares and penates of the home, guarding the stores and giving children. In their plurality and near anonymity, they were far more important to the common people than was the official image of Tlazolteotl cared for by the priests.

Even the containers in which portable images were kept could be treated as fetishes—such was the *toptli*, the ark or box, and the *tlaquimilolli* ("the bundle"). The latter particularly was of great importance in Aztec religious life.[5] It was thought to have been the god's cloak that he had left among men at the time of his disappearance.[6] Wrapped up in these swatches of cloth were relics of the god, a jawbone perhaps, a piece of worked jade representing a heart, a flint knife, quartz crystals, or perhaps ashes. In the lake city of Cuitlahuac the patron god of Mixcoatl. The legendary tlaquimilolli of the god kept there was a most sacred bundle that reputedly contained the ashes of the demonic goddess Itzpapalotl.[7] This, in brief, was a sophisticated kind of medicine bundle, originally used on the tribal wanderings. In the succeeding centuries when the tribes had settled down to urban living, these bundles were finally deposited in the great temples of the land. On a smaller scale the genius and protection of the family lineage was generally passed down from father to son in smaller swatches of cloth.[8] These held the talismans, idols, hallucinogens, and memorabilia that contained the life of the family and gave it historic continuity.

Idols of all kinds proliferated among the Aztecs.[9] One has the feeling that as a people they would have collapsed without them—they suffered indeed from a kind of iconomania. This mind set of theirs is quite different—let us say—from that of the early Romans who looked at the supernatural world as one in which they had an independent status and where their roles, though greatly inferior to those of the gods, were defined and guaranteed by contract. To them, images were not of the paramount importance that they were to the Aztecs. To the latter, idols were constantly leaking points of the divine electricity. In their cosmic constitution, the Romans saw themselves as having a bill of rights, and they could properly expect future repayment for services to the god. The Aztecs approached the gods laden down with gifts and expectant of little. They needed idols before all else lest their gifts be lost in a spiritual vacuity.

THE INCONSTANT NATURE OF THE AZTEC IDOL

The idols were of course also ixiptlas, "likenesses," a designation that we have earlier restricted to indicate a living person who had been chosen to represent the god, act out his myths where they existed, and offer themselves for worship and slaughter. But the idols possessed one power that the living ixiptla did not have—they could exude near facsimilies whenever a crisis or a drastic need arose. New statues of the gods could be figuratively peeled off the old ones, the new images thereby becoming avatars. The Aztec habit of naming the sacred images helped in this—for instance, the fire god Xiuhteuctli acquired a new avatar when one of his idols was named *Milintoc*. In such a dynamic system, gods often haunted the forms of several idols. Tezcatlipoca in Mexico had two particularly important idols; one was a likeness depicted standing and made of black volcanic stone obsidian[10]; the other was a seated and threatening representation that sent drought, famine, and pestilence. In the nearby community of Tlapitzahuayan there was kept a most holy image of that god made of wood.[11] In Tezcoco he was a tlaquimilolli.

Idols could be linked as father and son. In Huexotzinco, there was a small idol of the city god Camaxtli, patron of hunting. When clad as the god Quetzalcoatl of Cholula, this image then became affiliated to Camaxtli as a son.[12] And yet these two gods essentially have little in common! The ultimate in coalescence occurred when the idols of Camaxtli and Quetzalcoatl actually exchanged regalia. In Mexico-Tenochtitlan Huitzilopochtli's main image appears to have been that one named "Blue Sky."[13] He also had in that city two dough images, one of which was a well-known avatar called *Tlacahuepan* that was housed in a temple apparently outside the temenos, or sacred enclosure.[14] In the city of Tezcoco, Huitzilopochtli appeared in a medicine bundle as two maguey thorns.[15] Such changes and partial duplications in the end could produce different gods entirely, though which came first, the fully developed god or an image, oftentimes is moot. A final example of this plasticity can be seen in the fact that the great state gods, housed permanently in central temples, could be invoked by individuals in pursuance of a vow made, modeled by them in miniature, and kept at home.[16] There, of course, they were minimized to suit the family's needs.

In Aztec thought all of the preceding idols and fetishes were subject to the iron laws of time and decay. Every fifty-two years the Aztec calendar came to its crisis, at which moment cosmic vitality ceased altogether—a totally new temporal regime might or might not succeed it.[17] The vitality inhering in the things of man's manufacture, his tools, clothing, weapons, and pots, at this point all weakened and died. In Aztec households everywhere household idols were smashed or cast into running water and replaced with ones newly made. The statues of the great gods in the temples were refashioned or had their regalia and finery replaced. It should not surprise us that, although the fifty-two-year calendar round exhausted an idol and necessitated its replacement, the god in myth was in no way subjected to this particular cycle of time. He did not weaken, and he experienced no diminution. The fifty-two-year cycle affected cult only. This would seem to point to a clear distinction made by the Aztecs between the divine and its many appearances to men.

THE ITHUALLI OR SACRED ENCLOSURE—GENERAL REMARKS

Idols and fetishes were the points in the Aztecs' world from which there flickered those electric currents of the divine that produce those religious oscillations we call rituals. Pyramid temples, because they were oriented directionally into the cosmic structure, were static artifacts and were essentially display platforms on which the gods' houses were sited. Each temple, however, represented a somewhat different cosmic situation. The central temple in Tenochtitlan, for instance, was named *Coatepetl* after the world mountain, and it therefore housed not only the original mountain god Tlaloc but also the hero Huitzilopochtli who in myth fought off his enemies from the summit of that sacred eminence. More will be said about this later. Tlalxicco was the place where the perpetual fire burned, representing Xiuhteuctli, the fire god. It was an open fire pit and appropriately was attached to the temple of the Earth Mother, for fire lived in the earth's center; Tlalxicco means in Nahuatl "the place in the earth's navel." A rock garden, planted with cactuses and strewn with the dry litter of the desert, was another of the temples in Mexico. This was a small walled enclosure called Teotlalpan ("Godland") and was sacred to the god of hunting, Mixcoatl. It was named after the limitless northern steppe country out of which the god had led the Aztec tribes in the early days, and it represented the cosmic "place from which."

The Tochinco was a low square platform with stairs on each side. Here victims were sacrificed to the gods of strong drink. Other examples could be adduced of the various orientations and even the architecture of these Aztec temples. It is certainly true that the Aztec temple was more than a house for the god—it was first and foremost a crystallization out of the universe. Whereas an idol allowed only a particular god to manifest himself in concrete terms to men, the Aztec temple always hinted at a cosmos where other gods might exist.

In any consideration of Aztec temples one has to begin with the temenos, or sacred enclosure (*ithualli*). In this discussion, I shall use as a model the great enclosure in Tenochtitlan. We can be sure that according to their size and resources all the other Aztec cities had, or at least attempted, something similar.[18]

Aztec shrines and temples can be placed in two categories: first, those included in the ithualli, and then those scattered about in the various city wards, at important road crossings, or on hills and crags outside the city.[19] Inclusion within the temenos meant that the deity was considered a support to the state, either because of an original tribal patronage and history, or because of identification with the ruling family and noble lines. The gods with temples in the environs outside could be—and often were—of great significance, with colorful and complicated rites, deities, like Coyotlinahual or Huixtocihuatl, but they were unrelated to the Mexica claims to dominion. In fact, they were often gods brought into Mexico-Tenochtitlan by foreign groups settling there. Their rites, however, might be included in the ritual calendar in the same fashion and to the same extent as those in the temenos group. Inclusion in the temenos was therefore not always a sign of wide support among the people, but was rather a lock on social and political prestige.

In the temenos were gathered together the deities without whom the claims of the ruling group would have been in jeopardy: Huitzilopochtli for his victory bringing and his omens during the years of wandering; Tezcatlipoca for his gift of supreme authority and power; Cihuacoatl for her blood thirst that continually fanned the fires of war and thereby supported the knightly quest; Tlaloc for his territoriality that gave the Mexicans the right to inhabit the sweet water part of the lake; Chicomecoatl for the food supplies from the tributary environs that supported and magnified the city; Xochiquetzal for luxuries, the arts, and the sexual prerogatives held by knights and rulers; Quetzal-coatl as the first Toltec ruler and therefore the fount of royal legitimacy and control of the priesthood; Mixcoatl for his patronage of the hunt, a nobleman's pursuit; and Tonatiuh (Xipe) for his patronage of the knightly orders.

The temenos was a square, walled enclosure of vast size in the city's center.[20] The wall was of stone and represented the limits of the Aztec cosmos. Up against the circuit wall on the inside were ranged buildings used for fasting and other religious purposes by various Mexican groups.[21] As examples, we can cite the pound where the children waiting to be sacrificed to Tlaloc were kept, and the (probably adjoining) one for the adults. The latter edifice was also a kitchen where the sacrificed victims were brought, cut up in pieces, and cooked in stews of squash flowers for the nobles.[22]

In terms of urban architecture, however, the ithualli with its high surrounding walls was a rallying point in time of crisis, a fortress and an armory. Near three of the four gates were buildings in which were stored great quantities of weapons that the city might need to defend itself when under attack—bows, arrows, atlatls, darts, sword clubs, and the like. It was a way of admitting the vulnerability of the gods. As sound defensive architecture, the ithualli was a piece of military nonsense. It may seem strange that such an aggressive and bellicose people as the Aztecs should encase the most vital parts of their community within such weak and indefensible palisades. If anything it is a tribute to their ferocity—upon which they ultimately depended.

The vast area contained some eight or nine temples (according to Durán), but there were also adjunct edifices, at least five priestly apartments, and shrines of some of the city wards[23]; in all, some five thousand people were housed there.[24] No layperson could live there—even a ruler could not. Access to the area was via four portals, each oriented at one of the cardinal directions.[25] From the gates, straight and wide roads stretched away to the four directions, though the eastern one ended abruptly at a busy wharf at the nearby water's edge. The three other avenues were carried over the lake on causeways.

This basic urban architecture symbolized the supernatural influences that affected the outside world, flowing outward from Tenochtitlan in the four directions and filling the cosmos. The effect was that of a theology supporting a polity. The gods are at home in the center (by definition here, the city of Mexico-Tenochtitlan), whereas beyond lies the world into which Mexico is invited to march and conquer. This march has been ordered for the purpose of bringing back hearts and blood to sustain the gods, who in turn will look with favor on the Mexicans, furthering their aggrandizement outward and their prosperity within. Thus the center of the city was not so much an urban concept as it was an Olympus, in the suburbs of which resided an elite class of mortals.

We cannot give a definitive list of the gods dwelling in the enclosure for the sources are unclear on that point. Even the numbers that they give fluctuate; the commonest tallies run from eight to thirteen.[26] We assume the following ten: Huitzilopochtli, Tezcatlipoca, Quetzalcoatl, Tlaloc, Xipe, Xochiquetzal, Chicomecoatl, Cihuacoatl, Mixcoatl, and Xiuhteuctli. Each one of these ten prime deities possessed his or her house or symbolic place within the walled area, but there were numerous other edifices there as well. First were the several groups of priestly apartments (the *calmecacs*), under Quetzalcoatl's patronage, where lived the five thousand who served the temples and taught their calendrical and cabalistic arts to the upcoming generation of priests and nobles.[27] I have mentioned the arsenals that were considered to be not only repositories of arms but were also temples. There were chambers attached to the main temple and reserved for the ruler and ranking nobles who went there to perform religious retreats and fasts. There were also the indispensable ball courts used in at least two of the annual cults. There was the place where the human skins worn in several of the festivals were finally deposited (*netlatiloyan*). There was the famous pair of round sculptured stones, set up on daises, upon which selected war captives fought gladiatorial combats and where they died sacrificially. And there was more than one skull rack (*tzompantli*), which was a raised rectangular armature of horizontal poles upon which were threaded the skulls of the victims sacrificed to the gods. Besides these, there were basins and enclosed springs used for sacred purposes as well as a desert rock garden where the god Mixcoatl was immanent. These monuments and constructions will be commented on more fully; here they are mentioned only to emphasize the variety to be found in the great enclosure.

This variety precluded belief in an all-pervasive supernatural situation. The gods had no synod house where they met to pronounce words of command. It was true that the divine was everywhere, but it lay about in glittering sherds, each a unique piece. God to the Aztecs could not be seen as One. Aztec temples were thus in no way exponents of that numinous quality that we assign to the concept of "God."

THE AZTEC TEMPLE

Confusion about the typical Aztec temple is caused by the tendency of the English word "pyramid" to evoke in the mind of the reader an Egyptian archetype. The Egyptian and Aztec pyramids were quite distinct, for the latter always had on their exteriors an ascent of steeply pitched stairs and were thus designed to be climbed. The Egyptian pyramid was nothing more than a tumulus that covered a tomb and was not designed for climbing. What we generally refer to as the pyramid is the heavy, sloped base upon which the actual Aztec temple stood. In Nahuatl it is a *tzacualli*. The meaning of tzacualli is "something covered or closed over." Several interpretations of what this means are possible—I prefer to think that it is meant to call to mind an antrum or something similar over which the pyramid was erected in the first place and that it thus represented the simultaneous sequestration and concentration of a tabued spot. This was accomplished by building over the original site a mound that became in time the classical stepped pyramid found all over Mesoamerica.

This interpretation of the Aztec pyramid as a covering for a sacred place in or on the earth might seem to contradict an alternative and generally accepted theory that the tzacualli was really a mountain (*tepetl*). The Olmec pyramid at La Venta (long preceding Aztec times), in the opinion of the archaeologists, presumably reproduced the shape of one of the Tuxtla volcanoes.[28] And we definitely know that the tzacualli of Huitzilopochtli in Tenochtitlan was a facsimile of the world mountain called *Coatepetl* and that the ashes of the Aztec rulers could be interred in the body of that monument. Actually, there is no disparity at all between the two concepts—a mountain after all is a natural stopper over the hollows and caves in the earth below.[29] We thus do not have any difficulty understanding the logic whereby the deity or spirit connected with the buried cell or cave in the earth also had his "god house" (*teocalli*) erected on the mountain's peak, a duplication in the open air of the original chamber or dwelling below.

In most cases, the body of the Aztec pyramid was stepped into several levels or terraces, each with a pronounced batter. The number of these superimposed quasi-terraces was important, for it was not necessarily a random number but could be taken as the number of firmaments above (if the god in point were celestial) or the number of subimposed or reversed underworlds below (if the god were chthonic). If one likened the sky to a crystal mountain, the number of terraces in it could total thirteen if a simple ladderlike ascent to the summit was all that was taken into account. If, however, one were thinking of both ascent and descent, as in the case of the sun's path, then the pyramid could be constructed of six setbacks with the teocalli platform at the top as the zenith and seventh level, and the descent to the bottom coming out finally to make a total of thirteen, the usual number of heavens talked about in myth. Correspondingly, if an underworld god were in question, his temple could have five terraces, the total to come out to nine, the usual number of underworlds. Such permutations were a part of the Aztec lore of temples, but we do not know how consistently the rules were applied in the temenos temples —or indeed elsewhere.

THE COATEPETL

There were within the enclosure various temples, altars, fonts, cloisters, and stations of various types, but for the state and the myth that supported the state there was a nuclear group—all served by the same priesthood. These were the three temples: Coatepec (Huitzilopochtli), Tlalocan (Tlaloc), and Tlillan (Cihuacoatl), and if one reads them loosely in the order of nature, they stand for the heavens, the earth, and the underworld.

The city of Mexico-Tenochtitlan concentrated heavily on the cults of the gods resident in these three shrines, but within the ithualli we find that other deities were also important. Our major source for the gods and their shrines in the sacred enclosure is Sahagún, as previously mentioned, but owing to the fact that gods' names and the names of their statues often differ, he is sometimes a confusing guide. Notwithstanding this, he seems to be saying what I deduce below. I will begin here with the first two of the nuclear group and present the remaining shrines in the succeeding section.

Only one of the large temenos temples has been completely excavated so far. This is the tzacualli, which reared up well over a hundred feet above the level of the patio floor and had two fronting stairways leading up to the shrines of Tlaloc and of Huitzilopochtli on top. A word must be said about this famous structure that was called, from the myth of the latter god, Coatepetl, or "Snake Mountain."

Briefly, the great tzacualli was a doubled version of the world mountain on top of which took place the cults of the two quite different gods—Tlaloc and Huitzilopochtli. Although dispensing rain was his chief function, Tlaloc was an earth god, specifically a mountain king. He was that complex of activity that goes on around the mountain, the rolling movement of clouds, the tornadic onset of the rain, and the flash and fall of the thunderbolt. Even before he was a god with definition, Tlaloc was thus a numen in the realm of nature, for which reason we are not surprised to learn that he had no myths, or at least none that have come down to us. Huitzilopochtli was a deity formulated as an avatar of the sun, one of the significant objects in nature; yet his ties with the world of nature were minimal. He spoke not of nature but of culture, specifically of the culture of the Mexica Aztecs. In the case of Tlaloc, cult was the worshipper's sole way of knowing and proclaiming the god. In the case of Huitzilopochtli, one knew the god first through tribal legend and myth and then proclaimed him through cult.

Huitzilopochtli stood for and protected the city of Tenochtitlan and led it to its victories. Tlaloc belonged to the world at large, brought rain for the farmer, and therefore life to all. Thus side by side on the summit of the world mountain sat the god who represented the day as bright sunshine (one of Huitzilopochtli's names was "Blue Sky") and the older god, Tlaloc, the dark and lowering sky.

What placed Huitzilopochtli by the side of the more venerable Tlaloc in Tenochtitlan was the fact that Huitzilopochtli's mythic victory over his enemies took place—as it had to—on the world mountain.[30] Sun, moon, and stars (Huitzilopochtli, Coyolxauhqui, and the Four Hundred Huitznahua, respectively) in the tale did battle at the gates of dawn, which is to say, at the world mountain. Tlaloc was the mountain itself conceived of as the home of clouds. Huitzilopochtli was the sun rising out of that mountain. So of necessity they coexisted cheek by jowl on the summit of Coatepetl.

Statements as to how this juxtaposition came about are at the moment suppositious. I myself believe that it came about as a compromise between an original territorial jurisdiction in the lake (Tlaloc's) and a tribal settlement there (Huitzilopochtli's)[31]; other factors as well could have been at work at the time. When the Mexica Aztecs settled in the shoals of Lake Tezcoco they naturally brought with them their tribal god. But out there in the lake and along the near shore they were met by this more established god who was lord in the rock of Chapultepec and its flowing spring as well as a power over the waters of the lake. In Mexican telling, the muddy site in the water over which they were later to claim proprietary rights was first under Tlaloc's aegis. As god of the ingressing tribe, Huitzilopochtli had therefore to consult with Tlaloc before the settlement of the people could be sanctioned. So ran the legend. Historically it was probably an agreement between neo-Toltec priests of Tlaloc who were resident at the sacred spring of Chapultepec and the *teomama*, or carrying priest, of Huitzilopochtli. Threats and force of arms might also have been used. Out of this grew the first primitive shrine in the reed thickets and mud flats of the lake, a simple dais of sods on top of which stood two thatched, wooden huts, side by side.[32]

Concomitantly with the growth of the city of Tenochtitlan, and its twin island settlement Tlatilulco, the shrines expanded. Each ruler embellished the edifice, probably at his accession or at the beginning of one of the fifty-two-year cycles, but other renovations were also made, possibly every fourth year. The foundation of the first of these temples is lost as it lies below water level and cannot be reclaimed from the mud. The deepest one yet recovered is probably referrable to the reign of Huitzilihuitl, generally dated to 1396–1417.[33] The most pretentious rebuilding (which ended with Ahuitzotl's famous dedication) was begun by Moteuczoma I, the project in all spanning three reigns.

As finally designed at the time of the Spanish entry, the edifice was flanked on both north and south sides by three small shrines, two being similar in their decoration and recalling in their design the architecture of Teotihuacan. These two are referred to in the latest archaeological reports as the "Red Temples."[34] As for the great pyramid in its final form, the surface area of its top was approximately a hundred feet above ground level; the ascent was made via the two separate but adjoining staircases, each staircase having 114 steps.[35]

Two ever-burning braziers stood at the forward corners of the summit, whereas farther back and set against the façades of the temples were placed figures holding tall poles from which fluttered flags. The whole edifice faced west. Tlaloc inhabited the northernmost shrine, Huitzilopochtli the southernmost, or the one on the right hand of a person facing the temple. This placement comports with the fact that the sun was known to live in the south.

The two shrines were set back toward the east edge of the flat area at the pyramid top. Fronting each was a sacrificial stone.[36] That in front of the early Tlaloc temple (of the time of Huitzilihuitl) was what is referred to as a *chacmool*, a name arbitrarily given by archaeologists to a sculptured Toltec figure semireclining on his back while holding on his belly an offertory plate or bowl.[37] In front of Huitzilopochtli's shrine and even closer to the forward edge of the platform stood the all-purpose *techcatl*, a conic stone coming to a rounded point over which the victims were stretched for slaughter. At an earlier period that item had been shaped differently, being then a low stone slab with its flattened side facing the stairs. It is not known why the earlier techcatl gave way to the later conic version. Flanking each shrine entrance there stood in rigid attention the two stone standard bearers, naked but for their loincloths. These custodians with their staring shell eyes and brutal witless faces must have made a strong impression on all who saw them.[38]

The shrines also differed. They had contrasting façades with the tops edged with merlons. Their floor plans, however, were the same, with the doors placed in the long facing side of a rectangle. Inside in the high comb of each building there was a three-storied loft for the storage of weapons, access to these levels being gained by ladders.[39] The possibility that the central shrine of a city was designed as an armory of last resort specifies perfectly the Aztec concept of war. No city was defeated until its defenders had been driven back to their last eminence, the city pyramid. And no matter how well the battle might be going elsewhere, if the temple of the patron god was seized or set on fire, all resistance came to a sudden end. The heart of the city had been broken.

The Coatepetl was more than a primate church housing the god of Tenochtitlan—it was a congelation in stone of the central myth of the Mexican people, a sculpted tale wherein Huitzilopochtli played the role of the sun king in the sky. Around it, other edifices and iconic pieces filled out additional passages in the myth considered to be important. Not all of these adjuncts can today be understood. For instance, the three shrines closely flanking the great temple on the north and south sides, respectively, are tantalizing in their possible references, but otherwise opaque in meaning. It has been suggested that one of the northern three that was designed as a great altar of skulls was both a chapel to the God of the Dead and a hellmouth. The north was traditionally the direction of the dead.

The axial myth told how the goddess Coyolxauhqui led her swarming minions, the Four Hundred Huitznahua, to an attack upon the world mountain held by Huitzilopochtli (just born from his mother Coatlicue). At the onset the god hurled down upon them his weapon, a blazing dragon, the Xiuhcoatl. Then, in single combat, he successfully engaged the fierce goddess, decapitating her as she was reaching the summit of the mountain. Her body, hewn in pieces, he toppled down the slopes to the bottom. Finally, in a great victory he sacrificed the captured Huitznahua and ate them. By right of that victory he could assume their name and be called himself Huitznahua.

All of the preceding could be read in imperishable stone. A magnificent diorite head of Coyolxauhqui was seen on the pyramid's top near the techcatl,[40] whereas her dismembered body was sculptured in high relief on a flat round stone of great size placed (in the reign of Axayacatl) on the platform (*apetlac*) at the bottom of the stairway,[41] the very spot where the bodies of sacrificed victims pitched over the edge came to rest below.[42] The fact that this remarkable work of art was designed as a circular plaque symbolized the lunar nature of the goddess. Both of these Coyolxauhqui monuments now form part of the national treasures of modern Mexico. In addition, a colossal head of the Xiuhcoatl, the Fire Serpent, a masterpiece in stone of near-abstract design, was also placed at the pyramid's base to portray the deadly ophidian dart that the god had flung against the Four Hundred Huitznahua.[43] Directly in front of the round Coyolxauhqui Stone, set into the forward lip of the platform there was a flat tabular stone that may have been the god's abattoir block whereon the tumbled bodies of sacrificial victims were cut up preparatory to distribution.

As a statue called "Blue Sky," Huitzilopochtli himself occupied the house on the summit. And because this house was a celestial edifice, there were placed at the corners statues of those demonic caryatids that in Aztec myth supported the sky.[44]

The shibboleth in stone that finally completed the myth was a gigantic statue of Coatlicue, the Earth Mother who bore Huitzilopochtli.[45] This piece, which is incontestably the most noteworthy of all images from the whole pre-Columbian world, along with the Coyolxauhqui stones, stands today in the Muséo Nacional. It is impossible to assess it aesthetically, so devastating is its whole aspect, and so monstrous are its parts. Where it stood when the Spaniards first entered the sacred enclosure is an unresolved problem; we know only that Moteuczoma dedicated the shrine of Coatlicue in 1518 and that it was in close proximity to the Coatepetl. It was called the Coatlan ("Serpent's Lair").

We may have given to the reader the impression that on the Coatepetl only the cult of Huitzilopochtli mattered. Yet judging from Sahagún, as well as from artifacts from the recent excavations, the rites for Tlaloc were only a little less ornate, and they were surely more popular. Tlaloc represented life. Everywhere in the recent excavations were found quantities of marine and lucastrine offerings dear to Tlaloc: cockleshells, conch shells, sharks' teeth, turtle carapaces, coral, and cayman skulls. One cist offering in particular was notable.[46] It was an underground recess located precisely at the foot of the Tlaloc staircase and contained stone figurines and masks from the Pacific area of the Aztec empire, all similarly oriented and liberally mixed with seashells. The excavators believe that each piece may have stood for a subject community in Guerrero in the person of its local god. The cache thus may have represented homage paid by foreign supernaturals to Tlaloc at some important ritual. For this particular ceremony a caged jaguar had been brought all the way up from those lowlands and here on the foot of the stairway sacrificed, the carcass then being dumped into the cist on top of the multiple offerings— after which the cist was sealed up. There can be no doubt that the jaguar represented the god Tepeyollotl, a powerful and ancient god who dwelt in the dark, inner chambers of the mountain. It was also somewhere close to the foot of the great stairs where early excavators found the remarkable *cuauhxicalli*, carved like a jaguar, which now greets the visitor to the Aztec hall in the Museo Nacional. The jaguar was a denizen of the rainy land and therefore close to Tlaloc. Its presence within the Coatepetl was thus natural.

This double temple, the Coatepetl, with its overpowering visual symbolism, was surely one of mankind's most majestic architectural creations. Stuccoed and then painted in rich reds, greens, blues, and ochers, intermittently flashing pure white surfaces, facing outward with dangerously pitched stairs, and flanked around the apron at ground level with huge somber frogs and undulating serpents horribly alive with their eternal grimaces, it is hard to see how any people could have fitted an edifice so perfectly to their needs and their beliefs.

At his accession, Moteuczoma II, a man of intense piety, began to renovate the structure, but was put off or delayed by a series of evil omens connected with rumors from the far Caribbean waters of the disquieting Spanish presence. As the years crowded upon 1519, the annus mirabilis, tensions focused on the temple, confirming it even more centrally in the lives of the Mexican Aztecs.

Flanking the Coatepetl and the six shrines clustered at its sides, were two other interesting buildings, apparently with closely related functions. The one on the north side of the Coatepetl, called by the excavators the "House of the Eagles," is equated by Cecelia Klein with the Tlacochcalco mentioned frequently in the sources.[47] It was a clubhouse for the Eagle knights, a colonnaded building where they met, transacted their business, and performed certain austerities. Its twin, south of the Coatepetl, was probably reserved for the Jaguar knights, the other commandery. This would then be the Tlacatecco. In these buildings were kept the sacred bundles of both Huitzilopochtli and Tezcatlipoca, and here too the newly elected *tlatoani* and his council of princes carried out their initiatory four-day fast and vigil.[48] These two commanderies were of the utmost importance because in them, and through the rituals practiced therein, the elite warrior class was given control of the nuclear cult of the state religion.

THE TLILLAN COMPLEX

Inevitably, the shrine of the Earth Mother was connected with the great temple.[49] We have seen that in the myth the world mountain was named Coatepetl, a direct reference to the earth goddess Cihuacoatl ("Snake Woman") who lived on the mountain and there conceived the heroic youth Huitzilopochtli from a feather (the symbol of air or sky). Cihuacoatl was the vast earth itself, expressed for most purposes as a ponderous mountain. In the temenos her temple was appropriately called Tlillan ("Place of Darkness"), referring to the earth's interior.[50] This shrine was placed on a very low tzacualli, really a platform, and was a depressed structure with a door so low that one had to cringe to enter—all of this in keeping with the lumpiness and gloom of the earth. Inside was the idol, never seen by the people and only dimly seen by the groveling priests who served her. The floor was said by one Spanish source to have been encrusted with a pavement of dried blood some nine inches thick. Out of this malodorous den came the oracles that guided the Mexican state. And just as important to the state as her oracles was the goddess's appetite, which was unceasing. Every eight days her priests went to the palace to complain that she was hungry, and inevitably a victim was released to her from the pool of prisoners. After the arm or haunch of human meat and the bowl of blood had been introduced into her den, the gnawed-on bone at the expiration of an appropriate time would be hurled out the door as the goddess shouted from within, "There it is, all eaten up!"[51]

Three other edifices were included in the Tlillan complex: the fire pit (Tlalxicco), the dungeon of the captured gods (Coacalco), and a retreat for the ruler and priests where they could receive oracles (Tlillan calmecac). Myth had it, as we have seen, that the fire god was essentially a chthonic being who lived in the subterranean regions, in fact in the "earth's navel" (*tlalxicco*). This connection between earth and volcanic fire explains why a stone-lined pit filled with an ever-burning fire, constantly tended by the priests, should stand in close proximity to the Tlillan.[52]

Actually, there was a well-defined fire cult in the ithualli that can be viewed as apart from the Tlillan and its chthonic ceremonies.[53] The god of fire, Xiuhteuctli, was also god of time and the cosmic years. His shrine in the temenos became exceedingly active during the closing month of each calendar year. It was called the Tzonmalco, but we have no details about it. Possibly it was an enclosed dais with steps leading up all four sides. There was another fire temple called Tetlanman[54] that the fire god shared with the goddess Chantico.

The Coacalco also stood near the Tlillan and was logically related

to it."[55] Cihuacoatl could be thought of as the "land" itself, in this instance the land of Mexico. Whenever Mexico-Tenochtitlan directed
her armies against some foreign nation or city, that community was
first given the opportunity of surrendering without a fight. Refusal to
do so, when added to its final defeat, ensured that the enemy god
would be taken captive. The desperation and fury that the enemy
might show while resisting was seen as an enchantment by the enemy
god, namely the spirit of its "land," and properly called for the immunization of that deity. Taken into custody, the enemy idol was escorted back to Mexico as a war captive and ensconced, with a greatly
reduced cult, in a long low building much like the Tlillan. This was
the Coacalco, a prison with many small entrances and cagelike cells.
Thus, these diverse and potentially treacherous "lands" were kept
under the watchful eye of the "land" par excellence, the mighty
earth goddess Cihuacoatl who in her role as custodian was first of all a
Mexican. After holocausts of victims in the important festivals, these
captive gods were allowed to drink limited quantities of blood—in
other words, they did not starve, yet neither did they flourish. If at
any time it became politically desirable to increase the service of such
and such an idol, it could be taken out of its cage and returned temporarily to its home mountain or other holy place. But generally it
was brought back, as there was no other way to insure permanent vassalage of a people.

There were two other temples about which something must be
said here because they were also shrines of the Earth Mother, but in
quite different capacities. It is apparent that the Mexica did not know
exactly how to connect the two goddesses, Xochiquetzal and Chicomecoatl, with the state ritual, for neither goddess played any part in
the Huitzilapochtli myth. Yet the two could not be neglected either,
for they were venerable and belonged to all the people, not just to the
state. Their subordination is marked by the fact that their shrines and
services were performed by the state priests attached to the Coatepetl.

Chicomecoatl was the patroness of cultivated foods, the produce
of gardens and milpas, and as such she was primary. Without her favors no state could survive. Xochiquetzal, though she was also the
mother of corn, ruled more widely, standing for all aspects of womankind, the skills of weaving and dyeing, and empire over birth and all
things sexual.

We know little about their temples except that they were close to the Coatepetl, that they were modest in their dimensions, and that they were adorned with a profusion of jewels and colorful textiles. The parts they played in the cults of the calendar year were far more impressive than the size of their shrines would indicate.

THE ASSOCIATED BUILDINGS

We have seen in the myth that the Four Hundred Huitznahua were the stars and that they were thought of as demonic forces challenging Huitzilopochtli, who was the sun. A structure of some size existed within the temenos, serving both as the locus of their service and as a kind of trophy house recalling Huitzilopochtli's great victory over them.[56] We know the name of this shrine. It was called the *Huitznahuac*, and it was a statement in stone that the young hero who slew the innumerable stars could, by the fact of that cosmic victory, assume their name and powers, calling himself *the* Huitznahuatl god. There is no doubt that this god was a form of Tezcatlipoca and that the temple Huitznahuac therefore belonged to Tezcatlipoca (possibly under his name of Omacatl). Attached to the Huitznahuac was a special ball court called the Tezcatlachco, which name effectively confirms the Tezcatlipoca connection. In the state celebration of the Panquetzaliztli, as we have seen, many victims were sacrificed here as ixiptlas of the stellar gods. Their skulls could be seen strung out by the hundreds on the nearby skull rack.

There was another version of the Aztec myth of the gigantomachy. Here one single star substituted for Coyolxauhqui and her stellar host; this was the planet Venus who was thought to be the elder brother of Tonatiuh, the sun, and comparable to him in all respects. In this myth the sun refuses to rise unless the assembled gods turn over to him their powers and prerogatives. A champion arises to defend their cause and challenge Tonatiuh. This is Ce Acatl, the morning star. The contest takes place in the dawning; the sun defeats Ce Acatl and after he has triumphed he rises in glory. He casts his defeated opponent down into the underworld and then proceeds to sacrifice all the bystanding gods and devours their hearts. Thus did the sun achieve his dominion over the heavens.

This myth spun off a different set of cults within the sacred enclosure, therefore demanding edifices other than those so far described.

One of these monuments was a large pillar topped with a conical cap of thatch and called Ilhuicatitlan, which means "In the Midst of the Heavens." Basically it was an outsized stela dedicated to the morning star whose features appeared on it. Carried on here was a special subcult not directly connected with that of Huitzilopochtli. In the darkness just before the planet's heliacal rising his ixiptla was brought to the foot of the pillar and there slaughtered. Numerous other victims were sacrificed to the pillar during the year, for the morning star was among the most feared of the gods.[57] Because the morning star was the "Great Star" and in himself represented all the stars of heaven, he was potentially evil. Certainly he was dangerous. The priests were well aware of the phases of Venus and could easily predict its heliacal rising. That day in fact stood as the most dreaded augural sign of the entire year, for on it always rode calamity.[58] If the planet appeared in the trecena of One Reed, the star would turn its deadly rays upon rulers and great men and slay them. If, in the trecena of One Movement, then youths and maidens would die. If in One Rain, then the morning star shot at and wounded Tlaloc— whereupon drought ensued. And there were other baleful possibilities—never, in fact, did the god bring blessings. As a consequence his cult was purely placatory.

Close to the pillar was a related edifice, a skull rack reserved for victims sacrificed in that cult. On the day when the planet Venus first appeared as the morning star a pretentious feast followed a holocaust of victims—one of the sources reports that the morning star received more human blood than any god other than the sun itself. The two celestial deities, sun and morning star, younger and older brother, respectively, were bound closely together in myth, but this relationship did not receive expression in this cult. Furthermore, we must realize that in this case we are dealing with the sun as Tonatiuh, not as Huitzilopochtli.

There was another temple within the temenos that was dedicated to the sun god in his avatar as Xipe. This shrine was unusual in the fact that its version of the sun cult was the property of one class only, the knights.[59] Huitzilopochtli was the sun indeed, but only after he had been translated into a mascot for all the Mexican people. Tezcatlipoca was also the sun but in the form of an assigner of destinies and a dark "otherness." But Tonatiuh was the actual sun disc —removed from all cultural associations—as it coursed across the face of day. The cult in this temple belonged not to the state, but to the dual order of elite warriors, the Eagle and Jaguar knights. These were clubs found in all Aztec cities and in most of the rest of Mesoamerica as well; the cult carried on by them here was thus international rather than specifically Mexican in flavor. The temple of Tonatiuh (referred to as Yopico) was relatively modest in size but had its own calmecac and skull rack. It was set within a compact stuccoed courtyard enclosing many inward-facing cells in each of which could be stored a human skin worn during the rites of Xipe. The shrine itself contained the god, not as an idol but as a depiction of the rayed sun identified with the hieroglyph Four Movement that was his date name as a celestial warrior needing hearts and blood to sustain him. This was the famous Sun Stone.

The Sun Stone is perhaps the best-known motif of Aztec culture.[60] It has been reproduced in prints, ceramics, and photographs an excessive number of times and presently stands in the place of honor in the great Aztec hall of the Museo Nacional de Antropología. Durán says that the stone was designed in the reign of Axayacatl during the days when the Mexica were planning their Matlatzinca campaign, and he adds that it was then placed on the top of a structure called a *cuauhxicalco* where it was used in sacrificial rites of a special nature.[61] This is not the place to enter into the controversy that still today surrounds the Sun Stone. Suffice it to say that the Sun Stone celebrating Four Movement was undoubtedly the centerpiece of the knights' worship of Tonatiuh, especially at the annual Flaying of Men. If this is true, then the stone was referred to by the Aztecs as the *huey cuauhxicalli* ("the *great* eagle-vessel"). The stone was laid flat, looking up to the zenith, and was protected from the weather when not in use by a rich awning stretched over it.[62] It was thus designed to fulfill its ritual purpose under the open sky. The wonderful complications and symbolism displayed on its face had to do with the sun as the focus and initiator of all horological mysteries. It was meticulously painted in several bright colors and probably rarely if ever served as a sacrificial block.

There was no techcatl in front of this shrine. Rather there was a sizable square stone dais out in the forecourt.[63] This had on each of its four sides a short access stairway. On top of the dais were two round stones, also laid flat, and together these two formed an elaborate and dual techcatl.[64] On the one stone (the *temalacatl*), captive warriors were tied by several feet of rope and forced into hopeless battle with their Eagle and Jaguar adversaries—dramatic and tragic duels with the upshot never in doubt. On the second stone (a cuauhxicalli), the victim who had been just struck down on the first stone was finally dispatched in a sacrificial killing—his heart was torn out. The more impressive Sun Stone that I mentioned in the preceding paragraph was a cuauhxicalli much more elaborate than this second one.

Somewhere in this general area also stood an adjunct building. It was called the Yopicalco, and here foreign rulers sojourned and watched, hidden from the sight of the populace, the rhythmic plunging of the sacrificial knife.[65]

Closely related to the Coatepetl in meaning was another structure, one related closely to a cult we have been discussing. This was the sacred ball court (*teotlachco*).[66] In one version of the Huitzilopochtli myth the god was said to have beheaded Coyolxauhqui in the middle of the ball court, whereas in his festival of the fifteenth month victims were slaughtered to him at dawn in the teotlachco.

The ground plan of the Mexican teotlachco has not been recovered as it is buried under crowded city blocks behind the cathedral in downtown Mexico City. We can, however, describe it with a fair degree of accuracy by analogy with other ball courts as a long, narrow playing field with stone walls. The audience stood on the wall tops and end courts looking down at the game being played beneath them—this was symbolic of the fact that the *tlachco*, or ball court, was a model of the celestial underworld, and represented the nocturnal concourse through which the sun had to run after his setting. The game itself was a contest between two teams, the one playing the role of the sun and his allies, the other the role of the planet Venus (Quetzalcoatl) and his stellar allies.

All over Mesoamerica and in much of the peripheral area including even some Carribbean islands, *tlachtli* was played with a rubber ball by opposing sides. Here within the Mexican temenos we can be even more specific regarding the game. It was played as a ritual of great solemnity miming the agonized struggle of the midnight sun, the final death of the stars, and the world's first sunrise. For such a dramatic contest the court had to be specially dedicated by the priests. This took place at midnight with the throwing of the ball four times into the court. There is the strong possibility that the priests set fire to the ball as it was flung into the court, thus identifying the ball as the sun flaming out in the underworld—alternatively the ball could symbolize the severed head of the game's loser, Coyolxauhqui, the moon. The actors in this miracle play were earth, sun, and the planet Venus (or alternatively the moon) leading the host of stars. In its classic form, this game, when played as a chapter in cult wherein the players of necessity wagered their heads, always ended with death to the losing side. He, or they, were beheaded in the center of the court.

THE SKULL RACK

One skull rack served both the Coatepetl and the Tlillan.[67] This was the great skull rack (huey tzompantli) that displayed the heads of persons sacrificed in the rites of Huitzilopochtli and his mother Cihuacoatl, as well as most of those who died in the Tlaloc cult. There were other skull racks in Mexico that were attached to temples of the greater gods. They were indeed necessary parts of Aztec cult practices, especially in this cult where the myth of the sun god culminated in the slaughter of his many enemies and the taking of their heads. A display of these was the proof of the god's victory, and thus completed the original statement given by the Coatepetl itself.

The huey tzompantli was a low, elongated dais on which stood an open lattice of great size. It was constructed of long poles, the number of vertical ones exceeding sixty. Before the meals commonly made on the flesh of the victims, their heads had been severed from the bodies and taken back to the skull rack where, broken through at the temples, they were threaded onto the horizontal stretchers. The end pieces of this vast armature were two high piers of outward-facing skulls bonded into a heavy cement to form an interestingly stippled surface when seen from afar. The number of skulls seen and counted by the first Spaniards ranges from estimates of 72,000 to 136,000, the former perhaps being preferable.[68] "Wherever man turned his eyes," wrote Herrera, "they fell on death."[69]

The tzompantli in a true sense was a shrine. It was dedicated to the Omacatzitzin, the gods of feasting, for it was after all a visual record of the remnants of the greatest victory banquet in Aztec myth.

The tzompantli was in short a symbol of victory and plentitude done in espaliered heads.

Thus do the major buildings of the Huitzilopochtli group interlock, and the key to their understanding is the myth of the gigantomachy. The Tlillan—the womb of earth out of which the hero comes—sets the stage for the fateful contest that is told in two parallel versions. In one version the Coatepec, the mountain above the earth, serves as the battleground, and the defeated die in war. In the other version, the battleground is discovered in the halls of night under the earth, the teotlachco, and the defeated die as losers in the ball game. In both cases the hero is the sun, and in both cases the defeated are the stars led either by the morning star or the moon. The final victory of the rising sun is celebrated by a cannibal meal and a display of the skulls of the defeated in the tzompantli, whereas the hero's claim to be the one who rightly took possession of their name and perquisites was made evident in the Huitznahuac.

THE TEMPLES OF TEZCATLIPOCA AND QUETZALCOATL

The reader is by now aware of the statist orientation of the buildings so far described. There were two other important temples within the temenos that were connected to the state cult but not through the myth of the gigantomachy. These were the shrines of Tezcatlipoca and Quetzalcoatl, the two gods so persistently at variance with each other in Aztec myth. Perhaps more than any of the others these two stood for Mexico's Toltec past—and thus for her legitimacy. Tezcatlipoca was the model upon which the state god Huitzilopochtli had been originally fashioned, whereas Quetzalcoatl was the archetype of every pious Aztec ruler. The first had earlier been a sun god and warrior, the second a god of the morning star and a priest. Attached to Tezcatlipoca's temple was the main *telpochcalli* or college for the training of young men in the arts of war.[70] Attached to Quetzalcoatl's shrine in the sacred enclosure was the calmecac where the young men who showed the requisite talents were trained for the priesthood and high office.

The Mexica were well aware that their national god, Huitzilopochtli, was modeled on one greater, namely Tezcatlipoca. This fact, when they were constructing the temenos, might well have caused them architectural problems. They were spared embarrassment, however, when they selected the myth of the gigantomachy as the centering device for the placement of temples—Tezcatlipoca does not appear in that myth. Thus Tezcatlipoca does not dominate the ithualli area; he is presented as simply another great Aztec god. It is possible that his temple may have been that one called the Huitznahuac and that he may have been worshipped there as the god Omacatl. Whatever it was called, his temple pyramid rose to an impressive eighty steps but still could not compare in grandeur with the Coatepetl.[71]

Tezcatlipoca was also the patron god of the Tlacochcalco, the House of Darts, or the armory, that may have been the meeting-house of the Eagle knights. He probably appeared there in his avatar as Yaotl, the god of discord or more literally "the Enemy." Everything about Tezcatlipoca was perilous, and for an Aztec to stand at his shrine was like being forced to the edge of a frightening eminence.

> Well I know that I am on a very high place and I am speaking with a person of great majesty, in whose presence runs a river deep in a gorge. Sheer cliffs loom above it. Being in your presence is like that—a sliding place from which many are hung.[72]

Nearby, as we have noted, was the city's main telpochcalli or bachelor house where at stated times there assembled that apprentice order so beloved of the god and referred to as "the Young." Also attached was an edifice where the god was honored under the title "Our Lord Five" (*Macuiltotec*) where victims could be sacrificed to the spirit of war, and where the ruler and his greater nobles performed certain penitential acts.[73] This may have been one of the portal arsenals.

Rulers and Tezcatlipoca were known to have a peculiar relationship, for the god spoke through the mouth of every legitimate tlatoani. Whereas Huitzilopochtli represented the military dominance of the Mexican state by right of conquest, Tezcatlipoca supported the prerogatives of the ruler and his entourage, validating their monopoly of warfare.

The Temple of Quetzalcoatl (probably called the *Chililico*)[74] appears to have stood in the center of the temenos facing the great pyramid, but there is no independent confirmation of this. The pyramid base had sixty steps and was very steeply pitched, but what distinguished the teocalli on top from all other temples was the fact that it was circular in ground plan, was beautifully thatched, and peaked in a high and narrow cone.[75] Entry into this shrine was through a doorway framed as a dragon's maw. It faced east and thus openly confronted the Coatepetl that faced west. This conforms to the mythic confrontation of the morning star with the sun. The Chililico, in fact, may have acted here as an astronomical observatory, possibly pinpointing the equinoctial sunrise between the two shrines on the Coatepetl.[76]

Inasmuch as Quetzalcoatl was the archetypal priest, it is not surprising that there was a calmecac attached to his shrine, a low building that housed the acolytes and the senior priests who guided and trained them. In front of the temple was a square stone podium on which at certain times a ritual theater depicting various diseases was performed.[77] In one impressive way the Chililico regulated the entire city of Tenochtitlan. At sunrise and at sunset a large drum with a distinctive tone and range was beaten from the upper platform of the shrine. This drum was the voice of the wind god calling to curfew or to its lifting, and in the dark streets of night no one but the guards stirred once the god had spoken.

This temple housed a universal, rather than a national, god. It was the home of the complex arts of computation, of the painting of books, and of the reading of omens in the almanac. It was therefore the guardian of the skills and secrets of the state; more will be said about this in a succeeding chapter.

THE CALMECAC

The institution that coordinated, timed, and shaped all of the aforementioned cults, and therefore administered the various shrines, was the calmecac, translated as "the file of dwellings," or "the cloisters." These were low blocks of buildings each with inner courts faced with cells and storage rooms. We have already alluded to the one attached to Quetzalcoatl's temple. Every temple offering a major cult, as a matter of fact, possessed one of these buildings that did duty as a priestly dormitory, a repository for cult paraphernalia, and a center of discipline and learning. Each calmecac was responsible for the carrying out of its particular cult or cults. In all of the city of Tenochtitlan there were at least seven calmecacs, of which some appear to have been outside the temenos.[78]

Two calmecacs within the temenos were of special note. The first was the Mexico calmecac that served most of the shrines. It was thus pivotal in all affairs of state. Within it was kept a famous statue of Quetzalcoatl, god of priests, here worshipped under the name of *Tlilpotonqui*.[79] Thus the Mexico calmecac was not only a service institution for the Coatepetl, but was specifically also a temple of the god Quetzalcoatl. However, it did not in any sense duplicate Chililico, the round temple of Quetzalcoatl, for its purpose was to accept certain children offered to the god from the purely Mexican wards of the city and to train them in chastity, obedience, and propriety. The curriculum at the highest level included training in hymnody, in day reckoning, in reading the histories of the Mexicans, in the painting of sacred books, and in the computation of horoscopes and auguries.[80] The second calmecac of note was the Tlillan calmecac that served the temple of that name and was in some senses an adjunct of the palace.[81] Special apartments were kept there for the retreats and fasting of the ruler and magnates.

THE MEANING OF THE ITHUALLI

It should be possible to elucidate the meaning of this remarkable patio, a locus that we have spoken of as the temenos, or sacred enclosure.

Of the goddesses worshipped here only one, Cihuacoatl, was integrated into the central myth of the state, the myth of Huitzilopochtli. Though this myth had been redesigned by the Mexica to validate the claims of the Aztec state and its main enterprise of war, it had earlier been a common nature myth.

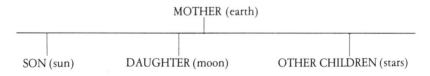

It was in the cults of the two other major goddesses, Xochiquetzal and Chicomecoatl, that the populace worshipped the earth. In these two the uniqueness and venerability of the earth goddess could be maintained, quite apart from the cult of Cihuacoatl. Sex, parturition, crafts, and food was the matter of their rituals, and therefore they represented no threat to the previously mentioned statist interpretation of the Mother. In Cihuacoatl, the Mother had had her *terribilità* so exaggerated that she could thenceforth serve only power. Thus in the ithualli the Mother was displayed not as one but as many.

So too with the male gods and their cults. In spite of the fact that a broad sun worship stood behind each of the cults (exclusive of that of Quetzalcoatl), their disparity was what was emphasized. During the pre-Aztec times there must have occurred constant speculation on the nature and jurisdictions of the gods. Yet, in spite of that, only a modest effort was made by the Aztecs to link them closely together.

Now there is, of course, no necessity for a people to organize their cults under one rubric. The Homeric Greeks did so by listing their gods as inhabitants of Olympus, a loose feudal monarchy, all of them related to each other by blood or marriage. Nevertheless, the Greeks never built a park, such as was the ithualli, for the cults of all the gods.

So what was logically important to the Aztecs was not any imposed concept of unity, but a central place, a hearth as it were, or a campsite. The ithualli was a late architectural memory of a people's wandering through the sacred defiles of the earth. Here they made a campfire at the end of the day's trek; here they welcomed strangers seeking ties with the ragtag band; here they rose up with the dawn and the auspices of the bright planet; and here they kicked away the ashes as they prepared to leave. Wanderers know only one center, and that is the hearth.

This interpretation of the ithualli as an imaginary locus based on tribal memories is nothing that the historian can prove. It was certainly not a conscious decision taken in the minds of the Aztec builders; otherwise they would have understood Huehueteotl, the old fire god, as more central. He is indeed represented in the enclosure by the Tzonmolco and by the hearth next to the Tlillan, besides which there was Tetlanman of Chantico, a goddess connected with fire. Nevertheless, the ithualli remained a fortress within which were ensconced the gods. Nevertheless, fire and memories of the wandering were everywhere.

Perhaps we may put it in the following terms. The design of the ithualli was that of a sacred park within which the gods were situated, but its sacredness was guaranteed, not by their presences, but by the fact that it was the center of all things—and this, in Aztec myth, is the definition of fire. The meaning of the ithualli was thus ambivalent.

TEMPLES OUTSIDE THE SACRED ENCLOSURE

In my discussion of the temenos, I may have given the impression that the cultic life of the Aztecs was totally concentrated on the gods domiciled within. This would be an erroneous impression as it would imply that only the state-approved canon of gods counted. Every ward (calpulli) in the great Aztec cities had its own parochial deity or fetish that commanded a full allegiance from its parishioners. Everywhere in the Aztec world there were temples (teocalli). One of the early friars marveled at the abundance of these structures.

> In every town and district and at distances of every quarter-league they had other small patios with three or four *teocallis*, in some places more and in others only one, and on every cliff or hillock, one or two; and along the road and in the corn fields there were many other little ones. All these *teocallis* were white and kept whitewashed, so that they were very visible.[82]

To catch the flavor of the ongoing religious life of the city we need to mention a few of these shrines, keeping in mind that the rather diverse ethnic groups and the guilds always clustered around particular shrines. Thus, each of the city's wards was centered in a cult peculiar to it.

As examples we may cite the following. The fire god was worshipped in his ward and shrine called Tzonmulco—this was of course distinct from the fire pit that we saw as an appendage to the Tlillan within the temenos. Here the god was revered, and here the tlatoani came for new fire whenever he needed to cense one of the gods. In the merchants' quarter, Yacateuctli, the god of travelers and commerce, received his due. In fact so many were the victims offered to him by the successful merchants that a special tzompantli was set up nearby to display their skulls. Izquitecatl, the god of intoxicating drink, possessed a shrine with a basin in front of it that brimmed to overflowing with octli on the days of his festivals. Xipe, who was at once the sun, a warrior, the spring season, and the patron of gold workers, had his temple pyramid in the ward of Yopico. We have seen him represented within the temenos in the gladiator cult, but here he received daily ongoing service. In the ward of Tlamatzinco, the young god of the Matlatzinca people from over the western range was worshipped. After the Mexica had conquered the capital city of those people, they had allowed some of them in as settlers, and in the event they brought with them their god. Again, those who grew flowers, sold them, and arranged them for displays lived in the ward of Coatlan and worshipped the goddess Coatlicue there. We have previously noted that the great lowland Earth Mother, Toci, was a captive in the Coacalco, which was in the ithualli, but we also found that she had for festival purposes a temple called the "House of the Goddess" (*Cihuateocalli*) on the south side of the city. In front of it was the elevated wooden rack where as a straw image the Great Mother Tlazolteotl was worshipped in the savage Ochpaniztli festival.[83] Just to the north of the city, worshippers of the earth mother Tonan greeted this deity as the rock of Tepeyac, the site being presently preempted by her lineal successor the Virgin of Guadalupe. The hunting god Mixcoatl had a well-known pyramid shrine in the city as well as his artificial desert garden in the temenos. There were altogether five temples of the corn deity in the city. We have already seen the central one co-opted by the state and placed within the temenos, but each of the four quarters of the city also had a shrine to maize, a *cinteopan*[84]; the basic food obviously could not be overvalued. Thus, the goddess of corn appears as either one or five, depending on whether we view her as state oriented or as belonging to all the people.

And so we could go on, adducing many temples and crossroad shrines within and just outside the city.[85] It was an unbelievable religious picture, suffocating in its cultic richness.

We should advance a caveat here—that the sources are never clear on the exact number of temples within the city, their locations, or the names of the gods worshipped there. Some are obvious but others are not, so there is always a sizable margin of error in any statement made on the subject.

4

The Mediators

In a study such as this it is worth repeating that an organized priesthood acts not only as custodian of religion but as interpreter as well. This is obvious. What is not so obvious is that a priesthood is normally a dumping ground for religious, magical, and supernatural offices of all kinds that have come down to it through the centuries. If we should care to guess that priests in Mesoamerica appeared as long ago as the rise of Olmec culture—say roughly in the middle of the second millennium B.C.—we would then be saying that they were simply the latest of the many professors of the supernatural in that area at that time. And we should then be prepared to see the highly specialized office of the Olmec priest as involved in a constant battle to absorb the powers of the earlier and more individualistic stargazers, seers, dream interpreters, fortune-tellers, shape changers, and others —but without ever any clear-cut successes. For the earlier shamans and wonder workers would never be eliminated and would continue on in their development even as the priesthood evolved.

The priestly office was designed to maintain and manipulate the orientation of the supernatural world in favor of the chiefdom or state. Yet we find constant contamination of the priesthood from the professions of the sorcerers and curers. The reader should keep the distinction in mind. Without it he or she will see the Aztec priesthood as badly muddled or ill defined. We shall point out these contaminations as we go along.

SORCERERS

There was a well-defined group of individuals in Aztec culture known as the *nahualli*s whose profession came down from the earliest times. Their special power was their ability to change themselves into animals or into dangerous forces such as fire and blood, and they were accordingly feared. Their profession was later given a divine prototype in the god Tezcatlipoca who was said to have been a nahualli. The same, though with less relevance, could be applied to the God Quetzalcoatl. The former most particularly could shift into any shape he pleased. His preferred animal alter ego was the jaguar, and when he appeared as such he was Tepeyollotl, a god of night who lurked in dark caves.

The nahualli is a shaman in all respects save the important feature that his practices do not primarily center about the spirit journey that is typically taken in the shamanic trance.[1] Nevertheless, like the shaman, the nahualli knows the heavens and the places of the dead. He knows also about droughts and rain, plagues and hunger, and as such can be of use to society. He has power to foresee the death of princes and the fall of cities. We thus see him as a seer and a shape shifter, not always but generally evil and dangerous. His supernatural powers appear when he is in the womb, and they can be confirmed by the almanac for he is often born under the sign of One Wind or One Rain, both of them days of occult power.[2] And if he was inclined to evil sorceries, for putting his plans into effect, he would always choose a *tonalpohualli* day that had the coefficient nine.[3] The number nine was congenial to magicians.

Now it is obvious that such a practitioner is not in any formal sense a priest, for his practices were not frozen into any cult patterns in which the state had an interest. Even though the ruler might retain a famous nahualli as a member of his entourage, such a person was not expected to perform the penances and offerings characteristic of a priest. The nahualli was thought of as *atlaca*, "nonhuman," perhaps even "inhuman."[4] On the contrary, the priest was a recognized member of the human society, even when he might engage in some of the magician's practices.

As in so many preliterate societies, black magic was pervasive and greatly feared among the Aztecs. Moteuczoma II repeatedly ordered his sorcerers to cast their enchantments against the incoming Spaniards hoping to thus demoralize the strangers and frustrate their designs. The sorcerer (*texoxqui*), was so much in demand, on the one hand, and so feared, on the other, that his work became highly compartmentalized.[5] There were sorcerers for almost every conceivable type of magic. There were rainmakers and those who arrested the hail; there were those who divined under the influence of various hallucinogenic drugs; there were those who destroyed or maddened people by magically removing their vital organs. There were those who blew fire from their mouths, who poisoned people, or killed them by throwing images of them into the fire. Some interpreted dreams or divined by scattering maize kernels on the ground and then reading their patterns. The Nahuatl vocabulary devoted to sorcery and specifying its types of practitioners is large.[6]

All of the preceding escape the definition of priest because of their social unaccountability. A priest could be, and often was, trained to foretell things or be the custodian of esoterica. The priest who was also a *tonalpouhqui* could read a person's fate from the sacred almanac (*tonalamatl*) and advise him on it exactly as if he were a person who divined things through demonic connections. But the priest was always a member of a social order, and thus he was known to accept a responsibility in carrying out the proper intentions of that order. As a priest, he could make errors or be lax in the performance of his duties, but he could not conceive of acting on his own as a way of life.

CURERS

He bewitches; he is a sorcerer (*nahualli*), a soothsayer (*tlapouhqui*) a caster of lots (*tlapoani*), a diagnostician by means of knots.

So runs the definition of the curer in Colonial Aztec society, obviously weighted by the newly Christianized mind as it looked back into its pagan past.[7]

What interests us in this definition is not that it is derogatory but that it classes the curer basically as a shaman and sorcerer. The Nahuatl word here being defined is *ticitl* that can mean equally a curer or a midwife, but in any case an expert in the adjustment of the human person caught in some corporeal crisis. The ticitl was excluded from the definition of priest by the Aztecs themselves; yet in a curious way he or she stands between the shaman and the priest. On the one hand, the methods of the ticitl could depend heavily on "counting" or reading from the painted books, a priestly monopoly and therefore implying a priest's training. When he consulted the Book of Destiny Days for the efficacy of a cure regarding a certain patient, he was a tonalpouhqui, or more generally a tlapouhqui.[8] On the other hand, the ticitl was not attached to any particular temple cult but operated in the interstices of society with a personal reputation to maintain. Curing in the early stages of man's life everywhere seems to have been one of the shaman's greatest arts, but inevitably as time went on some of it shifted into the priestly realm, simply because of the priest's more corporate and therefore more aggrandizing way of life. The Aztec ticitls were in a sense both shamans and priests, though they were not confused with either.

Curing and darkness went together. The supernatural patron of the ticitls was the mother goddess Yohualticitl,[9] said to be the spouse of the male spirit of the night, Yohualteuctli, who himself was a figuration of the sun in the underworld. These two deities do not appear in any of the public festivals with which I am familiar, and as a consequence may be thought of as mainly emanations of the popular imagination. This does not reduce their importance.

Yohualticitl was the deity of the *temazcalli*, or steam house, whose purpose was fundamentally curative.[10] These were low-domed mud structures entered through crawl holes and could contain, according to their size, up to ten people. The steam inside was produced by pouring water over stones heated in a fire. The cure or strengthening induced by the sweat bath resulted from the fact that the temazcalli was the original matrix, the dark womb from which all beings had emerged; a reentry into that womb was a death, and the reemergence was a rebirth into full vigor. A special group of curers, much revered, would accompany the parturient mother or diseased person into the steam house in order to fan him or her, thus blowing away all noxious emanations.[11]

Because of his reputation for wisdom, the wind god Quetzalcoatl presided over that aspect of curing that also included the prognosis of a disease.[12] The curer came in the night to where the sick person was and placed a small statue of Quetzalcoatl on the ground near him. He then cast maize kernels—some twenty of them—onto a white cloak laid on the ground.[13] According to the configurations made by the kernels, it could be seen whether the patient would survive or not. The twenty kernels probably stood for the twenty day signs of the tonalpohualli.

The preceding ministrations were offered not to society as a whole but to individuals, and thus they had no clear cultic connections. Occasionally, however, the ticitls did become active participants in cult as in the Ochpaniztli festival where they swarmed around the ixiptla of Toci, amusing and flattering her before her death. The goddess Yohualticitl is simply an avatar of Toci, who was revered by all midwives.[14] Thus, the ticitls shuttled back and forth between the shaman's world and that of the priest.

THE PRIESTHOOD

The Aztec priest may have come down from a prototypal Mesoamerican priest who was either a surrogate sufferer for the group, a calendric expert, or a vicarious appearance of the spirit. We cannot make a definite statement, and in fact we may even be putting the whole problem of origins too simply. We know that the Spaniards were appalled at the abuse to which the Aztec priests subjected themselves and the excruciating and bloody exercises that they regularly performed. It was thus the penitential aspects of the Aztec priesthood that the Spanish friars stressed, but there was of course far more.

Generally, the priest was called *tlamacazqui*, which means literally "he who gives things"—a "giver" in short. Thus defined, it is obvious that he is conceptually unrelated to the shaman or sorcerer, however much of his thunder he may have stolen. Another word for priest is *teopixqui*, which means "he who keeps or guards the god." These two designations have different implications. The first presents the priest as a placatory go-between, one who in person serves the god, approaching him with offerings from the state—this further defines donation as the central act in Aztec cult, and it sees the supernatural as competent to accept the spirit of the offering. The second title is quite different. It depicts the priest as the sole guarantor of the security and purity of the god who is here thought of as simply the animation of the idol. The first implies the capriciousness of the supernatural and its frequent rejections of man's petitions. The second specifies that the priest is privy to the god and is aware of his intentions. Here the god will accept only such petitions as come to him through his priest. Thus the priest has a monopoly on the god, and the state must sue through him.

The preceding implications were naturally not formulated in so many words by the Aztecs, and I have advanced them here only to

develop further pertinent questions. Overall, does Aztec cult display
for us a priest whose duties stress only one of the preceding readings,
or both? Or both in unequal quantity? It is my impression that the
Aztec priest more nearly resembles the sacerdotal servant implied in
the term *tlamacazqui* than in the term *teopixqui*. The fact, however,
that the second term was used at all to describe the Aztec priest shows
that to some extent it also reflects a truth about him.

The teopixqui, as a matter of fact, is closely related to the divine
office called *teomama* ("he who carries the god on his back"), an
early oracle giver who, through controlling the important taboos,
could carry the god about in a backpack while leading the tribe in
wandering or on the warpath. These peripatetic priests were true
"guardians" whose close contacts with the supernatural were in some
ways almost shamanistic. But the moment the tribe settled into an
urban context, the teomama became the teopixqui.

The important aspect of the Aztec priesthood that is not hinted
at in either of the previously mentioned denominations was penitential or surrogate suffering for the community.[15] The true priest could
always be referred to as *tlamaceuhqui*, a performer of meritorious actions such as dangerous pilgrimages or night journeys, cruel fasts, and
deprivations, or autosacrifice and self-mutilation.[16] Lay individuals
could also be referred to as tlamaceuhqui, but in such a case their
suffering was a conscious choice made to influence or thank one of the
gods. The penitential life for the priest was a duty that probably
ranked as high as that of service to the god. Thus, the Aztec priest
stood at the fulcrum point of the supernatural, halfway between the
Aztecs and their gods, that point that we have defined as cult.

Two features out of the Mesoamerican past clarify for us the
office of the Aztec priest. The first is the influence of an ancient Tlaloc
cult in Teotihuacan; the other is the effect made by the person of
Topiltzin Quetzalcoatl, a figure from the Toltec past.

In regard to the former, we notice first the fact that the word
tlamacazqui, which as we have seen means priest, is also used to
designate the god Tlaloc.[17] He is, as it were, the original "donor,"
the giver of storms and rain that in turn bring verdure and the growth
of corn. It appears that tlamacazqui might have been first of all a designation of Tlaloc himself, and only after that did his early priests assume it also, on the theory of the identity of master and servant. In
myth we find that *tlamacazqui* was a word used to describe "the

uncles" of the god Huitzilopochtli, namely the Four Hundred Huitznahua whom he defeated in the cosmic battle—and here the word
speaks again of identity.[18] We shall see later that the priests of several
of the Aztec gods carry the same names and wear the same clothing as
the gods whom they served. This close identification could mean that
the various Aztec priesthoods as a whole were modeled on one particular cultus out of the distant past, namely that one dedicated to the
storm king resident in the mountains—the deity who would become
known to the Aztecs much later as Tlaloc.

We must pause here briefly to consider Tlaloc. If it was, indeed,
he out of whose worship the first priesthood in Mesoamerica evolved,
then he certainly deserves our attention. The famous stone idol of the
god on the mountain behind Tezcoco (still today called "Mount Tlaloc") was reputed to have been the most ancient in the land, long
preceding the advent of the Aztecs.[19] In fact he was remembered as
having been the god of the Quinametin who were, in Aztec lore, the
early people of Teotihuacan.[20] In Teotihuacan art we see the god in
one of his manifestations wearing the year sign as a headpiece,
thereby announcing himself as a lord of the calendar and of all annual
computations—as such he was patron of those skilled in chronology,
namely the priests.[21]

Tlaloc's cult is probably implicated in the very foundations of
Mesoamerican civilization. Thus, we need not be surprised to find
him sitting in his Mexican temple as a coequal lord next to the great
Huitzilopochtli. One source even defines the relationship of Tlaloc to
Huitzilopochtli as that of father to son.[22] Such centrality and such
power of tradition inhered in the god that it would not be extreme to
advance the hypothesis that his priesthood, the tlamacazquis, was the
sacerdotal model for all other cults that would arise.

If we wish to further understand the god's priesthood, we must
look as well into another part of the past, this time to the Toltec
period, which followed Teotihuacan and preceded the rise of the Aztecs. The appearance at that time of a priest called *Topiltzin* is often
alluded to. We note that he was a devotee, not of Tlaloc, but of the
related god Quetzalcoatl. Both gods were essentially storm gods, but
Quetzalcoatl was particularly the wind, and he was depicted as a
"dragon" or "feathered serpent," which is exactly what the name
Quetzalcoatl means.

In legend, Topiltzin was a famous holy man who, after a period of wandering, settled in Tula, the Toltec capital, to become there the high priest of the god Quetzalcoatl.[23] By his position as well as by his exceptional holiness, he assumed the god's name as his own, thus becoming Topiltzin Quetzalcoatl. Later in Aztec times every high priest was called a *quetzalcoatl*.

The impact of this man (or men—if the legend has condensed several generations of high priests) on Toltec religious life and on the Aztec experience that followed it was enormous. Thenceforth he filled the role of archetypical priest subtly blended into the figure of his god Quetzalcoatl. Thus, whereas the priesthood had probably been formed on a Tlaloc template, it was now further enriched and endowed with new definition and personality by a religious genius from a related cult.

Both gods mentioned before were patrons of chronology but with differences. The line coming down from Tlaloc specified that it was the calendrical (solar) year that was the charge of priests, and it was only they who could compute seasons, festivals, and day counts. The line coming from Quetzalcoatl specified on the contrary the almanac, namely the tonalpohualli, as the charge of the priesthood whose members could read horoscopes, note the luck or ill fortune of a day, and in general guide the future. Both of these exercises involved expert knowledge and the imagination of the exceptional priest. Each skill belonged to a different god; yet they were gods who had been closely connected (perhaps even identical) in the distant past, both of them embodiments of the storm. In Aztec cult the similarity translates into the feature that Quetzalcoatl was the patron god of the calmecac, which is the school and home of the priests who are epithetically referred to as *Tlaloque*, namely the tlamacazquis.

I do not wish to suggest in this passage that the Aztec priesthood was immune to influences from other important cult conglomerations in Mesoamerican history. It is in fact probable that the gods Xipe, Xiuhteuctli, and the Great Mother herself all impinged upon the development of the office of the priest and on his later performances. Our texts, however, give us no details. As a working hypothesis, I have assumed that the worship of Tlaloc and Quetzalcoatl was the truly creative influence on the development of the Aztec priest.

The preceding discussion may also have clarified the role of the ixiptla. We have seen that the ixiptla was the "image" or "likeness" of a god. He did not fill the role of servant and had no connections with the calmecac. He was therefore a cult object, not a priest.

THE RULER AS A RELIGIOUS FIGURE

The Aztec ruler was generally referred to as *tlatoani* (literally "he who says things"). The concept of a speaker or of one who gives orders is in no way necessarily religious, and the Aztec state was quite aware of all the dynamics of command and political success. Basically therefore the tlatoani was a political officer, ruling as the first among equals in a Council of Five. At the time of his installation four princes were elected to serve as his councilors. The tlatoani's power fluctuated therefore according to the support or opposition that he received from this inner group and from other magnates around them. The tlatoani thus acted as a recognizable politico-military leader.

There is, however, an aspect of the office of tlatoani that is certainly religious—over and above the cult duties always associated with rulers in preliterate societies. In Mexico the dogma was that the tlatoani was chosen by the god Tezcatlipoca.[24] He was considered to be the very presence of the god whose divine words issued from his mouth. Rulership as an abstraction belonged only to Tezcatlipoca, and the tlatoani was thus only a simulacrum of him. Tutored by the god, the ruler knew all about the dangers of his office:

> In truth, the rulership is not a peaceful place, a good place, for things slip, things slide. And there remain piled up words of stone, words which are clubs. Those of the city remain grumbling, howling. His cities which remain about, remain menacing.[25]

As if to tie this down, it was Tezcatlipoca who also decided when the ruler had to die. If during his tenure, the ruler turned out to be inept or evil, only a high priest with Tezcatlipoca's backing could officially pronounce him deposed.[26] The relationship between the god and the ruler in fact was so close that the latter was understood to be in person responsible for rain, sunshine, and abundance in general.[27]

His also was the responsibility of maintaining the worship of the gods and of punishing sacrilege. When an enemy one dark night mounted a lightning raid from across the lake, burning down Toci's wooden shrine on the south side of Tenochtitlan, Moteuczoma ordered all of her attendant priests punished for not instantly alerting the city.[28] They were forced into box cages so small that they could not stand up. The floors were set with obsidian knives so that even the slightest movement drew blood. Fed on a limited diet to keep them barely alive but suffering as long as possible, these priests were objects of public ridicule and outrage until they mercifully died. The incident gives us the measure of the tlatoani's control over, and responsibility for, the priesthood.

In thus defining the office of the tlatoani, we are close to presenting him as if he were an ixiptla of Tezcatlipoca, the only one known in Aztec cult who was not sacrificed. If so, then the Aztec state existed in the aura of two manifestations of Tezcatlipoca active side by side throughout the year.

From the preceding it is obvious that the office of tlatoani was sacred, but was the ruler thereby divine? Or was the tlatoani merely the highest pontiff in the state? The answer to this must be that the Aztec tlatoani had indeed advanced in the popular estimation a certain distance toward being accepted as divine, but he had not yet been able to insert his palace into the ithualli where the gods lived. And surely the reason for this was that the charisma of the ruler could be as suddenly withdrawn by Tezcatlipoca as it may have been suddenly granted in the first place.

The Aztecs were accustomed to treating their rulers as "godlike"; yet, however exalted their social position, the rulers were not truly gods.[29] Death for them was almost, but not quite, a moment of transfiguration. As the Mexican ruler lay dying, a mask of the god Tezcatlipoca was placed on his face, and it was not removed until either he recovered or died.[30] This was probably a case of divine protection as much as identification with the god. As a follow-up of their deaths, small effigies of the deceased rulers might be placed among the statues of the greater gods.[31]

An address to the ruler on his installation is illustrative of the ambiguity mentioned previously. We hear the following being spoken to him:

> Although the common folk have gladdened you, although your younger brother, your older brother, have put their trust in you, now you are deified. Although you are human, as we are, although you are our friend, our son, our younger brother, our older brother, no more are

you human as we are. We do not look to you as human. Already you represent, you replace one.[32]

At the time of his installation, the new tlatoani chose one of the great gods to sponsor him, one whom he himself might represent. From that time on he would participate in that god's renown sometimes wearing his regalia, and when he died the officiating priest at the obsequies wore that god's vestments—whether it was Xipe, Mixcoatl, Huitzilopochtli or some other.[33] This did not in any way contradict the ruler's automatic identification with Tezcatlipoca already mentioned, for that was a continuing dogma of the state. The one god he never claimed to represent was Quetzalcoatl—that deity had already been preempted to fill the role of dynastic founder, the original Toltec ruler from whom all Aztec rulers descended and from whom they received their legitimacy.

In the sections that follow we will be able to see clearly the role that the ruler played vis-à-vis the priesthood.

THE HIERARCHY—THE NEOPHYTES

A certain Colonial source estimated that one out of every six Mexicans was a priest.[34] We have no way of checking the accuracy of this statement, and it is surely excessive. Nevertheless, we have no doubt whatsoever that priests were numerous in all the greater Aztec cities.

There appear to have been four ranks in the priesthood.[35] There was first the body of the neophytes (*tlamacaztoton*) and lay votaries, a fluctuating group out of which the professional priest would eventually come. This latter, as we have already seen, was called *tlamacazqui*, a generic title. Like our own word "priest," it can be used generally to mean any person with rights of manipulation in cult. Above the commonalty of priests was the *tlenamacac* (literally the "fire vender" but generally referred to in the literature as the fire priest). The rank of fire priest was prestigious and from this class the administrators and high priests came. The preceding is a simple schema, corresponding to our understanding of the way a priesthood is structured today, namely acolytes, priests, and then bishops topped by the archbishop or high priest (in Nahuatl, the *hueytlamacazqui*). I shall describe each in some detail in order to bring out the sophistication of Aztec cult.

There were several methods by which the Aztec priesthood recruited its members. The first was by devotion, an act where typically the parents of a child who had suffered some illness or impairment and then recovered pledged the child to the god responsible for the cure.[36] At an early age the child was taken to the appropriate temple and formally offered to the priest in charge, who then returned the child to its parents to raise until of age to enter the establishment, the tlamacazcalli. The period of indenture was generally for one year.

A more stringent system of recruitment obtained in the state cult centered around Huitzilopochtli.[37] In the city of Mexico-Tenochtitlan there were only six out of a score or so of wards (*calpulli*) that could claim to have been the habitations of the descendants of the original Mexica, the founders of the first settlement in the lake—all the other wards were descended from later increments to the population, sometimes even people of alien tongues.[38] Annually at the Panquetzaliztli festival the leaders of the aforementioned six wards designated some fifty calpulli youths and an equal number of calpulli girls to fill the quota of neophytes.[39] Being pure-blooded Mexicans, they could legitimately serve the tribal god and his associated deities in the central complex. Until the next Panquetzaliztli they were then domiciled in the adjoining calmecac. Here they lived chaste and painful lives, the young men in groups of four to six begging about the city for their food and engaged in constant bloodletting; the girls on the contrary were practically incarcerated. Beside this selected group of fifty, other youths from other calpullis could be sent by their noble fathers to the calmecac almost as day boarders to learn propriety, humility, and service to the state.[40] Their indoctrination, however, seems to have been just as intense, and formal application for their entry was made at a banquet where the higher priests were entertained and where the noble fathers pledged rich gifts to Quetzalcoatl, the god of the calmecac.

There was a marked difference between the neophytes of Tezcatlipoca and those of Huitzilopochtli. The former god had a special feeling for, and appreciation of, young people, for he himself was the "Youth" (*telpochtli*); he was in fact the youngest of the gods. The young people who were organized in his cult lived at home but daily came together in the *telpochcalli*, the bachelor house, there being one in each ward.[41] Besides their activities during the day in the work forces, during the evenings they were trained in the complex choric dances beloved of the gods. Young people serving out their apprenticeships to Huitzilopochtli lived in the calmecac, as we have said, but the tyros of Tezcatlipoca lived at home.

As far as we can ascertain, most young men received training either in a telpochcalli or a calmecac, the latter institution being reserved for nobles, princes, and other highly placed people, the former for all others. We do hear, however, of exceptions where the sons of lowly parents might be in the calmecac. But whether they were sons of commoners or nobles, the young men in any case formed the labor cadres of the state; those in the telpochcalli being used on state building projects, maintenance, repairs on aqueducts, collection of firewood, backup battalions in war emergencies, and so on. The neophytes in the calmecacs served their year mainly in temple service, bringing in wood from the forests, rushes from the lake, maguey thorns, rattlesnakes, scorpions, and so forth.[42] They performed the nightly vigils and watches and served in menial attendance upon the priests. The girls wove textiles to be used in the ceremonies, cooked the food of the gods, and attended the goddesses when called on. Thus, through the novitiate, the state tied both elite and common youths to its purposes.

At the end of their assigned year, most of the youths were released to marry and begin families, or to further their training for war and court life. But some youths from both schools who showed an aptitude for a life of religious learning and asceticism moved up in the calmecac into the class of priests, the tlamacazquis. At this point they would let their hair grow long.

Inasmuch as there were seven calmecacs in Mexico alone, each attached to one of the great temples, there may have been some difficulties in maintaining full priestly rosters—we do not know. We can certainly suspect competition among them. Cihuacoatl's calmecac was closely attached to the palace and therefore received the sons of the ruler and his magnates. The priests there had certain privileges. The "Mexico" calmecac, which we have already mentioned, belonged to Quetzalcoatl and served the central gods—it was probably the largest. The fire god had his calmecac as did Xipe and two of Tezcatlipoca's avatars. Thus, each god in the pantheon who was considered to be crucial in supporting the claims of the ruling class was provided with a calmecac where his prestige could be protected and his cult enhanced. Other gods who were not included in the state group and who were not supported by a calmecac had to ask for services from the seven.

THE HIERARCHY—THE PRIESTS

Any discussion of the Aztec priesthood must begin with the role played therein by the god Quetzalcoatl. In one myth the high god Tonacateuctli is said to have sent down his son Quetzalcoatl from the heavens to reform the human race at a time when they had become witless and evil. Quetzalcoatl first became aware of the full extent of men's sinfulness with the onset of a four-year drought that almost destroyed the Toltec empire. So gracious and humble were his petitions to Tlaloc and the other deities of water, and so severe his self-mutilations that the gods were pleased and sent down as a revelation a lizard to scratch in the earth, for that animal was a symbol of abundance.

Quetzalcoatl was the first priest, and he was therefore the first man to properly invoke the gods and to offer sacrifices to them.[43] It was he who built the first temples, it was he who instituted in Tula a new order of penitential priests to perform his austerities, and it was he who invented the art of divination from sacred books. But perhaps his most important cult innovations were certain acts of autosacrifice performed by both laymen and priests.

In Mexico Quetzalcoatl's priests numbered four.[44] Each one of them for a span of thirteen days presided over the rites and over the instruction of the youths in the calmecac. They could be referred to as the "conch heads," so called because on certain occasions they wore on their heads large conch shells, Quetzalcoatl's preferred insignia.[45] Whether they were the same as the quetzalcoatls mentioned elsewhere is unclear. Girls served as priestesses in the god's cult[46]—this was unusual in that priestesses appear to have been generally restricted to the cults of the goddesses. It is probable that these catechumens, both young men and girls alike, came from the six Mexican wards and thus represented the privileged group. In that case, they would have been a part of the fifty whom we have seen annually selected for the state cult. The role of the priests of Quetzalcoatl as instructors of the young was obviously of prime importance to the smooth functioning of the social structure.

We have seen that there were two major groups of priests, ordinary ones, or tlamacazquis, and the superior class, or the tlenamacacs. The role of the latter included the censing of the god in special festivals, the right to wear the god's distinguishing regalia and masks,[47] and finally the privilege of sacrificing victims.[48] Translated into our nomenclature he could be thought of as having episcopal standing. High priests were always of this rank.

The *tlamacazcayotl*,[49] or body of priests serving for life, was an extremely varied group, and our sources do not give us much in the way of detail concerning them. It is possible—even probable—that most of them were centered in the Huitzilopochtli/Tlaloc core of rituals that was of such overriding importance to the state. We know, for instance, that the goddess Xochiquetzal had no priests of her own—her cult was operated by the priests and priestesses of the Coatepetl.[50] Even the cult of the greatest of the goddesses, Cihuacoatl, was included in the charge of the priests of Huitzilopochtli.[51]

Most of the priests were, for reasons of birth, aptitude, or whatever, rooted in their positions. At the end of every four years the high priests and the tlatoani selected those whose service or holiness recommended them for advancement.[52] In some cases, for older and experienced men, this advancement meant separation from strictly priestly duties and assignment into the ranks of ambassadors, tribute experts, or judges.[53] As for the priest who on his own decided to leave the priesthood at the end of the four-year period, he was obliged to cut off the long hair that up to that time had distinguished him.

Cult includes a larger personnel than priests alone, however. Numerous lay groups played important roles and had to be worked into the festivals and penances under the jurisdiction of the priests. Toci, for instance, had a group of devotees serving her as a penance and referred to as "her Huaxtecs." They were under the charge of Toci's *teohua* who instructed them in the mock battles fought during the Ochpaniztli.[54] Huitzilopochtli had a group of men who had made vows to fast a year in his service, ending their penance at the feast of Toxcatl.[55] They were called the "Elder Brothers of Huitzilopochtli" and were much feared for their holiness. Service in this particular group was painful and costly.[56] The extent of participation by commoners, merchants, and others in Aztec cult was exceptional.

Priests who had grown old in temple service were known as *cuacuillis*, a compound word whose meaning is disputed.[57] They

could be of high rank, and several had crucial duties. The so-called
epcoacuacuilli belonged to the cult of Tlaloc (one of whose names was
Epcoatl, or Mother-of-Pearl Dragon).[58] In his charge was the entire
ceremonial calendar and the astronomical observations that supported it. When shifts were necessary in the observance of the festivals of the eighteen months, it was he who promulgated them. He
was aided by a subordinate, a priest whose charge was to preview and
license all dances and songs projected for the Tlaloque cults.[59]
Though possessing seniority and experience the cuacuillis were not
called on for particularly active roles; oftentimes they merely formed
an escort for some tlenamacac in the performance of his duties.[60]
Because of their age, they were exempt from some of the more brutal
types of autosacrifices.

Whether or not deities had a cadre of priests devoted to them
alone, they did at least have one priest to represent their cult, he being generally referred to as a *teohua*. Thus, there were roughly as
many teohuas as there were cults, and those serving the major gods
were of the rank of tlenamacac.[61] The teohua of the highest rank was
naturally the one assigned to Huitzilopochtli.[62] He was called the
Mexicatl teohua and was responsible for the proper observance of
Huitzilopochtli's daily service and the good order of the central calmecac. In this latter duty, he was assisted by the Teohua Uitznahuac
who was the priest of the god Omacatl, (a form of Tezcatlipoca). A
third, called the "Teohua of the Others," filled in with a similar
jurisdiction over the remaining cults in the ithualli. It was the Mexicatl teohua, acting in concert with Tlaloc's teohua, who recommended priests in the central cult for promotion. Another teohua
performed like custodial and supervisory duties for the gods referred
to collectively as the "Four Hundred Rabbits," a group of allied or
subject community gods outside Mexico-Tenochtitlan whose cults
were orgiastic. The controlling teohua who supervised them all was
the one called by the name of the god Two Rabbit; he was the most
prestigious of those foreign gods of drink and fertility.

There were two classes of priests who had to do with human sacrifice. The first were priests who were at the same time high-ranking
and fully recognized warriors.[63] It is curious that they were considered
to be attached to the Tlaloc cult (this might pose a problem for us
were it not for the fact that the priests of Huitzilopochtli and Tlaloc

formed one conjoined body). These priests accompanied the armies into battle, participated in the fray, and in all respects were typical warriors.[64] They were called *Tonatiuh Itlacahuan*, the "Sun's Men" and were umpires of sorts.[65] Besides performing certain rites leading to the onset of battle and animating the warriors, when all was over they adjudicated quarrels among claimant captors—for the taking of prisoners was the very purpose of war, and the competition in that deadly skill was immense and often led to disputes. Finally, they presided over the burning of the corpses of their own dead on the battlefield, a significant ritual. These strange sacerdotal figures licensed the captured warriors for future sacrifices, each one properly accredited to his rightful captor or captors.

Then there were the sacrificing priests themselves. In the Coatepetl cult there were six of these at any one time. They were the gruesome Chachalmecas whose posts ran in families and could only be claimed through inheritance.[66] They were considered to be of extraordinary holiness, and in token of that, their disheveled locks, never washed, were matted with soot and dried blood from thousands of past sacrifices.[67] The most distinguished of them all was the topiltzin, the man who actually wielded the knife. Although he represented the god Quetzalcoatl (i.e., Topiltzin), the first of all priests, he also changed his name to that of the god or goddess in whose cult he might be acting, while always remaining necessarily the quetzalcoatl.

It should be made clear at this point that our knowledge of the grades and duties of the Aztec priests is not firm. What has been presented here is simply one possible reconstruction.

THE HIERARCHY—THE HIGH PRIESTHOOD

Our knowledge of the high priesthood among the Aztecs is also inadequate. Each city appears to have defined the office differently and to have fitted it into the state in contrasting ways. In Cholula, during Toltec times we hear of a dual, and later a quadruple, division of the office. In Cuauhtitlan we hear of a priest-king of Mixcoatl.[68] From the important city of Huexotzinco comes a curious example of the high priesthood that is well worth reporting in full.[69] There appeared a notable warrior from among the Huexotzincas in the late days when that people were locked in bitter battle with Mexico. The exploits of this man, Toltecatl by name, were so sensational on the

field of battle that a grateful people raised him to a commanding position among their princes. At that time the priesthood of the city's
patron god Camaxtli were tyrannizing over the inhabitants of the
city, molesting the women, looting homes of accumulated food
stores, and in armed array even threatening the city's leadership. Toltecatl attempted to resist the disorderly priests, but even though he
was supported by a majority in the city, he and his party were
defeated. The high priest who, as a teohua, had the sacred bundle of
Camaxtli in his charge, used his sacerdotal prestige to the full, casting
public spells against Toltecatl and magically bringing fire out of a
stone pot. Faced with such supernatural terrors, Toltecatl and his followers had no choice but to flee into exile, leaving the field to the politically demented priesthood. It was then easy for Mexico, the inveterate enemy of Huexotzinco, to dispose of Toltecatl and his demor-
alized retainers who had been so tragically deprived of their base.
Such an incident gives us a clear view of the volatile nature of Aztec
religion in general and of the influence of the leading priests in particular.

For Mexico our sources are contradictory, although the probable
configuration of the office was dual. We hear of two Mexican high
priests, each one in rank a quetzalcoatl, a word which has the conno-
tation, as we have seen, of superior holiness. Not unexpectedly the two
represented Huitzilopochtli and Tlaloc, respectively; the first was the
Totec tlamacazqui, the second the Tlaloc tlamacazqui.[70] The exalted
level of this office did not allow the incumbents to directly administer
the affairs of the priesthood, which were the charge respectively of the
Mexicatl teohua and two of his coadjutors. In the preceding section
we briefly mentioned the three teohuas who administered the state
rituals and the training of the priests, and we guessed that, in spite of
their high charges, they were still not the high priests.

If the preceding reconstruction is correct, the two quetzalcoatls
had little or nothing to do with the administration of cult, leaving
this to their delegates. Their offices carried the ultimate taboos. For
instance a high priest, who was always celibate, could never enter a
private house for fear of contamination and the weakening of his
charisma. He could however visit the palace.[71] The two high priests
before important festivals had to fast and purify themselves in a small
shrine, Poyauhtlan, used almost exclusively for that purpose.[72] Or-

acles delivered in the temples could be carried to the ruler only by the cihuacoatl or by one of the quetzalcoatls, and on state occasions it would be a quetzalcoatl who would ceremoniously admonish the ruler, remind him of his subservience to the gods, and finally exhort the commons to obedience and virtue. One of his other supreme duties was to wield the knife in important sacrifices, at which time he took the name of the god to whom he made the offering. The two quetzalcoatls, who were always fire priests, were chosen in the first instance by the ruler, his magnates, and the leading teohuas,[73] and they were invariably members of the royal house or one of its associated lines.[74] The symmetry between Mexican cult and Mexican rule is thus evident.

In Mexico, a third figure confuses this picture. This is the cihuacoatl, an office that also existed in cities other than Mexico.[75] The name of the office, which is the same as the name of the state goddess Cihuacoatl, appears to have been instituted or at least greatly magnified during the Tepaneca War, by the appearance of that most remarkable man, Tlacaelel.[76]

Tlacaelel was a half-brother of the greatest of all Mexican rulers, Moteuczoma I. These two heroic and frightening figures created a dynamic partnership wherein the office of cihuacoatl, essentially viceregal, became the cornerstone of the Mexican genius in the use of terror and led to her subsequent rise to power. Invested with the office of cihuacoatl, Tlacaelel became to all intents and purposes an alternate ruler, a vizier, a supreme judge, and president of the inner council of state.[77] The essence of the office, however, was its tight connection with the sacrificial cult, for whenever the war sinews of the Mexicans seemed about to slacken, or whenever peace around the empire seemed imminent, the cihuacoatl appeared formally before the tlatoani with the latest oracle of the goddess. The content of these oracles was simple: the goddess was hungry. And so the armies were sent forth, and captives were brought back for the relish of the goddess and others in the pantheon.

Questions, of course, arise in connection with this office. Was the cihuacoatl one of the high priests and, if so, did he outrank them? Or was the office only collateral to the priesthood and not directly connected? We do not have any ready answers, but the fact that when he was young Tlacaelel was one of the most feared of Aztec warriors leads us to guess that the office of cihuacoatl, with which he appears invested at a later time, was only quasi priestly and was essentially a creation of the war policy of the state, exalting the goddess Cihuacoatl, who was also Yaocihuatl ("Warrior Woman"). At any rate, we can be certain that Aztec cult was not static but swayed back and forth in its course reflecting the personalities of its leaders.

PRIESTLY DUTIES

The priest normally made two types of offerings to the gods. In the first, he was a surrogate of the society or of some individuals in the society. He was, in other words, not the true donor of this gift but only a professional agent; he offered service, fire, and comestibles in the daily cults as well as special services at festivals. In the second type, whenever he donated his own blood in an act of autosacrifice, he was acting sui generis.

Most temples had no more than four or five priests, but the great ones might have forty and over.[78] Depending on their size, the temples could vary widely in the number and richness of their customary services. Let us give a resume of the ritual at the Coatepetl, as this could be considered as the norm.

The day began when devout mothers in the city awakened their children before dawn to take offerings to the temple. These young people shuffled rapidly along the dark and silent streets and along the cold canals, the girls carrying steaming bowls of corn mush to deliver to the priests, the boys carrying glowing coals in hand braziers and balls of copal to be added as incense.[79] With the latter, the priests would cense the four directions and the gods. These offerings brought merit or paid off debts owed to the god by certain households. Meanwhile, the priests had come out of their cells in the calmecac to ascend the temple steps and sweep the patio before the shrine. Others had seized their conch-shell trumpets and with them signaled the red light of the dawn. Throughout the city, the sonorous grunting of the great conch-shells along with the reedy sound of whistles made an eerie and insistent din. Then there was added the thudding of the drum from the temple of Quetzalcoatl, this officially beginning the workaday lives of the people. Then, as the sun appeared, the officiating priest stood before the shrine and greeted the god with words that were designed to read nothing into his intentions, for to claim knowledge would have been presumptuous. "The sun has come forth, the heat-maker, the precious youth, the ascending, soaring eagle. In what manner will he pursue his course? How will he spend the day? Perhaps something evil will befall his common people." And then the priest would add, "Deign to fulfill your office and complete your mission."[80]

That said, the priest twisted off the heads of some quail, the sun's birds, and threw the flapping bodies on the floor in front of the idol so that the rapid spattering of blood might be for the sun a pre-prandial refreshment. After that, the priest offered the hot food that had been prepared in the city below. While this was happening, priests were drawing blood from themselves and offering the thick maguey thorns with which they had pierced themselves.

So began the day on the temple top. Four times during the day, beginning with the dawn, incense was burned to the god while flutes and whistles shrilled.[81] During the night the priests arose five times to cense the god.

As the sun was going under, the priest saluted his departure intoning the formula, "The Lord of the Night has come to take over, the sharpnosed one [Yacahuitzli]. And what may we expect from him this night?"[82] The two huge braziers at the forward corners of the pyramid top were recharged with wood for burning as was the line of braziers leading up to the foot of the temple in the patio below. Some priests were delegated to remain there near the shrine throughout the night lest the god be unattended. Others departed into the night to keep vigil or to make offerings at road crossings and elsewhere. Periodically, the night broke into an uproar as the drums, the whistles, and the conch-shell trumpets began again, all signalling the beginning of one of the watches.[83] As the midnight watch was sounded, all the priests arose to draw their blood, while the leading officiant bathed in the nearby sacred spring of ice cold water.[84] Failure to perform these penances resulted in cruel and extreme punishments at the hands of one's fellow priests.

Fire, hearts, and blood were the three things most wanted by the god, and his need was greatest at midnight. Midnight was that crucial hiatus in time when the possibility existed that the sun might permanently die or not be able to revive himself sufficiently to emerge from the underworld. Priests were the assistants in that momentous emergency. In fact, so closely was the priest identified with the rekindling of the sun that in token of it he could show tattooing burned into his wrist that, as a row of dots, duplicated on his flesh the board (*mamalhuaztli*) from which new fire was drawn.[85] Festival days and new supernatural terrors of course brought human sacrifices into the picture to add to the preceding.

So austere was the life of the average tlamacazqui that his can be viewed as a penitential office in all of its aspects. Some of those exercises will be described in the next chapter—only one will be described here, the "placing of the thorns" (*nehuitztlatiliztli*).

In the late afternoon and dusk, certain of the acolytes had gone out into the environs to gather spines of the maguey plant for use during the coming night. After the sun had set and no light was left, some of the priests pierced themselves with these in various parts of their bodies and then inserted the bloodied points into a wadded ball of grass. After this, they plunged into the bitterly cold waters of the sacred walled spring of the temenos, and then, naked, took up a journey outward bound, whether under the stars in a clear night or in the rain or hail.[86] The purpose of this nocturnal excursion was to place the wadded balls, which attested to their piety, in some lonely and haunted spot in the environs or on some famous mountain shrine. Those undergoing this penance left the calmecac separately to move out of the dark city one by one. They carried torches, powdered tobacco to chew, and incense. As they jogged along the causeways and over to the lakeside, they blew intermittently on their conch-shell trumpets. Some of the hardier ones traveled as far as six miles out and could end up at one of the many *momoztlis* set up on the hilltops lining the lake. At the chosen spot, the priest would deposit the record of his autosacrifice, worship the spirit of the place, and then retrace his footsteps. Along the entire way he was expected to blow on his shell in answer to the watches being sounded in the city far off and unseen in the darkness below him.

It is difficult for us to appreciate the physical misery of the penitent and the terror caused in him by the supernaturals lurking in the night. The exposure of these naked priests in the cold and often freezing weather of the Basin of Mexico must have brought on a high mortality. Whether it was spiritual desperation or mere priestly rou-

tine, the act seems extreme to us. Nevertheless, the sources imply that
the excursions occurred nightly.

THE SACRA

Everywhere in the world certain objects appear routinely in cult.
They are not idols, and yet they are more than signs. These objects
stand midway between gods and men. In one sense, cult is merely the
manipulation of these objects in the presence, but out of the reach, of
the average person. They belong to the priests who alone know their
uses. They cannot, like idols, stand for the god in his wholeness;
rather they specify distinct orientations of the numinous and are thus
applicable to certain supernatural situations rather than being rigidly
tied to any one deity as such.

By definition, a god can initiate an action or point to a direction
that can then crystallize into a bowl, a staff, a headdress, a mask.
Priests handle or wear the objects, moving them about, raising them
or lowering them in a kind of mime. The number of such objects is
legion. Only a very few of those found in Aztec cult will be commented on here, not for the purpose of revealing anything startling
concerning their nature, but to specify the priest's use of them, for
without them as the tools of his trade the priest could not exist as an
expert craftsman. Out of the many possibles, we shall consider only a
few of these sacra: the knife, the conch-shell, mirrors, rubber and
paper, the rattle staff, and human skins.

It is obvious that the knife had a long and complicated cult history before the Aztecs. They had two words for it, depending on the
stone of which it was made. If it was of obsidian with razor sharp and
brittle edges, it was *itztli*; if it was of flint, heavy duty, and thicker, it
was *tecpatl*. The former was used for dismemberment, skinning, and
auto-sacrifice, the latter exclusively for the slaying of the victims by
heart extraction. So central was the knife in Aztec cult that it came
down to them from the Toltecs already a god in itself.[87]

The tecpatl was the son of the goddess Cihuacoatl, and he was
carried about by her in a medicine bundle slung on her back. Whenever thirst and hunger moved her, the goddess would leave the gruesome and heavily swaddled infant in the crowded marketplace of the
city, there to be found as if it had been an abandoned child. This ad-

vertised the fact that the lords were lax in providing food and drink for the mighty mother. Whoever found it rushed to the palace to give the news that the little knife was being deprived of blood. And so the tlatoani would order a prisoner sacrificed for the appeasement of the Mother. Cihuacoatl was sometimes depicted with two knives protruding from her headband, for her name means equally "Serpent Woman" or "Woman of Twins." If the knife symbolized anything specific, it was the numinous connection established at the world's beginning between men and gods.

I know of no instance in Mesoamerican history where the knife was used as a weapon, so we should not think of the tecpatl as derived from the battlefield. It was evoked from cult alone and thus was sui generis and distinctive. It can be said that as a cult instrument used in every important festival and crisis in the life of the Aztec state, it bound all parts of the Aztec religion together making them one. The priest who wielded the knife was thus performing at the very pinnacle of priestly duties. More will be said of this in chapter 7.

The conch-shell (*teucciztli*) also spanned cults, and it too had a venerable history in Mesoamerica. It was a talisman of mighty power for it was the living voice of Ehecatl, the god of the wind.[88] As such it also was a god in its own right. The priest in Teotihuacan wore it as a pectoral dangling about his neck as a mark of association with Quetzalcoatl.[89] The meaning of the talsiman, however, overrides any association with one special god. It was used as a trumpet to salute all the gods and was easily the most haunting sound in all Aztec cult. With it the priest could separate time into sections—a power unknown to the common man—as in the nightly watches, or he could, as Quetzalcoatl's deputy, call down the gods to some desired confrontation. It may have also been a symbol of the underworld.

In Aztec cult the conch shell generally appears in one of two guises. It appears either as the whole shell, used most often as a trumpet, or it appears as a cross-section cut through the middle to reveal the convoluted interior. This latter, called the "wind jewel," had a tendency to assume a starlike shape and was then diagnostic of the god Quetzalcoatl and the cults built around him. This shell that was hung around the neck of the high priest had long since become an emblem of many meanings: water and wind, descent and regeneration, esoteric wisdom, and craftsmanship. In the whole corpus of world art there is surely no more beautiful rendering of the conch-shell than the huge one in white stone uncovered in 1980 at the foot of the Coatepetl.[90] Here the artist has gone beyond any reference to Quetzalcoatl's cult and is suggesting a wider application to the cult centered on the state—in which case the conch shell is one of the sacra supporting the legitimacy of Huitzilopochtli's rule.

Unlike the knife and the conch shell, the mirror was peculiar to only one of the cults, that of Tezcatlipoca ("Smoking Mirror"). This may have been historically dictated, for mirrors go back in Meso-american religion to Olmec times, and in those early days appear to have been specific to one deity only.[91] Tezcatlipoca in the late days of the Aztecs is associated with divination by means of mirrors.[92] When he led his people, the Huitznahua, out of the north, it was in re-sponse to oracles given by a sacred mirror that was carried or worn by his priest; a source describes it as "a magic mirror which clouds up all over like shadows on its surface." This was supposedly the mirror that was finally installed in the god's central shrine in Tezcoco, the Aztec city on the shores of the great lake. On occasions the god could be darkly seen in it, and from it came equally lurid hints of the future. Although this mirror is iconographically depicted as set in the god's tlachialoni, a round burnished plate fixed on the end of a shaft like a lorgnette, or pierced with an eye hole through which the priest carry-ing it could peer, it also occurs as a circular plate or ring suspended as a pendant from the neck.

This mirror, from which came oracles, was thus a sign of the god's power as the supreme seer. In this latter sense the priests of Tez-catlipoca were in competition with the priests of Quetzalcoatl who also claimed ultimate prophetic powers for their god. The mirror of Tezcatlipoca and the wind jewel of Quetzalcoatl were coequal talis-mans—the first recalled the shaman and his occult practices; the lat-ter was specific of the priest who consulted the painted books. The first stood for the sun in the underworld; the second for air and the whirlwind.

The use of rubber in cult, like the conch shell and the mirror, goes back for its origins to the civilizations of the Gulf Coast where the rubber tree was indigenous. And, also like them, it tended to be used mainly in ceremonies connected with one god—in this case Tlaloc. When rubber that has been allowed to harden is burned, dense black smoke pours out, a pefect analog to black storm clouds as they pour out of the mountains and spread over the land. This flammable characteristic of rubber early attracted it into a religion centered on rain and swollen rivers. The rubber that was collected by dripping and drying into large balls, however, suggested another application. As a black ball bouncing and springing about a playing court it was an analog to the black sun in the underworld with the players on the two sides representing the sun's retinue and his foes. Thus rubber was associated with the cult of the *tlachtli*, the ball game built around the scenario of the sun in the underworld.

In the Tlaloc cult rubber was remembered as the blood of trees. Ethnology has produced a host of instances from all parts of the preliterate world of the stress placed upon trees as sentient beings. Rubber trees, for instance, were bled, whereas other trees, like the *amatl*, were flayed. Paper came from the peeling of the skins of these latter trees and others. The paper bark could be bleached and then used in sheets, rolls, or screen-fold books. Rubber was the blood of the tree as paper was its skin—the two were intimately conjoined, and they came together particularly in the Tlaloc cult. In the ceremonies connected with rain, rubber was often shaped into small rough figures —these were the rubber gods (*ulteteo*) who as a finale were burned in some of the rituals.[93] Thus, as clouds, they ascended into the heavens to cast their rains over the land. Or a burning rubber ball could be held over paper, the liquid drops spattering on it again representing clouds. In the Etzalcualiztli festival,

> When they slashed open breasts, when they opened the breast of one of them, they seized his heart; they went to place it in a vessel painted blue, named the cloud-vessel, which was painted with rubber on four sides. And its accouterments were papers dotted with drops of liquid rubber, much rubber; they were covered with rubber.[94]

Paper conveyed sorrow, mourning, and reverence; we have already seen paper flags as signs pointing to a divine presence. In the cult just mentioned, rubber indicated that the hearts piled up in the bowl were those of ixiptlas of the Tlalocs, whereas the paper specified the individual sacrificial victims. In many of the cults, perhaps most of them, those unfortunates who had been selected for sacrifice marched to their deaths carrying paper banners, almost as if they were their passports to the other world. We have already mentioned that the children destroyed in Tlaloc's cult were called "paper banners," they having merged with the symbols of their passing. When the god Nanahuatl in the great solar myth volunteered to be the one who would cast himself into the fire in order to arise as the new and the Fifth Sun, "they covered his head with a paper headdress and put upon him a paper stole and a paper breechclout."[95] Such examples make clear the uses of paper in the rituals.

In Aztec cult many types of staves and scepters were used, each specially decorated according to its symbolic content. Here we will consider only the *chicahuaztli* (the "strengthener"), a fertility instrument used in many of the cults and often depicted in the hands of deities connected with water, vegetation, or growth. The chicahuaztli varies in details but was generally a baton of moderate length held in the hand. At the top was a point like an arrowhead with two sets of barbs, whereas below this two crosspieces were separated from each other by a circular object. When the priest carrying the staff pounded it on the ground it made a rattling sound—no doubt this was a piece of sympathetic magic designed to bring on thunder. Like our other sacra, this one also has a pre-Aztec history, appearing for the first time in Teotihuacan being held by Quetzalcoatl.[96]

There have been several suggestions as to what the chicahuaztli signifies. Some see it as going back to a sun ray, to a rattlesnake, to a digging stick, or even to a phallus. These are all acceptable interpretations, and I would suspect that more than one meaning is actually present in the object. The fact that the instrument is portrayed most prominently in the cult of Xipe, a solar deity, leads me to believe, however, that the first suggestion is primary, namely that the point of the staff represents a ray coming from the sun.[97] The circular object out of which the point emerges then will symbolize the sun, though this does not explain why sometimes the point is split in half. When carried by the *xipe*s in the festival of the second month or when placed in the hands of the dead at funerals, it clearly specified an accretion of strength that in turn would bring regeneration.

The last of the sacra I shall mention is the human skin that was worn by priests or by lay volunteers who thus gained merit. The skin always came from a sacrificed victim who had been flayed by experts; it was worn reversed, with the wet and bloody side out. The skin of the head was prepared separately and was drawn over the wearer's face and laced on along the occipital slit. The torso was skinned first by splitting it up the back. The hands were severed at the wrists and left to dangle off the skin of the forearms. Below, the skin was cut only down to the knees; unlike the hands, the feet were discarded. Thongs laced the skin onto the wearer up and down the line of the spine. Significantly, the front of the human skin as thus worn always showed a large horizontal tear in the middle of the breast—this was where the knife had been driven through the sternum allowing the extraction of the victim's heart.

In some cases the skin was worn just for the duration of a day, but in the Tlacaxipehualiztli festival it was worn throughout a full Aztec month of twenty days. At the end, the skin had dried out to a foul shagreen, cracked and fetid. At that point it was ceremoniously deposited in an artificial cave in Xipe's shrine.

The human tegument was of all artifacts in Aztec cult the most complex in its meaning. If thought of as a molt, the flaying of a victim and the donning of his skin by a priest pointed to the reappearance of the sacrificed being, namely to a regeneration. And the sacrificed person was, at least at the moment of sacrifice, an aspect of the god to whom he was being devoted. Thus it was the god who was being revived. This was over and above the type of renewal (explicit in all human sacrifice) that provided the standard food and drink for the god, that is, hearts and blood. Alimentation was a daily service, but the wearing of the god's skin was a reduction process performed annually wherein the priesthood could at second hand annihilate the god physically and then remake him as an actor subject to their instruction. It represented a high art of priestly daring, and the Aztecs found it so congenial that they extended its use to many cults other than that of Xipe, where it seems to have originated.

All of the sacra mentioned previously, and many others not mentioned, were fashioned or used by peoples long antecedent to the Aztecs. All of the Mesoamerican peoples neighboring the Aztecs, namely the Mixtecs, Zapotecs, Totonacs, Tarascans, and others also shared these sacra, and by the time of the Aztecs the articles had, as it were, become homogenized. Together they formed a set of related signs, many transferable from one cult to another, and some of them indispensable to all. They had, in fact, taken on a life of their own. They were not seen solely as symbols of life and death or the presence of a god; rather they were life and death dispensers—almost epiphanies. All of them, acting as metaphors in a language of cult, described the dark marriage, as seen by the Aztec mind, between death and new life.

5

The Dramatization
of Conflict and Hostility

THE KNIGHT AS A CRYPTOPRIEST

Aztec Priests were men who had been trained and confirmed by the state to become servants of the supernaturals. They formed a completed and an exclusive group, and in that sense they represented a vested interest of the elite class. In the preceding chapter we discussed their exercises as if they—and only they—were routinely involved in cult, but as it turns out, this is not so. All members of the society participated in cult whether they were magnates, lesser nobles, merchants, craftsmen, or commoners such as porters, fishers, and farmers. The attendance of the people at certain of the festivals was de rigueur, and by definition the priests who performed the cults were the surrogates of the whole people. The Aztecs had organized their religious life around the guiding principle of a people's total dependence upon the gods. The priestly tactic was intended to turn this into a reality.

Yet, however skillful and representative the functioning of the priesthood was, the Aztecs acted as if they had achieved nothing permanent in the way of a rapport with the divine. A sense of mutability plagued the Aztecs in every aspect of their lives. Overnight a person could be reduced to slavery. Treachery was the urban way of life, and the cities consequently lived in an almost demented atmosphere of war. But war was only one of the many extravaganzas caused by their fears—in cult also they organized hostility and conflict in dramatic ways, and here certain segments of the populace played leading roles.

One class of Aztec men is especially important for this inquiry. The Aztec knight, the *teuctli*, was—like the North American Indian brave—a warrior who on the surface delighted in endless tribal battle. This is our picture of him at the social level. At another and deeper level, however, he plays a pseudopriestly role. The understanding of the teuctli was that he died so that the gods might eat him. He was simply an item of food in a jungle of carnivorous gods; it was the knights who themselves were the ingesta. More will be said on this. Here I mention it in order to put before the reader the knight's undoubted natural hostility toward a system that locked him in and made him a priestly accessory to his own doom.

TEZCATLIPOCA AS THE ENEMY

The relationship of priest to knight at first does not seem close, but let us consider this prayer to Tezcatlipoca made by the priests at the outset of battle; it is a prayer in behalf of the warrior who is setting forth:

> May his heart not falter in fear. May he savor the fragrance, the sweetness of death by the obsidian blade. With his heart may he gladden Necoc tene, the ritual feathering, the goddess Itzpapalotl. May he desire, may he long for the flowery death by the obsidian blade. May he savor the scent, savor the fragrance, savor the sweetness of the darkness, the din of battle, the roar of the crowd. Take his part; be his friend."[1]

The priest who offers this prayer is the same priest who dispatches the captive knight on the sacrificial block. Here he adjures the knights of his own city as they go off to war that they view positively the fact that they may be captured by the enemy and accordingly slain by the priests of the enemy city. Quite obviously the relationship is complicated, but we cannot escape the conclusion that the warrior is related to the priest in the same way as are the sacra.

Aztec society did not envisage the priesthood as primarily an intercessory body dealing with the gods and presenting to them the tragic necessities of human beings. This was indeed one of the priest's duties. But the priests were also seen as stagehands who devised set pieces in cult that would display the convulsive nature of the gods and thereby explain man's antipathy to them. In their great dramatic presentations, the Aztec priests certainly captured the spirit of the dire, which seemed in turn to make violence in human life legitimate. In the prayer quoted previously, the tension between a fear of death, natural to all of us, and the virtue of embracing it as a positive good in battle can be plainly felt. The god's part is not to save the warrior from extinction, but to convince him that a bloody death is what he desires above all things. The life of violence is an end in itself, a positive consummation, for the knight.

There are in history as many human stances possible toward the divine as there are cultures and persons. Each age and each people takes up a stance inevitably tied to its history and to its strivings—which stance can be generally found stated in myths or implied in cult practices. Men sometimes meet their gods almost as social equals, or they can adopt a groveling and hopeless abasement. Again they may neglect the gods, perhaps by appointing surrogates from among themselves who will assume their responsibilities. Or they can accept the gods almost as business partners in some strenuous exercise. They can view them as hooded and mysterious, or as concrete and knowable. They can be known to be open and approachable, or to be withdrawing and almost feral. In whatever fashion men view the supernatural, it is in cult where we find the clearest signs of their reactions.

In their cults, the Aztecs were meeting the violence of the heavens with a bravura of their own. This is exemplified in that passage from a Cuauhtitlan ritual where two priests descend the pyramid steps clad in the dripping skins of women just sacrificed while flaunting their unfleshed forearms, all the time braying and roaring frighteningly; the crowd waiting below hypnotically chants over and over again, "Now at last our gods are coming!" Here the gods represent that which men can only find repulsive and horrible, and yet they acclaim and magnify it.

But such an obliteration of empathy (and its institutionalizing in cult performances) drives man into a secondary estrangement—and this too finds outlet in cult. Men's frustrations with the conditions of their life and with the gods who ordain them are never far below the surface of Aztec cult. This basic incongruity between the intentions of the supernaturals and the desires and needs of people was focused by the Aztecs in the figure of the god Tezcatlipoca.[2] He was the final statement with which they glossed the universe. We can see why he was the god most necessary to them out of the entire pantheon, for without him they could not have vented their hostilities or understood their place in the world. But we must not make the mistake of equating him with the Devil. The Medieval European devil was a childlike and mechanistic addendum to God—he existed to drain away from God whatever was tormenting and unacceptable. Tezcatlipoca is a vision of the divine as both godlike and diabolical at the same time.

No doubt this accounts for that god named Yaotl who was the

patron of war and a variant form of Tezcatlipoca. Yaotl means both "warrior" and "enemy," which linguistic ambivalence indeed points to a secret animus never openly acknowledged by the Aztecs. In myth, Tezcatlipoca is the god who introduces humiliation, insult, and discord into the life of human beings. In popular thought he, more than any other god, partook of the demonic. Many phantoms and goblins of the night in fact were apparitions of Tezcatlipoca, shroud-wrapped dead men, and one particularly horrifying demon called "Broken Face" who hopped along darkened roads on a single talon foot. In the following description of Tezcatlipoca, one can easily grasp the fact that he was a deity at loggerheads with men and unaffected in any way by their desperation:

> When he walked on the earth, he quickened vice and sin. He introduced anguish and affliction. He brought discord among people, wherefore he was called "the Enemy of Both Sides." He created, he brought down all things. He cast his shadow on one, he visited one with all the evils which befall men; he mocked, he ridiculed men. But sometimes he bestowed riches.[3]

It was indeed common for Aztecs who were afflicted or overturned in their fortunes and who felt deeply the injustice of life to curse the god as a sodomite and worse. Such ebullitions of hostility were not uncommon in Aztec society. They were very explicit statements of a set stance vis-à-vis the divine, but because they were the expressions of individuals, they were not codified in cult. One might have expected to find in the Toxcatl feast evidences of animosity, but such is not the case.

Every well-to-do Aztec household had an image of Tezcatlipoca.[4] It was as if they felt him in his capacity as the "Enemy" to be a very individual presence as well as a cosmic force. This aspect of Aztec ambivalence toward the divine is thus suggestive only; it is apprehended as a diffuse background.

Better examples of the Aztec's hostility to the divine are the two institutions known as the *xochiyaoyotl* and *tlachtli*, the first a tournament, the second a sport.

THE FLOWER WAR (XOCHIYAOYOTL)

Because of its profound implications, the flower war cannot be omitted from any survey of Aztec cult; yet on the surface it appears to be simply a tournament.[5]

The Nahuatl word for war meant "the business of the warrior" (*yaoyotl*) but in a more metaphorical manner war could be referred to as *teoatl tlachinolli*, which is translated literally as "divine liquid and burnt things," where the first item is to be glossed as 'blood' and the second as 'bonfire'—bonfire in the original sense of a cremation, or a fire of bones. All Aztec battles formally ended when the dead had been accounted for and ceremoniously burned on the battlefield. Battle was thus understood as an effusion of blood plus the release through fire of the souls of the dead heroes.

But there was a further refinement—the flower war, xochi-yaoyotl. In this type of confrontation warriors were thought of as exotic flowers, arrayed as they were in feathered bonnets, carrying beautiful shields painted with bright devices, and wearing jaguar skin anklets. As fields of flowers wave and surge in the wind, so the warriors in the tides of battle heaved to and fro in the melee, colorful and splendid.[6] The fallen who lay in their blood were likened to red flowers scythed down by the wind. The contrast between the symbolism of the "red rose" of our European Middle Ages and the red rose of the Aztecs could hardly be greater. It is obvious in this latter symbolism that death for the knight was not an evil, but was a good, and therefore it was a desired thing.

By virtue of the fact that the flower war was a link in the chain that led from war to human sacrifice, it was therefore a regularly observed and religiously oriented practice. In other words, it was a cult. It worked in the following way.

Through the priests, or through the *cihuacoatl*, the word would be taken from temple to palace that the deity was hungry and thirsty. It might be possible to satisfy such an appeal by the release of only one of the captives previously taken and held caged in the state pool against just such an exigency, or it might involve large numbers of victims. If the latter, the *tlatoani* could announce a flower war to be fought against the knights of an enemy city with which there was an understanding. Certain Aztec cities, which were enemies on an across-the-board scale, were often leagued informally to provide opportunities whereby the knights of each city could come together in battle. The league might even institute battle on a set schedule, such as the first day of each month. Tezcoco for instance fought Huexotzinco and Tlaxcala alternately every month.[7] These gatherings did not include a levee en masse or a previous reconnoitering of the other's military dispositions, and thus were completely different from wars of conquest. Only the teuctli fought in these wars—it was a part of his prerogative. Commoners were excluded.

Participation in the event was voluntary, and the number of warriors who marched out on successive flower wars must have fluctuated noticeably. Nor was any care taken of the fact that when it arrived on the field one side might be heavily outnumbered—such an imbalance simply increased the glory and danger of the enterprise for that side. Every city in the loose league of participating states had on its frontiers a field designated for flower wars and thus accounted as sacred ground.[8] For the state the flower war was a way of keeping shock troops continually exercised and therefore reliable, whereas for the teuctli it was an opportunity to rise in the scale of the heroic with either fame or death as a prospect; for the priests it was a way of replenishing the god's larder.

Following the ruler's call, the volunteers assembled. In many cases, contingents from allied communities came in also to pit themselves against their equals. The opposing city had been notified, and it, too, could march with knightly volunteers from its allies or tributaries.[9] Such gatherings were in no sense armies with national objectives. They were spontaneous escadrilles of individual knights whose only objective was personal glory, but whose actions have to be seen as being in the realm of cult.

The god Tezcatlipoca in his avatar as Yaotl led the formations out of the city. Carried on his *teomama*'s back he preceded the marching knights over the trails and through the defiles to the designated battle site. Having arrived, the teomama installed the god in a temporary shrine praying that he look favorably on what was about to ensue. The opening mood of the encounter was chivalric inasmuch as both sides recognized a close kinship in the service of the gods. The leaders greeted each other in honorific terms as "brother" and awaited the signal to commence the terrible game.[10] In what followed, the teomama acted as a kind of amicus curiae, and it was probably only his intervention that could end the carnage when loss of large numbers threatened one side or the other. At first, warriors were fed into the press individually to enable them to seek out famous champions on the other side and engage them in duel, but soon need would force the remainder of the warriors to enter the lists, group by group. The teuctli's objective was to wear down his opponent and capture him—if that was impossible he fought for the kill. When four or five succeeded in isolating an enemy, then capture generally resulted, and he would be dragged off the field. It was battle à outrance, and those taken were bleeding and battered and at the end of their endurance. During the hour or so of the intense combat, certain veteran captains moved with small groups from spot to spot on the field, viewing the engagement as a whole, shoring up the weak spots where apprentice warriors might be fighting for the first time, or setting up segregated duels for their mighty ones. None could leave the field until the priests, advised by the captains, decreed mutual withdrawals.[11] It was not unheard of for one side to lose, through death and capture, a significant part of the escadrille. Sometimes luck might compensate it for such grievous losses by allotting to it an equal number of captives similarly taken from the enemy.

The moment combat was broken off, the so-called "Sun's Men," or captains, immediately sat to hear the inevitably conflicting claims of capture put forward by their knights. These were serious and potentially divisive issues, for accuracy of reporting in the fury and blood lust of battle was negligible, either on the part of those involved, or those who by chance witnessed the action. A case could involve an unsuccessful warrior's only opportunity to recoup a dwindling momentum toward personal glory. Such hurt pride and passion on the part of the disputing participants must have demanded unquestioned authority on the part of the adjudicating captains. A captive could be adjudged to as many as four captors, each of whom thus possessed a portion of the prestige and a commensurate claim on the captive. The captains judged swiftly, and their decisions were final. When the awards had been made, the bodies of one's own dead were gathered up, and there, on the holy field stained with their blood, they were burned. An arrow or an *atlatl* of the dead teuctli would be returned to the family as a cult object that they could use in their rites of sepulture. Results of the battle, numbers killed, wounded and captured were sent back to the palace by swift runners.

Here is an example of what was probably a not uncommon ending for a flower war. One source has the Tlatelulca knights reporting back to the Mexican tlatoani as follows:

> They said to Moteuczoma how they had taken a goodly number of captives, and that alone they were able to take one hundred Tlascalan warriors. Of their own warriors 370 had died or been lost through cap-

ture. And Moteuczoma said to the embassy, "Behold, brothers, how true was the word of the ancestors who taught us that the sun, Tlalteuctli, the god of battles, feeds alike from both sides."[12]

So the flower war was strictly nonpartisan, and from the god's point of view neither side could win or lose. The state implicated in a loss might feel that loss, and certain families certainly would, but none of that affected the cosmos except to its advantage. All those who died or were cremated on the field spilled their blood on the bosom of mother earth and then in flames ascended to enter the sun god's entourage. Similarly, all those who had been captured were destined to be sacrificed and would also ascend to become followers of the sun. The valorous could not lose.

In this cult of the flower war we can now see more clearly how curious was the role of the teuctli. War is the ultimate confrontation in hostility in which men can engage; yet in this instance we find a type of war reworked into an action purely accessory to the well-known ritual of sacrifice. As such, the flower war was a sacrament for the individual knight.[13] By partaking of this sacrament with ferocity and skill, no matter what his tragic end might be he earned a heavenly reward, whereas the interests of the state were neither helped nor hindered by anything he did. The role of the ordinary Aztec priest was different. As we have said, he was a surrogate for his society, and in that profession he perforce suffered in the place of that society. Himself, he did not matter, and nothing was ever said of some glorious heaven awaiting him because of *his* devotion. Whereas the Aztec world depended upon the priest to cajole the gods, the teuctli offered himself bodily to the gods with the certainty that this would win their approval. Thus the flower war, which was his invention, was a cult with no immediate relevance to the state or its objectives but a cult that the state patronized because the rulers were themselves teuctlis and lived warrior's lives. The teuctli was a priest who was not commissioned by the society and who therefore did not perform in a civil context but rather in a context of international hostility and violence. That was the world of Tezcatlipoca, and it too was holy.

AZTEC CHIVALRY: THE PERSONNEL OF A CULT

The preceding concepts, when reduced to their cultural skeleton, specified quite simply war, killing, and capture. The difference between our view today of the flower war and the teuctli's certainties is impressive. The mind of man plays with institutions like these and imaginatively turns them around, on the one hand disguising them, on the other hand enriching them. So the Mesoamerican teuctli, as he and the priest together worked out the possibilities of giving new names and new lineaments to battle and death, conceived of casting them in the mould of the chivalric. Aztec chivalry, in fact, is of fundamental importance in any inquiry into Aztec cult.

Wherever chivalry appears in history, it is always a way of sublimating the open brutality of armed conflict and of giving a rationale to the chaos of the battlefield. In essence, it says that what looks like the extension of chiefly or state power through brute force is not that at all; rather it is the use of force mitigated by agreed-upon rules that are observed by both sides to the extent that a game or tournament results. Both sides understand and give assent to the rules because both believe the myth that enshrines them. The rules can be variously drawn up. The following short discussion of the chivalric elements in Aztec life will add to an understanding of the theme of this chapter.

Two orders of Aztec knighthood embodied the cosmic myth—these were the orders of the Eagle knights and the Jaguar knights. The first personified the diurnal sun; the second the sun in the underworld. There was no distinction made between the two in terms of prestige, however, for the nocturnal sun in Aztec myth was a magisterial figure, noble, tragic, and mysterious, in every sense a warrior's beau ideal. When referred to as a class, however, both orders of knights were referred to as Eagles. There were other orders, the Otomí, the mountain lions, and possibly others, though about these we know little beyond their names. Each had their special meeting hall in the palace, and clear distinctions were made among them. In European chivalry one thinks of the Knights of St. James, the Knights Templar, the Teutonic Knights, and so forth. The Aztec orders were lodges that crossed state borders, for we know of Eagle and Jaguar knights in many of the Mesoamerican cities. Although every knight had a tribal or city commitment that defined the army group he fought with, all were members of an international brotherhoood whose sole commitment was service to the sun.

War was in fact a sacred activity.[14] When the four original gods decided to create the sun and thus establish the fifth universe, they first had to create war so that the hearts and blood needed by the sun would be available. So mighty a project was the creation of war that it took the gods two years to effect it.

We note in European chivalry the fact that the knight had no prototype in Christian myth. To that extent the latter differed from his Aztec counterpart whose god, the sun, was a teuctli. The Aztec knight could therefore believe that he was cast in his role as a true religious duty. This is why the term "cult" precisely fits the activity of a teuctli, and also why it is less applicable to the Christian knight, if at all. The Medieval church was always more than a little embarrassed by knighthood.

A complicated heraldry distinguished both knighthoods. The Aztec teuctli who had acquired renown bore on his shield, as the ruler's gift, a device peculiar to himself but understandable by all. Just as was true in late Medieval Europe, these devices depicted birds, animals, dragons, butterflies, gods, geometrical forms, and other symbols. This device was the teuctli's record of killings and captures, as well as of other acts of courage and cleverness. For parade occasions he wore his hair in different ways; he could appear in a special costume, or with a frame strapped to his back or forearm bearing blazons of brilliantly colored feathers, mother-of-pearl, turquoise, etc. For his feat in rescuing Axayacatl, the ruler of Teotihuacan, for instance, was awarded the right to wear on his shield a device showing a leg from the buttock of which issued flame.[15] The types and colors of such emblems were classified and spoke a complicated heraldic language.

A monopoly of weapons and war gear, which so distinguished the European knight—horse, armor, sword, and lance—was not of such importance to the teuctli. His weapons, the obsidian-edged wooden sword club and the atlatl were certainly at times handled by commoners, but essentially they were limited to the teuctli. It was probably this relative lack of elitism in weaponry that led the Aztec knight to concentrate instead on elaborating his armorial bearings, decorations, and facial paint.

Both the European and the Aztec knights formed self-conscious castes, and there is no difference between their contemptuous view of the commoners—respectively, the churl and the *macehualli*. In the case of the Aztec, a good illustration of the difference maintained between the teuctli and the commoner appears in the difference of treatment accorded to them by the people of their own cities if, after capture, they succeeded in escaping and making their way back home. The macehualli was honored for his escape, whereas the nobleman was killed ignominiously and out of hand by his own people.[16] By his capture he had become the possession of a god, and he properly should have ended on the sacrificial block in the enemy's city—by escaping, he had reneged on his chosen role in the chivalric cult.[17] In brief, he had become a coward, a traitor to Tezcatlipoca, and unpleasing to all men who desired the contentment of the gods.

The subject of homage is interesting in this comparison. The role of the lord differed in the two cases. Liege lordship and vassalage on the European scene had as a powerful ingredient the initial choice by the vassal to become his lord's man. This introduced a rough equality, made more imposing because in theory it was based on a written contractual document. In the case of the teuctli, it is true that he was duty bound to support the tlatoani on the battlefield with his life, but he was in no sense his equal nor in the last analysis could he demand much of him. The Aztec tlatoani was not just another teuctli —he was also a superior being through whom the god Tezcatlipoca deigned to speak. The Aztec liege lord thus appeared as one of the facts of the supernatural. Aztec chivalry had no political side to it, and for that reason alone it would resemble a cult. Correspondingly, the Aztec liegeman or teuctli appeared more sacerdotal. There is nothing at all in the history of European chivalry to indicate that the knight in any way resembled the priest.

The training of the two differed considerably. The European knight was informally apprenticed in a knightly household, great or small as the case might be. The young Aztec went through a carefully supervised state curriculum under the guidance of proved warriors and priests. He thus emerged at a more standardized level and with a noticeably greater number of skills in the cultural field than his European counterpart. His indoctrination was tighter, and as an individual he was probably less free. One senses that it was more difficult for the ardent young Aztec to attain the status of the ideal knight than it was for the English, Flemish, or French squire.

Both sides evolved a practice field where their fighting skills could be honed in times of peace. The European knight produced the tournament whose object was the unhorsing and capture of the opponent and the seizure of his expensive arms. His ultimate goal was to hold his captive for ransom, after which he freed him to fight again. The Aztec knight produced the flower war, also a true tournament, but far more deadly than its European counterpart.

The Aztec knight differed also in the fact that his *cursus honorum* as he rose to the top had many stations, whereas once dubbed a knight by another knight the European had achieved all that he could in terms of chivalry—if he continued to be ambitious he would then have to shift into the political sphere where he could rise by marriage or appointment to become a count or duke. The Aztec knight's world made possible numerous heroic actions each of which were recognized and moved him up a notch.

Thus for the determined and the lucky warrior continuing advancement was possible—for instance when a teuctli had taken his fourth captive he became a *tequihua*, "one with a commitment." [18] For this occasion an elegant knighting ceremony took place in the presence of the ruler in the great temple compound. The teuctli's hair was trimmed in the permitted fashion, and he was given a new device and more splendid feather decorations. A banquet followed, and no doubt it was his fourth prisoner, just sacrificed, who was eaten by the guests in his honor. As a tequihua he could now sit in the war council and could begin a move up the line of appointments to high offices. Yet much of his remaining rise had still to be justified by his continuing performance on the field of battle.

Each of the levels of heroism above the station of tequihua was appropriately named and brought with it impressive emoluments. Then somewhere near the top of the ladder there was a hiatus; a much honored teuctli would be given the post of resident commissioner in a subject town or some comparable position, or simply retired as an "old eagle," but only close kin of the tlatoani could be appointed to the council of the four princes, the highest body in the state. With certain exceptions these princes had also to be redoubtable teuctlis.

The ultimate in knightly conduct and chivalric privilege could occur only at the top. One of the last independent tlatoanis of Tenochtitlan, in order to celebrate his coronation with special éclat, invited the rulers of cities with whom he was then engaged in hostilities to attend.[19] This was the acme of perverted courtesy, for these guests would witness in the lines of victims led to sacrifice some of their own great men who had been taken in battle against Mexico. From the bearing of these doomed ones being led up to sacrifice the kings could take back with them reports of either their valor or their collapse. The guest rulers meanwhile would be magnificently and secretly housed, then finally escorted incognito to their own borders by a Mexican retinue. They carried back with them splendid gifts from the Mexican tlatoani.

The ideal in all heroic societies gives rise to marvelous tales. Here are two that can be used to point up the similarities between European and Aztec knights.

In the cold and narrow pass at Roncevalles in the Pyrenees the count Roland, the last of his small rear guard, prepared himself to die in a manner befitting a liegeman. Surrounded by four hundred Saracens he first performed miracles of valor against them. Then, as he died, he bade farewell to his legendary sword, turned his face to Spain, the land of the enemy, and performed a last act of homage to God, offering Him his glove. A choir of angels thereupon carried him up into the heavens. After that the emperor Charlemagne arrived to lament the terrible loss. With a mere change of names and venue, and forgetting disparities in the two cultures, this could parallel the tale of Tlacahuepan, the famous Aztec knight and brother of the emperor Moteuczoma II.

In the year 1507 or thereabouts, Moteuczoma decided on a splendid flower war to exercise his knights and offer them opportunities to perform deeds pleasing to the sun god. Contingents of knights from allied and subject communities now came together under the command of the ruler's brother Tlacahuepan, who was the Achilles of that day.[20] In accordance with the pomp of the occasion the emperor allowed Tlacahuepan to carry the insignia of the god Xipe Totec, a most rare honor and an earnest sign of the fact that Tlacahuepan would be expected to perform miracles of hardihood that day.

By prearrangement, the Mexicans met their opponents, the knights of Tlaxcala and Huexotzinco, on a sacred field near Atlixco. Once begun, the tournament called in more and more of the restive knights waiting on the edges of the battle. When badly used, small city groups would be temporarily withdrawn, to be relieved by others.

Tlacahuepan and his Mexican retinue had grandly reserved themselves for the crisis sure to come. When it came, it showed the Mexican party radically reduced in numbers through death and capture, the remaining knights having now to face monstrous odds. Tlacahuepan thereupon hurled himself into the melee and predictably was soon surrounded by a hundred of the enemy. The tale has him in the upshot standing helpless on a pile of some fifty dead, unable to function further from exhaustion. "Cease now, Huexotzinca," he finally said, "for I see that I am yours." But he insisted that instead of hauling him off as a captive to be later sacrificed, that they dispatch him then and there as he stood on that altar of dead men that he had made with his own hands. The Huexotzinca warriors thereupon cut him down, and each one took away, as a wonderful relic, a part of his body to consume.

With the return of the beaten remnants to Mexico, Moteuczoma had wooden statues made of Tlacahuepan and two other brothers who had died with him. These were taken to the temple, publicly burned there with slaves to attend them, and the ashes buried under Xipe's *quauhxicalli*. This tragedy, so consciously contrived, was mourned by all in Mexico and was accounted a most solemn and meritorious event, the very acme of chivalry. And even as they mourned, those Mexican warriors who had been taken on the field where Tlacahuepan died were at that moment being sacrificed in the enemy cities. In any case, all ascended into the heavens to live with the sun, even as Roland was borne up in the arms of the angels into Paradise. Songs would be sung about Tlacahuepan just as minstrels on the pilgrim road in northern Spain would chant their lays about Roland.

TLACHTLI—THE BALL GAME

The flower war that we have just described, though it was the quintessence of combat, had powerful cultic overtones. We have treated it as a kind of preprandial ritual of the gods and its practitioners as cryptopriests. Even more curious as a form of cult was *tlachtli*, the Aztec ball game.[21]

The game early attracted the attention of the Spanish conquerors, but they were quick to see in it a pagan religious reference, and so they discouraged it—even while admiring its suspense and the incredible agility of its players. The skills required for the game were so extraordinary and the elitist tradition supporting it so formidable that, along with the disappearance of the Aztec nobility, so too disappeared the game.

By the time the Aztecs had appeared on the Mesoamerican scene, the tlachtli was already of great antiquity. In an already sophisticated form it can be traced well back into Preclassic times.[22] Then in the ensuing archaeological record we can see the game passing through many cultural changes, including an efflorescence in Middle Classic when it became a dominating cult. By the time of the Aztecs, therefore, it must have already passed through a rich history of meanings, and to have been to some extent attenuated as a cult performance. We can guess that with its superb drama the flower war, which sprang up later than the tlachtli, weakened the ball game's hold on the Mesoamerican peoples. Nevertheless, much about the earlier ball game was remembered by the Aztecs, and they played the game avidly. Its still impressive cultic importance can be seen in the fact that it was featured through the Aztec year. It was played in the sixth, the seventh, and the fifteenth months, on the movable feast of Two Reed, and every eighth year in the Atamalcualiztli festival.

Because the meaning of the game cannot be elicited without reference to the ball court (*tlachco*) where it was played, I am describing the cult at the same time as I describe the edifice. As stated in an earlier chapter, the tlachco was essentially a temple complex, though one unique in Mesoamerican architecture. Its architectural forms changed to a limited extent with the spread of the cult out of the Gulf lowlands, but what went on within its walls remained always a game with opposing teams. We have already described the court as elongated and either sunk into the ground or encased in masonry. One entered through the ends that were considered to be passageways into and out of the underworld. The mise-en-scène was the dark sky of the underworld; the rubber ball bouncing and spinning about was a celestial body. The basic narrative scenario was that of the sun and its pulsating journey through time, but the linkage between the sun and the planet Venus was so close that the scenario could waver at times, appearing now to concentrate on the sun, now on his planetary enemy. The ambivalence was contained in an astronomical calculation. The priests had computed that time span indicated by the heavenly combat as being five Venusian years, which exactly equaled eight solar years, a commensurability seldom seen in the heavens and therefore rich in meaning.

The game played in the tlachco was extravagant and theatrical to the core. As noted, it displayed the ultimate cosmic drama and enabled the viewer to enter into its mysteries. Not only did it focus on the hostility between the sun and the planet, but it also gave meaning to the movements of the moon and the stars. The players, generally two or three on a side, represented the celestial parties, the one guarding the sun as he moved through the sky in the underworld, the other, the demonic party of evil stars led by the planet Venus. The tlachco was thus a sidereal battlefield and the tlachtli was the battle itself.

There were actually several related scenarios that could be played out in the tlachtli cult. The most obvious and simple form of the play appears to have pitted Piltzinteuctli, the young emergent sun, against Old Xolotl, who is that form of the planet Venus known as the evening star and who was the patron god of the entire game.[23] This scenario therefore stresses the ominous presence of the chthonic in the person of Xolotl whose abode is the underworld and who attempts to destroy the sun as he courses through its dark passages. A fuller cult performance was also possible, this one featuring four divine players, Xochipilli and Ixtlilton on the one side against Quetzalcoatl and Cihuacoatl on the other.[24] The stripling Xochipilli is indeterminately either the returning sun in the spring or the young maize plant just pushing up out of the earth. His partner is a god affiliated with the unrisen sun and like Xochipilli, is also connected with children. Opposed to the young hero in the two forms indicated is the Earth Mother, no doubt to be understood as the moon, and her partner, Quetzalcoatl, who is of course the planet Venus and Xolotl's twin. Thus, the sun's enemy could be cast as the moon, the spirit of night, or as the evening star.

In the version approved by the Mexican state the young sun (Huitzilopochtli) opposes his sister the moon (Coyolxauhqui) and the hosts of stellar demons (the Huitznahua) that she leads. This scenario of the ball game was played by trained slaves in the Panquetzaliztli festival. It closely followed the myth, for at the end of the game the player representing Coyolxauhqui was beheaded over the center stone in the court.[25] Others representing the Huitznahua were also butchered in that narrow playing field. The dramatis personae can also be identified, with no change in meaning, as the Red Tezcatlipoca (sun) and Tlazolteotl (moon).

One may choose any of the preceding readings of the game, but in any case it had death built into it. In spite of the victory version given out by the city of Mexico, the fuller Mesoamerican myth had it that the sun was inevitably captured in the underworld and there ritually sacrificed. The mystery aspect of the game was that a new sun was born from that death and would rise out of the earth again whole and secure. Thus three interpretations of the tlachtli cult are possible. Either it was the renewal of light, the renewal of maize, or both.

Different Aztec cities certainly understood the cult in these several ways, yet in all cases the players were felt to be representations of astral gods who in mythical times were locked in combat. Even when the game was played purely for sport and wagering, its prototypal meaning lent a special intensity to it. When played as a part of certain festivals, the game became a surpassing theater of death, and at that time the ball court counted as a temple of the cosmic night.

We have mentioned as one of the actors the god Xochipilli whom we know to have been synonymous with youth and new vigor. He personifies the fertility aspects of the cult that are logical outcomes of the seasonal symbols employed. The Aztec mythographers saw the wrinkled and inert seed corn dropped into the dark earth as a homologue of the descent of the crippled westering sun, tragically fallen from his former splendor. And as a new sun would arise again, youthful and heroic, so too would the corn sprout appear, crowned with green plumes like the warrior with his bonnet of green quetzal feathers. The two otherwise dissimilar concepts, young sun and young corn, became one in a tale of conflict and heroism.

In the seventh month, priests clad as Xochipilli and Ixtlilton mimed a game of tlachtli against Quetzalcoatl and Cihuacoatl. Inasmuch as we know that this month honored Xochipilli, the young corn, we can thus correctly interpret the meaning of that game from the identities of the players. The spirit of the springing corn (Xochipilli), aided by a god of the young (Ixtlilton), pit their youth and vigor against two somber forces, the planet Venus (Quetzalcoatl), the sun's elder brother and eternal antagonist, and the Earth Mother herself (Cihuacoatl), the dark womb out of which Xochipilli hopes to escape. The versatility—or ambiguity—of the tlachtli as a theatrical cult is thus amply demonstrated.

The gods most persistently coupled in myth and iconography with the tlachtli are Quetzalcoatl and his avatar Xolotl.[26] When translated into astronomical terms, these are the two phases of the planet Venus, morning and evening star. We are thus led to believe that, however closely the tlachtli symbolized the course of the sun in the underworld, to just the same degree it symbolized the other protagonist in the astral myth, namely the planet Venus. Thus to say that the tlachtli is really a mystery play about the sun is only partially correct. We are forced to interpret the tlachtli in cult as a situation drama where there is no necessarily preferred hero and no specific villain. It is rather a tableau of the cosmogonic situation forever repeated. It affirms that what is done by way of creation must be done in the night, in the underworld, and by dark and sometimes demonic beings—and that all this is performed through hostility, mortal combat, suffering, and death. Night is older than day and is the true setting for any such drama.

THE CULTIC USES OF DARKNESS

A consideration of the tlachco leads us directly to the nocturnalism that was such a significant feature of Aztec cult. We already understand that the tlachco was a temple of the night sky in the underworld. It was an alley down which ran astral beings, plunging about and fighting in the darkness. The Tarascan Indians in fact had a version of the game that they actually played at night with a flaming grass ball.[27] On certain solemn occasions in Mexico-Tenochtitlan a ball to be used in the next day's game was sanctified by being thrown four times into the ball court at midnight,[28] and a mimic game in the Atamalcualiztli festival was staged at night.[29] We know that the teuctli as a sacerdotal figure had to perform in the daytime, so we see him fighting in the flower war as a priest of the daytime sun. The players of tlachtli on the contrary can be seen as quasi priests in a cult of the nighttime sun.

But tlachtli was only one of the many Aztec cults depicting darkness. Perhaps the dominant theme running throughout Aztec religion was the placing of darkness at the center of the cult. Night was thought to be the creative situation wherein all originations took place, a preferred dreaming time of the gods and demons, and a situation that, however hateful, had to be fully embraced by men. This was said about the ixiptla of Toci, as they led her to her death:

> And when midnight came, then they took her to the temple. No one at all spoke, none talked, nor did anyone cough; it was as if the earth lay dead. And everyone gathered around in the darkness.[30]

The Aztecs' hidden hostilities were well expressed by the nocturnalism in which their surrogates, the priests, wrapped themselves. Night is a time of danger and horrible crises; it is the cloak of Tezcatlipoca who was invoked by his worshippers as Night and Wind, the very spirit of that intangibility and daunting quality hidden in the heart of darkness, which is therefore to be feared, repelled, and if possible done away with or destroyed. For human beings would of course prefer to be surrounded by the light.

At each of his daily risings, the tlamacazqui went to a special vat (actually a canoe) wherein was made the black dye with which he painted himself from top to toe.[31] This was a preparation of soot, a sacred substance among the Aztecs that was made every night by the acolytes. The thousands of braziers continually burning in all Aztec cities made the collection of soot relatively easy.

Thus even by day the priest walked about in a skin of night. As for those priests who elected to go out into the environs on the nocturnal jaunts, I have already alluded to them. They smeared themselves, however, with a different substance.[32] This was called the "divine medicine" (teopahtli), and it was made from crushed and incinerated scorpions and rattlesnakes, and then mixed with tobacco and the hallucinatory mushroom. It was said to be a favorite food of Tezcatlipoca. When mixed with soot and applied to the skin, it cast the priest, who was about to meet the perils of the night, into a narcosis that made him fearless and that enchanted him into a state of the demonic where he could deal with whatever Tezcatlipoca might send against him. Because of its unusual efficacy, teopahtli was also used as a potion in curing.

In temple service there were five offices and time markers during the night, which number exceeded the four that were observed during the day.[33] During the night certain priests rose to greet and cense the statue of the deity, but it was at midnight when an uproar of shell trumpets and pipes awakened all the priests who thereupon each offered a bit of their blood to the god.[34] The midnight office was in fact known as "the time when trumpets are sounded and one cuts one's flesh." This midnight blood was of the greatest importance in maintaining the image of the priesthood as the suffering servant of the people.

But most telling of all in the tale of Aztec nocturnalism was the fact that many human sacrifices could only legitimately be made at midnight or just before the sun rose. From the theatrical point of view this appears logical, for the horror of death on the *techcatl* was obviously compounded by darkness and the dancing light of fires. But it was more than a sense of drama that drove the Aztecs to this inconvenience. It was thought that night was the womb of all great actions and that, by thus increasing the tension and the sense of repulsion in the ritual, it overwhelmed man's religious frustrations. In the sense of overemphasis it thus made profitable the works of man.

In dealing with this subject, one immediately thinks of those famous eighteen consecutive plates in the *Codex Borgia*, plates that together form one of the most magnificent and baroque of all the religious records from antiquity.[35] These relate to a frightful journey through the darkness, one that parallels what we have just seen in the tlachco cult. The mnemonic key to the exact meaning of this cluster of plates has long since been lost to us, so it will always remain to a great extent enigmatic. Nevertheless, it can be mined to some extent to give us the feel that the Aztecs had for darkness.

The document is thought to come from the religious tradition of Cholula, or one of its important outliers. Thus, we can be pretty sure that it expresses the thought and cult practices of the Cholula priesthood—a corporate body of men with a far richer and more venerable tradition than either Tezcoco or Tenochtitlan.

We do not know whether the plates report a single myth or cult story, or whether they add up to merely a series of unrelated episodes or rites. Most scholars disagree among themselves. I shall make the assumption that although rituals are here being alluded to, at the same time the *tlacuilo*, or priestly painter of the book, is presenting it conditioned and colored by his own immersion in a rich mythology. This section of the *Codex Borgia* is thus a chapbook and a cult manual at the same time. I do not think it possible to separate the two with any certainty.

From the cast of gods and demons depicted, we can state that the subject matter pertains to the night, the underworld, sacrificial acts, and the revival of the light through the kindling of new fire. The central figures are Quetzalcoatl, several of his avatars, and the nighttime sun. Prominent also are Tezcatlipoca and Tlazolteotl. Demons and spirits are also a constant furniture throughout the scenario, surrounding the action, as it were, by an aura of the macabre. The chthonic element is repeatedly expressed in the figure of the earth goddess who is generally shown as supine, her head a skull, and her body embroidered with stars and swirls of darkness. With these as the main characters, the sequence appears quite simply to set forth the adventures of the sun who, falling into the abyss, weakens and then is seized and held while a simulacrum is sacrificed to him. By the blood of this surrogate he is finally resuscitated, rising to light the world again.

The sequence of plates is certainly all of this. Nevertheless, its obvious allusion to the primacy of darkness does not keep it from being ambiguous in almost all of its details. From our Spanish sources we know that the Aztec priests quite correctly separated the planet Venus into a morning star and an evening star, the former divinized as Tlahuizcalpanteuctli, the latter as Xolotl.[36] But both are avatars of the god Quetzalcoatl who, under his date name "One Reed," was himself the god of the planet Venus. This richness of allusion becomes even more equivocal when we are told that Xolotl's date name, "Four Movement," is also the date name of Yohualteuctli, the sun in the underworld. In this latter understanding, therefore, once the sun and the evening star fall into the underworld, they ambiguously melt together as Four Movement. What allows them to do this is a sacrificial act at midnight that creates the new sun who will then arise. Nanahuatl (an avatar of Xolotl) is shown in the myth as a diseased and decrepit being who leaps into the fire to become the new sun, robust and glowing. Thus, in the sun and the two phases of Venus, we have a single celestial concept that encapsules the three deities and unites them as a process—the process of death transformed into life through sacrifice. What is particularly relevant to us is that all this takes place in the darkness.

In the Spanish texts that relate the previously mentioned Aztec myths, night as the final arbiter was represented by the *tzitzimime* who were skeletal demons and night's embodiment living in the sky. When the world should end, so the old people prophesied,

> that which is above us will fall in; the demons will descend, will come to destroy the earth, will come to eat the common folk; there will be eternal darkness on earth; nowhere will there be people on earth.[37]

The perfect symbol of the umbrageous world in which the Aztecs lived was the temple of the Great Mother, the so-called *Tlillan*, meaning the "Place of Darkness." This stood near the Coatepetl, the shrine of the vibrant lord of the daytime, Huitzilopochtli. The Tlillan was just as important to the state as was the Coatepetl.

THE CULT OF THE SKY WOMEN

The cult of the Sky Women appears to have been the most popular and widespread of all those that we have so far mentioned. This we gather from the ubiquity of their shrines in the Aztec world as well as the frequency of their feast days. These feasts taken all together formed a special cult of darkness.

The plural noun which is translated as "demons" in the preceding quotation is *tzitzimime*. A word must be said here about these creatures because, more than most other Aztec supernaturals, they personified the darkness.[38] The tzitzimime were one of the variant forms of the Sky Women and represented everything that people feared most.

One would have thought that the Aztecs might have imagined them as chthonic beings, but such was not the case—being denizens of the night sky, they were celestial. I have said earlier that demons did not evoke cult among the Nahuas, yet here is an instance of it. To understand why this was so, we must briefly identify the three forms of these demonic presences, all of whom could be referred to as "women of ill omen" (*tetzauhcihua*). They were perhaps not the ultimate in the Aztec nightmare, but they did make explicit for the Aztec the need to identify the features of divine malevolence. The basic fact about this class of Aztec demons is that, even though to some extent polymorphous, when given a sex they were always female, and as females they could be seen as one, four, five, or as many.

Considered as powers living in the sky, they were the skeletal tzitzimime, creatures who supported the four corners of the firmament and who would, on the day of doom, slide down from their dark eyries to devour all of mankind. When however the Aztecs turned their vision, not to final things, but to the present, the creatures were alluded to as the "princesses" (*cihuapipiltin*) or "goddesses" *cihuateteo*), women who raced unseen through the air to cast diseases and deformities on people, particularly on children.[39] Allied to these were the sinister *Ixcuinanme*, a word that may mean "bitches." These were more sexually oriented than the others for they could lure young men away to assignations and death. They were also known by the name of the great Huaxtec sex goddess when she was considered as plural, that is, the Tlazolteteo.

Most impressive was the understanding of this bevy of female demons as *Ilhuicacihua* ("Sky Women").[40] These were female warriors, or Amazons, grotesque travesties on the Aztec reality where war was a monopoly of the men and where the female was an ever-present symbol of cowardice. Although it was the male warriors dead in battle or later sacrificed who attended the sun as he made his way from his estate in the east to the zenith, it was the Sky Women who came up out of the west to meet the sun at that apical point, thence escorting him down to his setting. For this reason the west was called *cihuatlampa* ("land of women") by the Aztecs and others and was considered a direction somber, listless, and ugly.

Many centuries of myth making lay behind this rich speculation wherein the demonic elements resident in the sky were seen to be females, variously fragmented into seducers, devourers, and warriors. Yet however varied were the physical aspects of their demonic power, the cult was one thing and served them all.

Next to failure of their food supply, preliterate peoples probably looked upon disease and deformity as the most telling signs of their cosmic isolation. Starvation could result from the wrath of certain gods or from their indifference, but the presence of a person with running sores, or a wasting disease, the grimace of a paralytic, or the fumbling progress of a clubfoot, meant something even more—they were exemplars of a capriciousness beyond fathoming. Whether these derelicts moved about or sat in silent despair, they had all been touched by the malice of the Sky Women; they were overt signs of that casual hostility. This is not to say that the well-known and more individualized gods did not send diseases, for they did, but a certain disease was specific to, and diagnostic of, the jurisdiction of a known god. The princesses inflicted diseases and deformities generally.

> It was said that they were angered by men; they tricked men. When someone was under their spell, he was possessed, his mouth was twisted, his face contorted, he lacked use of a hand, his feet were misshapen, his feet were deadened, his hand trembled, he foamed at the mouth.[41]

Popular lore never accurately separated the various female specters into really clear categories. A tzitzimitl, for instance, could be found to be performing exactly as if she were one of the princesses or the Tlazolteteo. They all shared in the same quintuplicate constitution, and all were associated with the cardinal directions and their assigned colors. But it seems that the princesses were the preferred ones for most cult purposes.

It was priests of some pre-Aztec culture who had gathered up the popular cults of the princesses and had immersed them in the tonalpohualli where they finally appeared in five out of the twenty named days (house, deer, eagle, monkey, and rain), each further distinguished by the coefficient "one," and each separated in the almanac by a four-day interval. On three of these days in particular—One Rain, One Deer, and One Monkey—rites were celebrated in their honor.[42]

One Deer was a family festival particularly honored by husbands and wives who at that time prayed to the princesses that they might intercede with the appropriate gods to grant them healthy children. At this time married couples pierced themselves with thorns and then burned the thorns in front of the demons' shrines. In addition to this, the state or the city ward might provide a prostitute as a sacrifice. Condemned criminals also could be released by the state to spill their blood for the princesses. During One Rain families attempted to placate the furies by setting up small images of them in their homes and adorning them in garments of colored paper. One Monkey was celebrated by total avoidance, for on that day mothers kept their children inside the homes. Again the state could intervene on this occasion by presenting a child as a sacrifice to the demons. This last was a soundless celebration, joyless, and without dancing. Even the adults were silent and circumspect as they went about their chores under a fearful sky.

No other gods had as many days dedicated to them in the list of movable feasts. What this meant was that the priests had succeeded in taking over the cult of the Sky Women and in fitting it arbitrarily (and successfully) into the five-directional universe so congenial to all Mesoamericans. It was one of those more obvious priestly attempts to understand the cosmos through harnessing and rationalizing the scattered cults of the people.

The rites were carried out at special shrines that were often situated at crossroads or on lonely trails where the traveler was most at peril. The rites took place preferably at midnight. Each neighborhood had one of these shrines, called a *cihuateopan*, and to it individuals who feared for their children or who hoped for remission of their own afflictions, brought offerings.[43] On a low dais, the princesses were usually arranged as five idols, placed side by side.[44] They were lumpy stone blocks and were depicted seated in the customary female fashion with skull-like faces and with their talon-like hands clutched horribly in front of them. Their worshippers vowed to bring them paper streamers, white or colored.

A description of those Sky Women who in particular were warriors and mention of the method of their recruitment is in order here. Whenever a woman died in childbirth, retaining the foetus in her womb, she was likened to a warrior who had suffered agonies in battle and had died having captured an enemy (i.e., the unborn child). The dead woman was immediately transformed into a *mocihuaquetzqui*, which we can loosely translate as an "Amazon."[45] At midnight her body was taken on the back of the husband to one of the shrines for burial. It was customary for young warriors as well as those who had performed on the field of battle with little success to congregate around the funeral party in an attempt to cut off some portion of the corpse, preferable the hair, or middle finger of the left hand, talismans of courage and invulnerability. Once she was buried, her spirit ascended into the sky to take her place among the Sky Women.

In summary, the popular understanding of the Sky Women as bearers of disease and malformation was overriding, whereas the concept of them as warriors was mainly an aspect of mythology, not of cult. But in all cases these beings added to the world's stock of miseries.

I suspect that these spirit women were feared by one and all, nobles as well as commoners, even more than was Tezcatlipoca. If so, it tells us much about the sensitivity of the Aztecs to the presence of the divine. The biblical mind did not and does not characterize the Lord as a power inexplicably hostile to man. Rather, He is the just master who has been affronted by man's disobedience and the punishment He gives to him is therefore justified. His law was wrongfully broken, and the evils of life, such as disease and death, flow consequently from that. The Aztec did not produce such a statement of divine logic and saw the miseries of the human race as fluctuations in an ingenious hostility that was hidden in the darkness.

THREE

Sacrifice as a Substitute for Renewal

THE POSTULATES OF HUMAN SACRIFICE

There is no rejoicing, there is no contentment; there is torment, there is
pain, there is fatigue, there is want. Torment, pain dominate. Difficult
is the world, a place where one is caused to weep, a place where one is
caused pain. . . . And it is a place of thirst, it is a place of hunger. This
is the way things are.[1]

Out of such a world as is delineated here might well come an extreme cult.

It is very difficult to lead a modern reader to appreciate reality as
did the Aztec. Yet without something of this perception, understanding of their cult responses to the world is tentative at best. Many
might assume that the Aztec was a pessimist, but the word "pessimist" really does not fit. Some scholars might prefer to say that the
Aztecs had looked upon the naked truth and proclaimed it to be what
it was, nothing more, nothing less.

To the Aztec the universe was set in obsidian; it glistened with
an obdurate darkness that was indeed its inner nature. Light in the
darkness was spasmodic, perhaps even unnatural, a fitful glare here
and there that would reveal a god tensing over the scene, men sway-
ing back and forth over a battleground, the installation of a ruler or
his tumble into disgrace, or a man hunched against the chill wind.
Yet the Aztecs were not reduced to passivity simply because of their
life among the shadows. They created for themselves a stage of annually renewing colors and of measured movement among the shadows,
and on that artificial scaffold they played out their role.

The Aztecs were not dualists, persons who reduce categories of
being to two equal opposites, life and death, light and darkness, day
and night. On the contrary they believed that death, darkness, and
night were in a real sense positive qualities, that together they made

up a dynamic that could create forms and lend meaning. Yet they did not feel themselves an integral part of this. They could properly measure the reality of this world only because they were alien to it.

They made no attempt to devise a philosophy that would organize their thoughts concerning it. Instead they spoke their words of submission and rebuttal through the language of cult. I have already adverted to their cultic use of the night through which they accustomed themselves to beckon to the supernaturals. And this darkness, in consonance with its pseudopositive quality, showed periodicity and renewals, like cosmic pulse beats.

From the preceding chapter, it is obvious that a surreal quality characterized Aztec religion. Because they knew that no ultimate ransom would be offered to release them from their prison, some relief from the harshness of their life became a necessity. In their own cultic style, therefore, they substituted reprieve for what we in the Christian tradition know as salvation. The steps that they took to remedy their lot were not simple, and they formulated them in the astronomical, numerological, and chronological terms that meant so much to them.

Their myths taught them that things threatened to give up their spirit after a period defined as four, eight, thirteen, or fifty-two years. These culmination periods were to become for them preferably points of postponement. Temples would be repainted every fourth year, and certain festivals were at that time observed with increased emphasis. We have seen for instance that every fourth year the Toxcatl festival turned into a plenary remission of sins and crimes. All of such rituals might be considered as renewals. Certainly the Atamalcualiztli that was performed every eighth year was a renewal of the frayed spirit of the corn. The most pointed renewal came with the New Fire ceremony on the fifty-second year. When assured at that time that the daily and annual movement of the sun would continue and that life would not be eclipsed, the Aztecs took heart and projected their own continuation for at least another lustrum. Frequent cleansing of their lives and renewals of their vigor were necessary to this people who otherwise felt themselves to be fair game for the gods.

But the priests over the centuries had told the people of another renewal need, this one not human but divine. The gods also must be refreshed. Preliterate folk everywhere have projected onto gods and demons the need to eat and drink—there is nothing unusual in this.

They have offered to the supernaturals their most prized foods and prepared drinks, and often this collation has been human flesh and blood. Thus, the Aztecs were in no sense aberrant in the fact that they offered up their fellows as alimentation for the gods, but in the gross theater that they built up around the act, and in the astonishing numbers of men, women, and children they annually destroyed to maintain their cults, they were truly exceptional. More than any other people in history, they must have thought of themselves as mere caterers and butlers to gods whose hunger and thirst were never sated. Cults that grow up to express such a theology by definition have to be extreme.

The tradition of human sacrifice was old in Mesoamerica, and we have good reason to believe that it first appears among small hunting/gathering bands in the Tehuacan Valley around the middle of the sixth millennium B.C.[2] At such an early date human sacrifice could not have had the same meaning that it did later among the agriculturists and warriors, but certainly such a long projection from the past can explain in part the later Aztec extremism.

The Aztecs could define the art of human sacrifice as simply the "killing of men" (*tlacamictiliztli*). The verb "to make an offering [to a god]" is *huemana*. This verb conjures up the picture of a person's spreading offerings out on the ground before a statue, or placing them on an altar. Embedded in the verb is the noun *huentli* ("an offering or sacrifice").

One could also use the noun *nextlahualli* to refer to a human being who was sacrificed. Literally, the word means "a debt paid," where an original debt governing the relationship of man to the supernaturals is premised. One can only suppose that the debt here alluded to was that incurred when the god Quetzalcoatl descended into the underworld, returned with the bones of men long dead, and revived them by pouring over them an effusion of his own blood. The Aztec creation of man thus differs radically from the myth found in the book of Genesis where no quid pro quo is mentioned or implied. Adam before he falls owes nothing to his creator, being simply a living sign of God's goodness. And even after the fall, Adam is not in any way a debtor but is rather a disobedient servant, willful and therefore condignly punished. This comparison should enable us to feel more keenly the Aztecs' comprehension of human life as being originally encumbered with a debt that somehow must be discharged, though the creditor's surpassing rank made discharge almost impossible. Out of this profound disparity and the frustration felt by the Aztecs came their sacrificial cult.

The basic scenario, however, was quite simple. Ogres are always hungry; they must be fed, and it is man who must provide the food. In later times the priests could think of that refection as a cosmic renewal.

CHILD SACRIFICE IN THE CULT OF TLALOC

The Aztec priests performed several types of human sacrifice depending on the cult in question, but there was one method more frequently used than any of the others; this was heart extraction. We will be dealing with this at greater length in one of the following sections, so here it is mentioned only.

The second form of human sacrifice was indissolubly linked to the cult of the Tlalocs and thus was most in evidence during the early part of the calendrical year, which was the growing season. The victims here were small children from about three to six years of age. Such a convention as this clearly separates the cult of Tlaloc from all the others.

There can be no doubt that child sacrifice, long precedent to the Aztecs, comes from a very ancient level of Mesoamerican life, and that it was hallowed by tradition.[3] The Tlalocs were spirits of the high wilderness who were specifically the lords of the rain clouds. There were as many of them as there were mountains in the land, and all were conceived to be small people, gnomelike creatures, blue in color, whimsically beating on the jugs from which spilled the rain.[4] The rattle of the thunder was the breaking of the jugs. These rain spirits lived inside the mountains eternally feasting and surrounded with treasures. They were the local spirits whose ixiptlas had to be children.

The children were referred to as "debt payments," the reference being an acknowledgment by the folk of that which they owed to the gods, namely payment in kind, in this case small people who could be seen to be facsimiles of the Tlalocs. Thus, the children chosen for sacrifice were painted blue, the color of water, and they were spattered with liquid rubber, an old Mesoamerican substance used in rain magic.[5]

For certain of the more urgent ceremonies only children of the nobility would do,[6] but most of the children appear to have been purchased in the slave markets just outside Tenochtitlan.[7] Others were part of the regular tribute levied on selected communities that were under the domination of the major Aztec cities. In the growing season, when rain was all important, there was naturally a great demand by the state for these victims, and they were kept in a special pound until they were needed. We have already seen the various ways in which they were disposed of. In the Tozoztli festivals, for instance, four children were annually sealed up in a cave in the mountains. Some were sacrificed on those mountain peaks after which they had been ceremonially named; others were cast into the lake to drown. Bodies of water and mountains were the important loci in their cult.

A special instance of sacrifice and burial within the mountain was recently uncovered during the course of the excavations in the heart of Mexico City. Attached to the north side of the central temple (i.e., the Tlaloc side) there was found a small stepped altar with the skulls and bones of more than thirty-five children sealed up inside.[8] This may well be a testimony to the catastrophic drought that took place during the reign of Moteuczoma I, but it is the exact equivalent of the annual Cuahuitlehua sacrifices.

It is important to realize that these doomed children, so pathetic to us, were reverenced by the Aztecs as true ixiptlas, and it was believed that when they entered into the interior of the mountain, they there took up lives of eternal bliss. Through such sacrifices, the Aztecs hoped to further a continuous osmosis between the world of the mountain (which was the home of rain) and the world of man.

SOME BASIC SACRIFICIAL ACTS

Scalping and the taking of heads were endemic among the Stone Age cultures of the New World at the time when the first white settlers arrived. In the meeting of American Indians and whites in our Eastern Woodlands and, farther west, on the Great Plains, nothing so shocked our ancestors as the practice of scalping, and nothing gave them a more satisfying justification for their own acts of aggression.

The Aztecs had pushed the practice of head taking to the point where they had organized it finally into vast state-sponsored projects.[9] These blended so thoroughly into their religions that their original lack of relevance to the priestly cults was forgotten. By the time of the

Aztecs it was accepted as axiomatic that such activities of men were especially pleasing to the gods.

A warrior's valor was contained in his scalp lock and for this reason a captor, in the vigil preceding his captive's death, cut from the crown of the latter's head a lock of hair that thenceforth as a matter of pride he displayed hanging from the roof poles of his house.[10] Any gathering of guests in his home served the owner as an occasion for boasting of his coup. Scalping remained a completely private matter, but head-hunting, perhaps because of its greater visual impact, was integrated into the cults. This was publicized by means of the skull racks that stood beside the larger temples. The famous dance of the severed heads in the cult of Xipe will be described, but there were others in other months of the year. In every case where an adult was sacrificed, his or her head was testimony to the nourishment provided to the god, and all were accordingly threaded on the poles of the appropriate skull rack.

Sacrificial death by fire was a ritual particularly associated with the Tepanecs, some of whom formed part of the Mexican people.[11] Naturally it was used in the cult of the fire god, and its best known example comes from the Great Feast of the Dead. In this ghastly ceremony, the entire pantheon of gods, represented by their ixiptlas, were bound hand and foot, carried up to the sacred hearth on the backs of priests, and then severally were thrown into the fire pit. Each of these ixiptlas was accompanied by four or five slaves or captives to add to their dignity. Left in the coals to roast only a moment, they were then quickly hooked out to suffer heart extraction on the techcatl. These hearts were offered to Xiuhteuctli.

In the preceding we note that sacrifice by fire was felt to be incomplete unless mated to the more common death by heart extraction. This may have first occurred at the time when the Tlatilulca (a Tepanec group) joined with the Tenochcas to become the Mexican people.

SACRIFICES IN THE CULT OF XIPE

It was in the cult of Xipe where the most bizarre varieties of human sacrifice were to be found.[12] Xipe was old in Mesoamerica and had had time to accumulate cultic oddities from many varied sources.

Xipe was an international god whose original cult appears to have been one of solar renewal. Commonly, he is shown wearing the skin of a sacrificed victim. His very name seems to mean the "Skinned One." The wearing of skins, however, was not restricted to his cult. Among others, it can be found in the cult of the great goddess Toci, whereas in most cults where it was used, it identified the just-sacrificed ixiptla as the deity who was renewed.

Flaying did, however, reach its peak in the rites associated with Xipe for here all the gods, in the persons of their ixiptlas, were sacrificed and skinned. The priests who assumed the skins then roamed the city as Xipeme or avatars of the god. Thus for the time being all of the gods, representing the totality of nature, underwent renewal and were touched by the coming of spring. Xipe was the catalyst in this burgeoning of all things.

The skinning of human bodies was a special skill practiced by certain priests. Customarily, they took up their positions at the foot of the temple stairs to begin their work as soon as the discarded corpse came tumbling down to rest beside them. The speed with which they accomplished their task was considered a matter of amazement in one of the Colonial sources.[13] I have previously described the act of flaying. The skin was always worn inside out with the hands generally attached but not the feet. The skin from the head was pulled over the face like a mask and laced up the back. These skins were only doffed after twenty days of wear by volunteers, by which time they were brittle and smelled offensively. As holy objects, they nevertheless had to be reverently put away in a stone burial pit dug into Xipe's temple. The new year, beginning with the sun's swing north, was symbolized by the new skins worn at that time. They were auroral influences of considerable power.

There was a distinctive form of human sacrifice that was observed only in the cult of Xipe. It was unlike any other ritual in Aztec religion and was referred to as "the streaking [with blood]" (*tlahuahua-naliztli*). It will be described in our account of the second month of the calendar. Here we need only note its meaning.

The "streaking" was a late knightly addition (Toltec perhaps) to an earlier solar cult of renewal. It was a mock gladiatorial combat that was staged so as to reenact before the god the heroism displayed by the two antagonists, captor and captive, in their original and fateful encounter on the battlefield. This presacrificial battle rite was thought to enhance the value of the sacrifice itself that immediately followed.

By reproducing the bravery—or at least the combative posture —of the enemy warrior who had been captured, it allowed the spectators to see the one who now delivered him to the god, namely the captor, exulting and posturing before the place of sacrifice. The vainglory of the Aztec warrior was thus given an ultimate form of expression in this rite. But we have noted that this scene of the Indian brave vaunting his deed was imposed upon an older scenario more attuned to the needs of a whole community—the strife between the sun and his enemies. The outcome here in Xipe's cult was that the sun was subdued by his formidable opponent, the morning star. The four knights who fought against the tethered captive on the temalacatl represented the minions of the morning star, whereas the captive played the part of Xipe, the sun. The captive therefore had to die and in dying be resurrected as the new sun. This was the meaning for the community.

But no cult with so many centuries behind it is ever that easy to interpret. The reading I have given here probably refers to the cult as conceptualized during a certain period prior to the appearance of the Aztecs, but there can be no certainty that it maintained itself in that form. Mesoamerican cult was profound and fluid at the same time.

Here is what happened in the tlahuahuanaliztli insofar as we can reconstruct it. Once brought back from the battlefield the captive was spoken of as the "son" of his captor who was thus his "father."[14] It was this affiliation, in fact, that prevented the captor from partaking of the banquet that he offered to his kin at the culmination of the affair—for the human flesh consumed in that meal was that of his "son." No doubt this filiation was designed to cast over the capture and the resulting sacrifice an aura of quasi meaning that would absolve the captor from the blood guilt of his deed. In any case, this absolution must have been of small account, for the only figure in the transaction who really counted was the deity who was the first to taste the flesh and drink the blood of the captive. In the cult of the second month, as we have seen, that deity was the sun in his great spring avatar, Xipe, the Flayed One.

If we can accept this, then the captor's son must be the new (or the renewed) sun who is quite obviously not the morning star. This presents the modern scholar with a dilemma, but it was not the Aztecs' dilemma, for they had an ability to see behind all of the actors in a play—even a play of conflict and opposites—a whole situation. The roles of the sun and the morning star were of course known to them, but these roles could at times coalesce, bringing opposites together in a situational integrity. What does give it an easy logic for us is the late militaristic overlay we have analyzed here.

The victim was escorted up the dais fronting the sun's temple and there tied by a rope to a center ring in the great round stone, the temalacatl that represented the sun. He was armed with a sword club that had its inset obsidian blades removed and replaced with tufts of feathers. His opponents, two Eagle and two Jaguar knights, wielded the deadly cutting form of the weapon, but only one of them at a time confronted him. The desired denouement was for the victim to comport himself with valor and to continue the unequal struggle until its inevitable end. His energetic participation had two effects. It increased the prestige of the captor among his fellows, and at the same time it increased the value that the sun placed upon that captive—a hero's heart was far tastier to Tonatiuh than was the heart of a craven. Often however, the captive, full well knowing the hopelessness of his situation, simply crumpled on the stone and refused to defend himself. But whether he comported himself bravely or not, bleeding at last from a mortal blow he was untied and hauled over to the other stone, the *cuauhxicalli*. Onto this he was raised, and there had his heart torn out. Dying in this way, his blood flowed over the upraised face of the sun depicted on the stone, a case of the direct alimentation of the god.

All of the cult passages connected with the preceding festival are melodramatic. A priest clad in a bear skin accompanied each of the victims up to the gladiatorial stone. Called "Old Bear," he was considered to be a protective uncle to the doomed man. It was he who received him from the captor, bound him to the stone, and gave him his imitation weapons. In addition to Old Bear and the four knights, there was an entourage of four other warriors called the "Four Dawns." They were left-handed and therefore supremely dangerous to any foe. They undoubtedly represented the four cardinal directions of the world's first day. If many prisoners were to be fought and slain, these four could be called on to spell the weary Eagle and Jaguar knights. Watching over the whole procedure were priests representing the gods Ixcozauhqui ("Fire Face") and Titlacahuan, Tezcatli-poca's most pristine avatar. Respectively, these two deities stood for the day sun and the sun at night.

The sacrificing priest was an avatar of Xipe known as *Yohual-lahuan* ("He Who Is Drunken During the Night"). The name prob-ably refers to the night sun who is sacrificed in the underworld and then springs into life again. He was the chief sacrificial priest in Xipe's cult, and as he came up to the stone, he led a procession of all the gods who were represented by their high priests. Thus, the pan-theon shared in the renewal rites of the sun.

The blood of the dead man was sucked out of the open excava-tion in his chest through a reed and collected in a special bowl. This was given to the captor who was then privileged to go around to all the idols in the city, dressed in his finery, and to smear their mouths with the blood. The act cast him as the equivalent of a priest and cer-tainly brought him merit in the estimation of the gods. In the mean-while, as a coda to that particular set of sacrifices, all of the god impersonators along with the Yohuallahuan and Old Bear, the latter howling in simulated grief, danced about the stone, each carrying one of the severed heads.

But now to further involve ourselves in the maze of meanings we must look at another form of human sacrifice that often appeared in the Xipe cult along with the "streaking," but that could also be employed in other cults, notably in that of Chicomecoatl. This was "the shooting of men [with arrows]" (*tlacacaliliztli*), a type of sacrifi-cial death recalling the martyrdom of St. Sebastian, which was so fas-cinating to the painters of the Renaissance.[15] The only notable differ-ence between the two deaths was that, whereas the Christian saint was tied to a tree, the Aztec victim was lashed in spread-eagle fashion to a square and upright wooden frame and, thus immobilized, was trans-fixed with arrows. It was in fact a style of crucifixion. The blood drip-ping down from the victim fell upon the Earth Mother and impreg-nated (or nourished) her. This form of human sacrifice must also have had a respectable age for it is found all over Mesoamerica—in fact the North American Pawnee, far removed geographically, used it in their cult of the morning star.

In the Chicomecoatl cult, archers dressed as avatars of Tonatiuh, the sun, and the Four Dawns shot the crucified victims.[16] It has been suggested that the arrows, which on a primary level of symbolism must be the rays of the sun, on a deeper level are forms of the phallus. Both readings are probably right. The presence of the Four Dawns would lead us to see again in this rite the duel between the morning star and the sun. It would thus be a sun ritual somewhat akin to the "streaking" in the cult of Xipe, but whereas the streaking has reference only to the feeding of the sun, the "shooting" speaks of the copulation of sun and earth, in other words, of conception and fertility.

The joining of these two rites, originally quite separate, is significant as a priestly attempt to exhaust all the possibilities of meaning in the production of a central cult.

CATEGORIES OF SACRIFICIAL VICTIMS

A prisoner taken in war belonged, by that very fact, to the gods, and therefore he could end his life only as a sacrificial victim.[17] Nevertheless, once that irrevocable destiny was established for him, the captive could be traded between cities, offered to others as a gift, or more commonly, turned over to a superior city as a part of the subject city's tribute.[18] Whereas for most subject cities tribute was generally assessed in corn, clothing, or luxury items, for some others with an appropriate warlike reputation, tribute could be assessed at a certain number of captured knights to be delivered every eighty days. It would seem that the original captor, wherever it might be that his captive found his end, accompanied him there as an indispensable part of the cult. Captives were precious commodities, and the palace treasurer had ultimate responsibility for maintaining and guarding them until they were destroyed or transferred.[19]

Not all humans sacrificed were thought to be equal, and they were in fact divided into types. The highest grade of victims was "he who dies like a flower," a metaphor for one who dies with gallantry. An example of this status would be the enemy warrior who had been captured in battle and brought back to await sacrifice in some appropriate ritual or for some special state need. His bravery had been proven by his original presence in the press of battle, and he was therefore highly valued. His captor, whom we have seen as the prisoner's "father," turned him over to the state that kept him closely guarded along with others in "the captives' hall" (*malcalli*), a stronghold or cellar probably adjunct to the palace.[20] This pound, so crucial for the state religion, was under the care of a special major-domo. We hear also of other prisoners as being guarded by the chiefs of the *calpullis* or wards of the city. Inasmuch as each ward worshipped its own god, these compounds were in effect warehouses where food and drink suitable to the gods were stored against the day when they were to be consumed.

One captive above all others was selected out for honors, that one who may have been taken by the ruler himself.[21] He was brought back from the battlefield carried in a litter by the great nobles and was splendidly clad. In fact, as he processed into the city at the head of the file of captives he was greeted by the populace as the son of the ruler, almost a god, and until the time of his sacrifice (generally some forty days later), he lived in the palace carefully guarded but surrounded by luxury. Great men came from far and near to participate in the rejoicings. Poets created new songs for the occasion. After his death, his skin was stuffed with cotton and kept in the palace as a distinguished trophy. On special occasions the *tlatoani* displayed his prowess by dancing in the skin.[22]

Another type of victim was the "bathed one" (*tlaaltilli*). Whereas it was the warrior who delivered his captive into the hands of the god as an offering, it was the merchant or rich artisan who did the same with the purchased slave whom he had turned into a bathed one. There seems to have been some distinction made between the slave and the captive; both victims, by dying on the sacrificial stone, died a "flower death," but the sacrificed warrior went to join the entourage of the sun god, whereas the sacrificed slave had to descend into the underworld.[23]

It is impossible to say in what order these two kinds of victims appeared in Mesoamerica. There can certainly be no doubt that the Aztecs inherited both from the Toltec past, but they may have been even older than that. Whereas the value of the war captive came solely from his activity and bravery on the field of battle, the value of the bathed one resided in the wealth and care lavished on him by his owner. It must be understood that great wealth and its expert accumulation were thought by the Aztecs to be certain signs of the favor of either Tezcatlipoca or Yacateuctli, the latter an avatar of Quetzalcoatl and the patron god of merchants. A wealthy man was thus almost as welcome a donor at the altar of the Aztec god as was a knight.

A rich man could offer a bathed one at whatever altar he wished, but his preferences lay in the cults either of Huitzilopochtli, Quetzalcoatl, or Xiuhteuctli. His procedures were set. When he went to the market at Azcapotzalco or Itzucan to buy a slave for sacrificial purposes, he particularly assessed the slave's ability to dance and walk elegantly, for the potential victim was to be in a sense an ixiptla of some deity and therefore had to be free of blemishes if possible and to offer a certain presence. But slavery itself was a stain and took great effort to overcome or erase.[24] Accordingly, the slave was subjected to a regimen of ceremonial daily bathing in warm water for a period sometimes as long as a year, or perhaps for only seven days depending on the amount of purity the merchant desired to attain for his bathed one.[25] These unfortunates were well fed, and, in fact, a public woman or whore was hired to tempt a male slave, who was being bathed, to gorge himself during the period of his purification—the sole purpose of this was to prepare him for the cooking pot. The woman was not sacrificed.[26]

The bathed one was donated beforehand by his or her owner to one of the approaching cults and therefore was identified with the deity involved, though the connection does not seem to have been as close as was the case with a state ixiptla. Throughout the cleansing period the slave was publicly displayed, dancing on rooftops clad in rich garments while smoking cigars and sniffing flowers. All of this added to the owner's prestige as a man of wealth.

In the Panquetzaliztli festival the merchants customarily offered many slaves and were themselves much in evidence, often dancing with these slaves in the running serpent dance.[27] When the time of sacrifice came, the merchants individually accompanied each of their bathed ones to the foot of the pyramid steps, carrying for them their paper banners of sacrifice and then staying there to claim the body when it tumbled down. With the aid of younger men, the merchant brought the appropriate parts of the body back to his residence to prepare it for the ensuing private banquet.

There were other offices filled by the victims at the time of their deaths. There were the so-called *pepechhuan*. The word *pepechtli* means a pad, a place to lie or sit on, and in a cultic sense it refers to victims who were sacrificed as a group introductory to one of greater note. They were therefore meant to serve as a ritual base or opener. In the Small Feast of the Lords, for instance, a group of captives were assigned to be sacrificed just before Huixtocihuatl's ixiptla was destroyed. Similarly, in the Etzalcualiztli festival, a group of captives were sacrificed as pepechhuan before the ixiptla of Tlaloc.[28] The appearance of such a class of victims must be thought of as a cult elaboration only, and not a novelty. Ixiptlas of the gods were magnified but not changed by such lavish use of victims.[29]

Another office filled by a person marked for sacrifice was that of messenger to the sun.[30] This was always a war prisoner who was taken to the temple of Tonatiuh and there adorned for sacrifice. At the foot of the steps, priests addressed him reverently, requesting that he greet the sun and intercede with him in behalf of the knights there assembled. He was given a walking staff, a shield, and token gifts wrapped in a bundle that he was to offer to the deity. If the scenario was properly observed, the captive would vocally assent to his mission and then mount the steps of the sun dais, pausing at each step as he simulated the measured and dignified rising of the sun. At the top he went over to the round sun stone (the *cuauhxicalli*) and standing on it delivered aloud the message entrusted to him, all the while facing the image of the sun that hung over the altar. The sacrificial priests took the gifts in behalf of the sun and then, forcing the captive over the cuauhxicalli, quickly slit his throat, allowing the blood to completely wash over the face of the sun embossed on the stone. Only after that did they perform heart extraction on him, offering his heart to the god. All of this took place at noon on the day Four Olin, the sun's day.

This ritual was designed to reestablish communication between the sun god and his preferred children, the knights. All of the commoners had to fast on that day, although no benefits accrued to them from doing so. They were summoned to the site of the drama by the big conch-shell trumpets blown from the pyramid tops.

A final sacrificial office was that of the persons destroyed in the obsequies of rulers, princes, and outstanding magnates. These, however, were not directly implicated with the supernaturals (in other words, they did not serve either as substitutes of the gods or as their food), so we shall leave a consideration of them for the final chapter.

SACRIFICE BY HEART EXTRACTION

Of all the skills of men that are recorded in history none can have exceeded in its combined expertise and frightfulness the Aztec extraction of hearts. They had not invented it. All of the peoples around them employed it in their cults, some, like the Aztecs, to excess. We do not know when it began in Mesoamerica, but it was certainly a feature of the Classic period, and it might have been earlier than that. By the time of the Aztecs, it was an old and hallowed custom.

The Aztec ritual, with which we are here concerned, was the business of the priesthood and was indissolubly connected with the design of the pyramid temple as it finally evolved. At the front of the open space on the pyramid top stood the *techcatl*, not more than two or three feet from the verge. On this, the victim was killed and then toppled over the edge. The extraordinary steepness of the steps was dictated by the need to have the body tumble without hindrance all the way down to the bottom. Thus, after a series of sacrifices, that part of the stairway directly under the techcatl would be stained with blood and too slippery either to mount or descend. Victims in that series would then have to be dragged up well over to the side of the cascade of blood at a point where the steps were dry. And from this the Aztec poets could interpret that treacherous frontal ascent as memorable and infinitely precious—the temple stairway became for them the "jade steps." At the bottom was the *apetlac*, a projecting masonry apron, itself with five or six steps leading up on its three sides—a flat area where the bodies came to rest. This was Huitzilopochtli's "dining table" (*tlacuayan*) where he consumed the essence of the victim's flesh before it was claimed by the captors and carried off to their tables. We have learned that the victim before his sacrifice was *teomicqui* or *xochimicqui* ("one who dies in a godlike way, or like a flower"). As soon as the body landed on the apetlac it became a *cuauhtecatl*, which means in full "an inhabitant of eagle land."[31] That was the fulfillment of an Aztec warrior's life and his desired apotheosis.

The actual sacrifice can be briefly described.[32] The victims could be prepared for the sacrifice by being displayed by the owner or captor in dances leading up to the rites.[33] Come the day of sacrifice, they were appropriately painted, generally with red-and-white streaks longitudinally applied to the body. Tufts of down were stuck on their heads—no doubt to represent them as fledgling eagles ready for their flight heavenward. Each carried a paper flag that announced him as a candidate for sacrifice, and he wore festooned over his shoulder a paper ribbon.[34] They were lined up for review in rows at the foot of the skull rack, each one pinioned and with his captor or owner beside him. At the foot of the ascent the captor delivered his captive over to the priests who then dragged him up by the hair if he did not himself make the ascent.[35] On reaching the level at the summit he was immediately thrown backward over the techcatl, four priests bearing heavily down on the limbs, while the fifth one crushed the throat with a special implement, in the instance of Huixtocihuatl's cult, a sawfish's bill.[36] The sixth priest, who was always a *tlenamacac*, struck a powerful blow into the center of the upthrust chest and broke through the sternum. Reaching into the wound he ripped out the still-beating heart and turning, held it skyward for a moment—an offering to the god. He then tossed the heart into a special bowl nearby. These hearts were called *cuauhnochtli*.[37] Nochtli is the plump, red, and edible fruit of the prickly pear cactus, often vaguely heartshaped. The compound word means "eagle-cactus fruit," and designated the ambrosial dish beloved of the sun. Sometimes the officiating priest would dip his hand into the gaping wound and then flip the blood toward each of the four directions, in this way giving to all the gods, wherever they were, a share in the offering. The body was then unceremoniously tipped off the stone, and the priests readied themselves for the next victim already on his way up.[38]

Waiting at the foot of the "jade steps" stood the captor and the old priests who were skilled at flaying and quick dismemberment. The corpse was decapitated on the apetlac and the limbs removed. The trunk was probably discarded, though we are not told much about the disposition of such gruesome remnants. After ceremonies where there had been many victims, they were probably heaped up in canoes and taken off to some deserted part of the lakeshore to be handed over to the vultures and coyotes.[39] The head, which belonged to the god, was immediately prepared for threading on the adjacent skull rack. The scalp lock belonged to the captor who prized it as a talisman of power and hung it ostentatiously from the rafters of his home[40]; additionally he hung a thighbone from a wooden post standing in the open patio of his home.[41] One of the thighs went to the palace kitchens, and one to the captor for the ceremonial cannibal meal that he served to his friends that night.

The cannibal meal was really not a part of the god's worship but was an appended rite performed by and for the individual warrior announcing the successful completion of his duel and validating the transferal of vital war power from captive to captor.[42] The flesh was cooked and diced with vegetables and herbs or squash flowers. It was served in the presence of the captor who was forbidden to partake of it, because it was deemed to be the flesh of his son. The gods had already consumed their portion, the heart and blood.

THE SACRIFICE OF THE YEAR EIGHT REED

On the day Seven Reed of the year Eight Reed (1487) occurred the greatest event in all Aztec history, the dedication of the new temple of Huitzilopochtli by the Mexican ruler Ahuitzotl.[43] The work of renewing and enlarging the edifice had been started four years earlier at the opening of the reign of the short-lived Tizoc. All the newly conquered peoples as well as the older tributary states had been earlier ordered to provide the labor and precious materials wherewith to build and adorn the temple—now they were called on to provide additionally great numbers of captives for the slaughter. Tenochtitlan, of course, had been accumulating her own supply in the interim, crowding them into a special pound and assigning the overflow to the various calpullis in the city. A brief description of this exceptional celebration is in order here for it brings out the extravagance and theatricality of Aztec cult with special clarity.

On his accession to the office of tlatoani, the new ruler had undertaken a campaign for the purpose of rounding up a supply of victims who were to be hoarded against the time of the dedication. Enormous numbers of victims were thus accrued. The lowest figure in our sources given for the number of victims is 4,000, the highest 80,400.[44] The job of guarding these men and women, of feeding and caring for them while alive, and of disposing of the cadavers afterwards must have called on all of Tenochtitlan's aptitude for organization. In anticipation of the hecatomb, Ahuitzotl ordered the skulls

that were at the time displayed on the great skull rack to be burned
and discarded, thus making room for the great addition to come.

Tenochtitlan introduced the festivities with a quixotic invitation.
Three of her most fearless captains were selected to carry greeting to
the rulers of Tlaxcala, Cholula, and Huexotzinco with the request
that they attend as honored guests. These cities were among Mexico's
inveterate enemies. Using the greatest stealth, the messengers
penetrated the enemy's defenses in the dead of night and were finally
able to approach the palace guards in all three cities, and to request to
be taken to the respective rulers in order to offer invitations. All of the
rulers on the other side of the mountains accepted, even though they
knew that they would be witnessing the sacrificial deaths of some of
their own knights taken previously by the Mexica. These rulers,
escorted to the borders by their own warriors, were met by parties of
Mexican knights who disguised them and thus were able to bring
them incognito into the heart of Tenochtitlan. They were housed for
the several days of the ceremonies in concealed roof apartments of the
Cihuatecpan overlooking the sacrificial area. From these rooftops they
were said to be able to view all of the ceremonies at their leisure. Two
hundred picked Mexican warriors guarded them against the possibility of popular tumults should their presences become known. Finally,
at the conclusion of the dedication, they were loaded down with
sumptuous gifts and again under the greatest secrecy taken back to
their own frontiers. Nothing could inform us more clearly concerning
the international character of Aztec sacrifice and the fact that worship
of the gods could in a sense prevail over the political interests of the
city.

The extraordinary ritual of the dedication of the new Coatepetl
involved not only Huitzilopochtli, but the entire pantheon of gods as
well. In the persons of their high priests all of the gods attended. Four
rulers presided over the sacrifices, the three kings of the Three City
League plus Tlacaelel, the aging but still powerful *cihuacoatl* of
Mexico. Each one of the four was stationed at a techcatl, Ahuitzotl
presiding at Huitzilopochtli's shrine, the others at the shrines of
Tlaloc, Xipe, and Tezcatlipoca. These four sacrificed the first victims
and then stepped back to give way to the high priests of the invited
gods who spelled each other in the sustained ordeal of killing. From
sunrise to sunset for four consecutive days the slaughter went on with

the waiting victims in four files leading to each of the temples mentioned and in some cases stretching back to well outside the temenos walls. So unforgettable was the sight that one spot on the causeway road leading across the lake from the south was ever after known as "The Tail End of the File of Prisoners" (*Malcuitlapilco*).[45] The waiting victims were grouped in lots according to the city, either subject or allied, that was donating them for sacrifice, and each of the victims was accompanied by the true donor, namely his captor, splendidly arrayed.

The fact that New Fire was made for the occasion shows us that the year 1487 was one of the renewal years, probably one that occurred every fourth year and therefore ritually sensitive.[46] The celebrations of other festivals normally coming on or near this time, with which popular or priestly sensibilities would have been concerned, must have presented a problem of organization and adjustment, as must have also the stockpiling of gifts and supplies and the deployment of people to avoid congestion. In the staging of this four-day spectacle, the entire Mexican state was transformed into an elaborate play with priests, rulers, and victims cast as the actors, and with the populace a captive audience.

THE PARAPHERNALIA OF SACRIFICE

Out of the ritual of heart extraction and the implements used in it grew a number of divine personations, fetishes, and in one case an actual god. In a few cases they even entered the mythology. Of all these none were more central than the *tecpatl ixcuahua* ("the wide-bladed sacrificial knife").[47] We have mentioned it earlier but more should be made of it here.

Myth had it that the firstborn son of the goddess Starskirt, queen of the heavens, was Tecpatl, the knife of sacrifice.[48] This mighty demon fell or was thrown down from the sky to become an earthling. From him sprang the gods, sixteen hundred of them, who were captained by Xolotl, the first god to perform blood sacrifices. In another myth, the knife was the beloved son of the horrid earth goddess Cihuacoatl, a son whom she carried about swaddled as a papoose. These myths state categorically the centrality of heart sacrifice in Aztec ritual.

The knife was traditionally of flint (*tecpatl*). Flint was less brittle than obsidian and although never as sharp, was heftier and, with a strong arm delivering the blow, could smash through the human sternum and ribs—the obsidian knife might have splintered in such a process.[49] The word for a chip or blade of obsidian is *itztli*, and this alternates with tecpatl to designate the god of the knife. The itztli was used, not only for autosacrifice, but for the flaying and dismemberment of victims. It could be looked upon as an accomplice of the tecpatl knife that had previously destroyed the victim.

As a divinized being the knife became the god Itztapaltotec, probably "Our Lord Obsidian Core."[50] In the codices he is shown as an anthropoid knife adorned as the sun god Xipe Totec. When designated as Itztli, however, the god is always an avatar of Tezcatlipoca. Obviously, there was much priestly speculation concerning the knife of sacrifice, son of the great goddess. The recent excavations in the Zócalo in Mexico City have produced splendid examples of these knives, some with mosaic hafts, inlaid mouth parts, and staring skeletal eyes made of shell.[51] The knife, thus cast as a demonic devourer, was not only one of the best-known icons in the Aztec cities, but throughout Mesoamerica as well. As the focal instrument in the cult, it signified a deathly dichotomy, horror and fascination both. Certainly, it was as unvarnished a statement of death as man has ever propounded.

In the minds of the Aztec priests the knife could even be made to undo itself. The sacrificial knife was customarily not washed after rituals as cleansing would deprive the god of some of the blood that was rightfully his. On occasions, however, the blood, dried and caked on the blade from previous killings, could be dissolved and the washings therefrom mixed with magical substances to produce a distillation known as *itzpatli* ("knife medicine").[52] This could be administered to warriors before battle or to an ixiptla about to be sacrificed who showed fear or despair. Partaking of it rendered a man brave and contemptuous of death.

Preliterate peoples, and we ourselves, usually wrap death up in formal, limited rituals, clearly distinguished from rites affirming life. Not so the Aztecs. The central act of their ritual life, the final knife thrust, became an omnipresent and tyrannical icon within whose aura men, women, and children were forced to live out their lives. It is most difficult for us to understand how the Aztecs could have so ardently embraced the livid presence of death as seen in this object.

Death was, of course, an enemy of the Aztecs, as is true for all men, yet continually and unfailingly they invited death into the rituals of their every day. I cannot to my own satisfaction understand such a thoroughgoing perversion of man's normal avoidance of death.

The profound effects of cult upon man's understanding of his place in the cosmos is nowhere more graphically displayed than here. An instrument invented and used originally for everyday utilitarian purposes ended by being imported into the center of a cult, and then, because of its conspicuousness and specificity as a tool, it became the symbol of the ritual act itself, overruling thought and dictating a way of life supportive of the cult. Nothing that I am aware of in other religions so vividly illustrates the independent power that inheres in cult.

The necessary complement of the tecpatl was the techcatl, the stone of sacrifice. This was a stone block two to three feet high and shaped into a rounded cone or sugarloaf. Unlike the knife, which was in its origin precult, the techcatl was a creation of that cult, and was designed no doubt after some centuries of trial and error, to make heart extraction easier. The stone was normally placed in front of the open door of the god's shrine and just a bit back of the top step of the temple stairway.

If the tecpatl was the hammer, the techcatl was the anvil; both were simply parts of the greater whole, and the two operating together produced for the god's table the cuauhnochtli, his ambrosia, the human heart. Like the knife, the block was supposed to have fallen from the skies, but in this case it was the work of Tezcatlipoca, god of war and sorcery, bent on driving the ancient Toltecs mad.[53] According to the Aztecs, the techcatl fell on the rock Chapultepec and on that spot was first used to undo the unwitting people.[54]

A third cult object was bound in with the knife and the block to form a completed trinity of cult objects that together fully defined the sacrificial act. This third item was the "eagle bowl" (*cuauhxicalli*), originally a shallow gourd vessel in which the heart was offered to the god. In that compound Nahuatl word, "eagle" stands for the sun— so the meaning was "the sun's dish," and this was iconographically defined by pasting eagle feathers around the lip of the receptacle. In late times the gourd was made of stone, often with the hieroglyphic name of the sun incised in the bottom of the dish.

Knife, block, and bowl thus defined a whole cult act going back to the most primitive levels of the hunt—the killing of the game, its dismemberment, and the offering of a selected tidbit from the carcass to a superior person or chief. In Aztec cult that chieftain was identified as Tonatiuh, the sun, whose *nahualli* was an eagle. We note that the farmer's life played no part at all in the designing of this cult —it harks back rather to preagricultural times.

A special twist in this ritual complex is to be noticed in Xipe's cult. Xipe is the sun, as is Tonatiuh, but one with a somewhat different set of cult objects. Here the method of killing was divided: gladiatorial combat on the *temalacatl* as proof of the vigor and savor of the victim to be offered, immediately followed by heart extraction, not on a techcatl but on another great round stone called, like the stone bowl, a cuauhxicalli. The victim here is thought of as being destroyed in the bowl itself, with the implication that the victim's body in its entirety, after being skinned, was consumed by the god. Thus, we could describe this great fixed outdoor stone as a ceremonial cauldron, and the subsequent wearing of the skin as the renewed strength, the renovation as it were, given by a substantial meal.

HUMAN SACRIFICE AS SEEN IN AZTEC HISTORY

A word remains to be said about the place of blood sacrifice in Aztec religious life. Were its truths apparent to all levels of Aztec society, or was it basically the property of the warriors? Did the people—the artisans, farmers, fishermen, and porters—feel themselves necessarily implicated in the ritual because the cosmos depended upon it? Or were they merely dumb and uncomprehending bystanders? Had the priests and rulers entered into a conspiracy to foster the cult as a way of disciplining the potentially troublesome, those who might want to take the fragile state apart? Surely there must be a way of assessing the depth of Aztec commitment to this cult that had infiltrated all the others and bent them to its will. Probably the surest way to find out is to consult the historical record. Even this is difficult for we have an adequate record only of the history of the Mexica people. Of other Aztec tribes, such as those of Tezcoco, Tlaxcala, Chalco, and Culhuacan, we have only unsatisfactory fragments. But let us assume for the sake of the argument that the Mexica were somehow typical of all the others.

Because the Mexica prided themselves on being the descendants of the hardy Chichimecs of the northern steppe country, it might be thought that their fascination with human sacrifice therefore came from the steppe. What casts some doubt on this is that the kind of sacrifice we are talking about appears to have been quite urban and war oriented. The Chichimecs were of all levels of savagery, but basically they were a bow-and-arrow people, and came from a raiding tradition, rather than that of mass capture. Those of the Chichimecs who lived adjacent to the northern peripheries of Mesoamerica certainly had adopted much from the great mother cultures of Teotihuacan and Tula—for instance, people like the Cazcanes of Zacatecas spoke a Nahua tongue, played tlachtli, worshipped the morning star, and sacrificed men by killing them on the steps of temples. Undoubtedly, they had borrowed these cultural traits from the urbanized warrior society of the Toltecs. This is not to say that some of the Chichimec peoples did not possess sacrificial rites—many probably did, but the rites must have been tied in with the large-scale warfare that was so congenial to the Toltecs. The Chichimecs who settled in the city of Tezcoco claimed to have had no traditions of sacrifice prior to accepting Nahua civilization from the Toltec city of Culhuacan. In fact, the Chichimec ruler Quinatzin forbad the Toltec cities that had fallen to his arrowmen to build temples or offer sacrifices.[55] The ruler who followed him reversed this as a part of a plan to wean his people away from their wild, free-roaming ways.[56] Human sacrifice was thus seen by this ruler and those that followed him to be an integral part of the culture that they had at first feared but then decided to acquire. In the process, the Acolhua Aztecs naturally had to accept also the Toltec concept of continuous war and organized armies without which sacrificial victims could not be accumulated.

The Mexica, who had also been a Chichimec people, were similarly introduced to the cult by the Toltecs then living in the Basin. Even when the Mexica resided under the rock of Chapultepec, the first of their several Basin foundations, their legends show them involved in the cultus[57]; their own chieftain, Huitzilihuitl, who had been captured by the warriors of the city of Culhuacan, was sacrificed on the techcatl. So quickly did the Mexica absorb the custom of human sacrifice that they were already ardent practitioners by the time they had founded the city of Tenochtitlan. The founding legend itself was warped around the theme of sacrifice. The sun god, so it ran, in his nahualli as an eagle, had alighted on a cactus plant on a small island in the lake, from which perch he screamed for war and the hearts that war would bring him. On this spot, where the eagle was first seen, was destined to arise the city of Mexico. The Mexica thus understood human sacrifice to be in the very basement of their history. We have already seen the lengths to which this could be carried in the dedication of the Temple of Huitzilopochtli in 1487.

By the end of their history, human sacrifice had evolved for the Aztecs into a footling enterprise. It had become a panacea. It meant everything and nothing. When Moteuczoma was awakened in the middle of the night to receive the news of his ambassadors' first meeting with the Spaniards, he had two captives sacrificed so that their blood could be sprinkled over the ambassadors before they began their report. The ambassadors had been made taboo by reason of their contact with the foreign gods, and had to be desanctified. Moteuczoma is then said to have dispatched victims down to the coast to be sacrificed in front of Cortés so that their hearts and blood might be offered to him. Cortés is reported, probably apocryphally, to have run the sacrificer through with his sword, thereby staggering the others in the embassy who could not have possibly understood such a refusal.

All students of New World history know how the Mexica, throughout the hopeless defense of their city, persisted in fighting the enemy in the rigid style dictated by the requirements of sacrifice. They even formally sacrificed what few Spanish horses they were able to seize, displaying their heads on the *tzompantli*. The city of Mexico foundered in part because of the tyrannical hold that the cult of sacrifice had acquired over the people. And if this was so at the end, the power of the cult throughout the peak years of Aztec history cannot be questioned.

The Aztecs' Statement
of Individuality through Cult

CULTS THAT CONCERNED ONLY THE INDIVIDUAL

The cults that we have been considering up to now have all pointed to the supernaturals as insurers of the Aztecs' social life. Most of those cults belonged to the state and were manipulated by the rulers, nobles, or priests. If they did not belong directly to the state, they still concerned community resources of food and the skills needed to produce them. In all of these cases, aggregations of individuals were in question.

But outside the state, the guilds, and the military orders, people continued to live out their private lives as well, and occasionally these found expression in cults existing outside the orbit of the state. Rites, such as those of burial or curing, made use of certain specific supernaturals as power sources, but always had their center in a discrete, individual person, a person who was to be named, or cured, or buried as the case might be. It is easy enough to posit such a cult area, but to find reliable source material for description and analysis of it is difficult. Therefore, this final chapter, more than the others, will contain an element of speculation. Its essential rightness will be seen only if it does not contradict what I have written previously.

When we talk about the Aztec individual, we are on shaky ground—the friars knew him only as a type to be catechized. It is my belief that Aztec individuals were separated out from the community only to the extent that they were implicated in such cults as are the subject of this chapter: birth, naming, baptism, confession, penance, narcotics, and burial. These cults were detached from Aztec communal interests and needs. They were available to the single person, and only through them could he be identified as a true individual. Some of the cults that also concern the individual (prayer and curing, for instance) have been omitted from consideration in this volume.

THE NAMED INDIVIDUAL

The birth of a child is an irreducible novelty. No knowledge can possibly be gained about the child as an individual previous to parturition. And even later, when the young person begins to emerge as discrete and unlike all others, even then the world of experience is recasting him with a Rhadamanthine hand in order to submerge him into that sea of expectations that we know to be a society. Out of this contest—often agonized—finally appears the mature individual, generally overwhelmed by his society, but never totally lost to his refractory self. This must have been true of preliterate communities as well as of our own.

Among the Aztecs the preceding was symbolized in their naming patterns. A newly born child possessed two names that had little or nothing to do with each other—one defining him as a member of society, the other defining him as a person in his own right.

As a fated creature, already immutably fixed, the individual was born with a name; this name was not given by anyone but was rather discovered by the priest who found it inscribed in the Book of Fates. This name, the *tonalli* name, was simply a date, namely that day when the child appeared out of the womb of the mother. We have alluded to this previously. At a minimum there were 260 different futures for the child (actually 261 counting the disastrous *nemontemi* days that were a part of the calendar but not of the almanac). Each one of the 260 *tonalpohualli* days was designated with a fortune, good, bad, or mixed, as the case might be. Knowledge of this fate accompanied the person throughout life.

But it was not that simple. Fate had many devices, and it was difficult, if not impossible, even for the most experienced *tonalpouhqui* to exhaust the full meaning of a person's fortune day.[1] There were influences that might ameliorate for the individual a tragic future. For instance each of the twenty thirteen-day packets (*trecenas*) into which the tonalpohualli was divided had a divine patron, and out of these several gods there vibrated unlike qualities. Let us assume that a child was born on the day Seven Monkey. Now Seven Monkey is to be found in the trecena that begins with One Snake. That particular trecena had as patrons the gods Tlahuizcalpanteuctli and Xiuhteuctli (sometimes Xuihcoatl), the gods of dawn and fire, respectively. Each or either of these gods can exert his own special aura, and additionally the whole trecena itself possessed a fate (good in this instance). Again, the number seven has a fate attached (good), and the sign "monkey" by itself has a fortune (indifferent). The tonalpouhqui would take all of these into account as well as other readings of fate, to come up with a compendious forecast of the child's future.

Numerous legitimate ways of modifying the basic fate of a child could be found by the learned tonalpouhqui. Most commonly a bad luck birthdate was offset by setting the naming ceremony on the first day following that carried with it a good fortune.[2] Thus fragments of fate could be jumbled together when needed to produce mitigations of future disaster or clarifications of an indifferent and therefore an ambiguous fate. So the child Seven Monkey arrived in this world already pigeonholed by society. And because that society held superior rights over him, his tonalli name was his most demanding and certainly his most important name. That name could never be changed throughout that person's life and his fate was thus irrevocable. This was true both of nobles and commoners.

In some cases, it might turn out that a child's tonalli name was by coincidence also the tonalli name of a god. Thus, if born on the day One Death (which was also the birth date of the god Tezcatlipoca), a boy would be given, as his second name, the name of one of Tezcatlipoca's many avatars, whether Omacatl, Yaotl, Titlacahuan, or some other.[3] Here the tonalli date would be the circumstance surrounding the child's birth and would thus indicate the second or personal name.

The second name designated the newly born child, not as a cosmic integer, but as a person.[4] It was called the "earthly name" (*tlalticpactocaitl*) and was quite separate from the date name that had an abstract and derived quality. These "second names" could be the names of great leaders or gods, names of places connected with the child, names of birds, animals, trees, common items in the culture, or occasionally references to some event occurring at the time of the birth. Girls were often named after specific flowers. This second name could also be designated as the "finished or completed name" (*itzonquizca tocaitl*) for a reason that I cannot fathom.[5] A person born on one of the nemontemi days automatically lacked a tonalli name. For his given name he would generally be called, if male,

Nentlacatl ("Useless Person") or, if a girl, the feminine of this.[6] If a child was born into an important family, he or she was often given the name of a revered grandparent.[7] Such a patronymic, substituting for the second name was called the "ancestral name" (*huehue tocaitl*).[8]

The earthly name was given to the child during the rite of baptism held at dawn in the family courtyard.[9] The midwife, who had some days previously officiated at the delivery, washed the child while invoking the goddess of water to dissolve any contamination still adhering to it. Quetzalcoatl, who created the child, was also invoked. The midwife then lifted the child four times to the heavens, calling first upon the supreme heavenly pair (Citlallicue and Citlallatonac), who apportioned the souls of the unborn, then to the Heavenly Children themselves (the as-yet-unborn) and finally to the sun in both his daily and his nocturnal forms (Tonatiuh and Tlalteuctli). It will be noticed that the preceding rite in no way involved the priesthood—only the extended family and the midwives participated.

This accomplished, the name of the child then appeared; the midwife was the first to pronounce it. At that point adolescent boys, here representing the heroic ancestral dead, rushed about shouting and publicizing the name, thus identifying the child and validating his existence. Gift giving among the relatives, parents, and midwives followed. We do not know whether the same was done in the case of a female child.

The naming ceremony would take place only on a fortunate day even though the assumption was that the newborn one was per se uncontaminated, and therefore lucky, having been selected by appropriate gods in the heavens and then sent down to assume form and an earthly name. Yet the fact that the newborn had an automatically pure and heavenly origin does not seem to have affected the Aztecs' thinking in regard to its ultimate lot—which was to be found in the tonalli.

The baptism by fire that we have mentioned previously appears to have had nothing to do with the naming. It took place in the month of Izcalli at which time all children born in the previous calendar year were taken to the fire god's temple and there passed through the fire by the old men of their *calpulli*. At that festival they were also given godparents and *octli* to drink. This was thus a rite de passage subsequent to the initial naming.

Confusion perhaps stems from the feature that when a young man, because of his prowess on the battlefield, became a knight, he was correspondingly given a new prestige name generally called "great name" or "name of fame" (*tenyotl*).[10] We know little about these names, beyond the fact that as a warrior or an official in the state moved upward in the roll of offices and honors, he often took a new name at each move. These new names may really have been titles or honorifics. Similarly, a merchant who had made a singularly splendid profit on some distant and perilous venture would take a new name commemorating the fact, which name was then solemnly proclaimed at a great banquet.[11]

From the preceding bits of information that we have about names and naming among the Aztecs we can see that ordinary individuals could appear to others ambiguously as themselves, namely discrete persons able to make a range of decisions, or as persons lost forever to freedom in their fate. Whether such an analysis distinguishes the Aztec from us today and other peoples in history is moot. It may be that the concept of an individual is in any case irremediably mixed. We had probably best assume here that the concept of the Aztec individual was to some extent similar to our own, though he could never have gone so far as to think of himself as autonomous.

CONFESSION

It was believed that when a baby first entered the world, it could carry traces of contamination from the parents. These were relatively minor, however, and they were washed away by the midwife in what amounted to a preliminary baptism at the time of birth. Having been created by the sage Quetzalcoatl the baby was basically well oriented and without sin. But the evolving individual had the power by his or her own volition to sully this pristine state, to commit crimes, become arrogant, or even neglect services owing to the supernaturals.

The connection between this freedom and a person's fate is unclear. The Aztecs did not try to accommodate this modest theory of free will to their belief in the tonalpohualli that, as we have seen, fated individuals beforehand to certain actions and qualities of life. Nevertheless, they were aware of the contradiction. All they could do was to commit themselves to one of the two theories, blotting out the other, as an occasion arose. Overriding both, however, was the Aztecs' special relation to the supernaturals and here they judged, not by the assumptions of their tonallis, but by what they felt was their ultimate responsibility for willed sins as well as for those sins stemming from their ignorance. As we shall see, however, the confessing priest could plead with Tezcatlipoca to take into account the sinner's dilemma, caught as he thus was between Scylla and Charybdis.

Most private rituals are magical in their intent and techniques and thus will not concern us here. They are mechanical and coercive acts and the individual who performs them is unrelated to the power that he unleashes. A private ritual, however, can involve both an individual and one of the supernaturals, in which case there is a definable relationship between them. What further distinguishes these private rituals is that all of them arise at the need of an individual—the city or the state are unconcerned.

The act of confession was described by the Aztecs as "setting the heart straight,"[12] and the priest who specialized in such offices was the *tlapouhqui*.[13] Only two deities were intimately involved in the confessional act, Tlazolteotl, goddess of sex and sexual excesses, and Tezcatlipoca, the deity to whom everything was revealed. As for this latter god we have seen that on every fourth celebration of his annual feast, the Toxcatl, he extended a plenary remission of sins to the entire population. This was an aspect of renewal and probably was not tied to confession. However, the individual could choose at any time to discover all his or her sins to the tlapouhqui who acted in the interests of Tezcatlipoca. Because this was a secret belonging to the god and therefore sacred, the tlapouhqui could never reveal it to others.[14]

We must not equate this profession of sins with the confessional known to us in the Western tradition. Aztec confession could not, for instance, help to effect a blessed afterlife for the individual; whatever he did or said, the Aztec still descended to Mictlan. Aztec confession was rather designed to persuade Tezcatlipoca to prevent any public discovery of one's sins. In the case of sexual sins, fornication and adultery, sinners confessed to Tlazolteotl, the deity who had in the first instance enticed them to give way to their sexual appetites.

But again it was not always a single sin that imperiled the individual and sent him to the deity—rather it could be a whole life of sin that needed expiation. Consequently, an individual's confession was a most serious business and was generally performed only once in a person's life, and that when he was fully mature or perhaps even old. The deity would cancel out his or her derelictions once but not a second time.[15]

The rite of confession could take the following form.[16] A favorable day would be designated by the tlapouhqui, one that would in and of itself conduce to forgiveness by the god. On that day the sinner would bring a new reed mat upon which he would sit to symbolize the new life he was to acquire. The tlapouhqui first invoked fire and then, acting in the name of Tezcatlipoca, adjured the sinner to omit no uncleanness in his tale of sins. The sinner then removed all his clothing and sat naked through his confession as a sign that nothing would be withheld by him from the god. Having heard the entire tale of offenses, the tlapouhqui then sentenced the sinner to a penance that would reflect the seriousness of his misdeeds. In his summation, the priest made reference to Tezcatlipoca as Lord of the Near and the Nigh, who could as easily cast down as raise up, and in the god's name he adjured the now forgiven sinner

> to clothe him who goes naked, who acquires not that which to hang from his neck, from his loins. For your body is also as his, especially the sick one, for he is the image of the Lord of the Near and the Nigh.
> Be careful, be yet careful. Pay close attention. May the Lord of the Near and the Nigh recreate you. This is all; take yourself hence.[17]

On returning home, the individual felt as if new life had been granted to him and that, unless he sinned again, the god would not persecute him—for which reason he would be safe from human retribution as well.[18]

PENANCE AND AUTOSACRIFICE

We have previously noted how the priest was cast as a surrogate who paid for the transgressions of the whole community, undergoing cruel penances and deprivations. These social accumulations of sin could also be handled by the community at large such as took place in the cult of Xochiquetzal, goddess of love and flowers.[19] Here people publicly announced themselves guilty of venial transgressions, but they did not specify the exact sins—instead they simply counted them by number, after which they performed the required penances. Just before dawn in that festival all the people, even including the small children, went down to the nearest riverbank for a public washing, after which they partook of the cereal *tzoalli*, known to be the flesh of the gods. Needless to say, the city as a whole benefited from this. But when a particularly heinous sin threatened some individual's peace of mind, then he sought the imposition of a penance on himself alone. This would be a case where the individual initiated a ritual confession and where he alone carried the penance to a successful conclusion. This would make it the concern of only one participant.

The complex of confession and penance was the *tlamacehualiztli*, a word that carried the implication of merit gained—in other words, a good work—but one that is otherwise ambiguous.[20] Washing was common after some penitential exercises and that would show that the penance by itself did not cleanse, but was only a necessary preliminary to ultimate cleansing. Disease, deformity, or psychic impediment were all thought to be the result of sin, actions committed either against the customs of the community or the rites of the gods. This direct link between illness and surreptitious sin is a commonplace in preliterate cultures. Among the Aztecs it was taken with great seriousness.

The penance was sometimes defined in a vow made by some ill or otherwise threatened individual. Such were vows of pilgrimage to holy sites, caves, springs or high peaks, or to sacred cities like Cholula. Or the vow might have promised nightly visits to named temples while carrying braziers filled with lighted coals on one's head—this perhaps for a whole year.[21] Or it might be a vow to acquire the wherewithal to banquet the god—sometimes to the economic ruin of the individual.[22] The possibilities were endless, and the Aztecs showed great invention in the penances that they performed.

A penance might be undertaken, not as a result of a person's vow, but because it was commanded by a priest after hearing a statement of the individual's guilt.[23] The priest might command, for instance, that the sinner purchase a slave for sacrifice to Tezcatlipoca, to be followed by a ceremonial meal where the slave would be eaten by the guests. In a different vein, the priest could order almsgiving to the poor. A penance for a mild sexual infraction might involve dancing in front of Tlazolteotl's statue. More drastic was a regimen of nocturnal immersions in freezingly cold springs. Or the penitent might be assigned various combinations of fasting, abstinence from sex, or going unwashed for long periods. A wealthy sinner could always hire a priest to perform his penance for him, a frequent occurrence so it would seem.[24]

A person involved in the preceding penitential practices would often mark his house with a laurel bough.[25] Where the penance involved a sedentary exercise, such as fasting, a small plot in the fields, forests, or along the shore of the lake could be set aside. This holy place was roped off from the world with cables of roughly woven grass hung with paper tassels.[26] Within this temporary sacred enclosure the penitent would remain until his torment was ended.

Many penances—and certainly the more serious ones—involved the shedding by individuals of their own blood—this was an act of autosacrifice that the individual agreed to or even initiated. Because it was one of the most conspicuous forms of Aztec cult, I shall go into some detail in presenting it.

For the Aztec, autosacrifice was *nextlahualli*, payment for something owed. The blood drawn here was thus coin paid by the individual human being to a supernatural creditor. Commonly individuals pierced their ears, arms or calves of their legs with spines collected from the maguey plantations. The blood extracted was blotted up with pieces of paper that were then collected reverently by a priest. There were times when all the inhabitants of the city of Mexico were called upon to do this, as on the movable feast of Four Movement, when even the very poor and babies in arms had their ears cut for blood.

This bloodletting was also an accepted form of offering for individuals when they approached a supernatural. In the case of the priesthood it was also an individual's choice, though we can easily understand that the priest, because of his profession, was under greater pressure to employ autosacrifice. His model in this was the patron god of his order, Quetzalcoatl, who first taught humans the need for bloodletting and the forms it should take, especially for the members of the priesthood.[27]

The rigors of some of these practices must be to us matters of amazement and sometimes of horror; yet the fact that they were so commonly practiced convinces us of their centrality in the Aztec cultus. To signal the time of midnight in the temple, flutes and conch shells (the voices of Tezcatlipoca and Quetzalcoatl, respectively) were blown to awaken the priests who then routinely pierced themselves with maguey thorns for the well-being of the deity. At this "hour of the blowing," autosacrifice was incumbent on the priests.

Not associated with this, because of their strictly voluntary nature, were two other common forms of autosacrifice.[28] The first was a logical outcome of the feeling that sexual activity was an offense to the gods because it was unclean. Ardent young priests who desired to attain a state of permanent chastity could, among other things, reduce themselves to a state of impotence. Such a devotee would either slit his penis in half, thus rendering erection impossible, or he would drive a hole through the member, pushing through the wound long rods, the greater the number the greater his holiness.[29] On special occasions several of these mutilated priests would thread through their penises a single long cord and, thus connected, would shuffle about in the performances of their common duties. The priests of the Valley of Tehuacan were noted for this practice. Needless to say, the merit for such extreme acts was prodigious.

Far commoner in the priesthood was a related type of self-mutilation—which could be practiced also by the lay individual. Here the tongue was perforated.[30] In preparation for these sessions the priests would chip from a block of obsidian many fine points, or lancets. Those among them who were experts in tongue drilling punched large holes through the tongues of their colleagues from the underside. In one of the rituals known to us from the city of Tlaxcala, the high priest was required to draw 405 long sticks through his tongue, and the lesser priests who had volunteered did the same with twenty rods apiece. This was repeated four times in an eighty-day period. If so desired, heavy cords with thorns transversely inserted in them at intervals could be substituted for the rods. Immediately following each such session, the priests with their ruined tongues would attempt to chant hymns of praise to the god. The bloody rods or cords coming out of the priests' mouths symbolized these words of praise. These discarded instruments of torture were then taken to the sacred city hearth there to be burnt and sent to their heavenly destination. Infection must have killed some of these priests, but still the number of Aztecs going about their business with shredded ears and uncouth tongues must have been considerable.

These cleansings, expiations, confessions, and remissions of sins were endless during the Aztec year. They were necessary, in the calculations of the Aztecs, because of the blood debt that they owed to the supernaturals. It was an endless paying, with the debt never liquidated. Save for the fallen warrior and the darlings of Tlaloc, the individual could look forward to no change in his condition of mortality, for whatever he might do of merit, he nevertheless descended in the end to Mictlan. The Aztecs lacked a myth that could have supported for the individual a hope for salvation and which could have provided him with a logic of transfiguration. For this reason, the autosacrificial practices had no end. The Aztecs did not envisage their debt as paid off or indeed as ultimately payable.

OTHERWORLDS

Funeral rites are inconceivable without an already existing idea of an otherworld that is there waiting to receive the deceased individual. Here cult and belief are so intertwined as to be almost inseparable. Because of this we must introduce our discussion of Aztec funeral cults with a roster of Aztec otherworlds. Additionally, we must investigate Aztec concepts of death.

There were at least seven Aztec otherworlds that we can isolate. They were the deathly underworld (Mictlan), a subdivision of this in the far north (Mictlampa), the Elysian Fields in the Sky (Tonatiuhixco), the ever-verdant land within the mountain (Tlalocan), a subdivision of this where gargantuan feasting took place (Cincalco), the heaven reserved for the souls of babies, and finally a place, probably in the mountain also, for the legendary heroes and famous rulers of the past (Xicco).

Mictlan, which means simply the "Land of the Dead," was the destination of the commoner, the *macehualli*. But the word *macehualli* has two meanings. It can mean a commoner only, and as such it was derogatory; again it can be used as an all-inclusive term for mankind in general. Thus Mictlan can be thought of as the catchall land for those without rank, with more desirable worlds being reserved for the members of elite classes. Or it can be thought of as "Our Common Home" (Tocenchan),[31] in which case the speaker accepts the fact that regardless of social rank, all men must finally descend into the unloved underworld.[32]

Mictlan was the abyss underground into which humans tumbled at the end. It is not a place of Dantesque torments but only of darkness and pseudobeing. People there are cold, remote, and dumb. It is ruled over by the skeletal Lord of the Dead and his spouse who is a deathly form of the earth goddess. In Mictlan all individuality is erased. Each shade is like another.

Mictlampa is the word for the direction north, a dire direction and always associated with darkness and evil. There the ancestors live, being thought of as stellar points fitfully blinking in the night sky.[33] Unlike the numbed souls in Mictlan, the dead in Mictlampa are to some extent hostile and can therefore be dangerous to the living. Their influence was historically conditioned—inasmuch as the Aztecs thought of themselves as having once been Chichimecs up in the country of the northern steppe, so also the massed ancestors in Mictlampa were thought of as Chichimecs.

Tonatiuhixco is a word for east and summons up thoughts of youth and splendor. It means the "Place of the Facing of the Sun." Only warriors who died in battle or on the block of sacrifice went there. Together they formed the noble entourage of the sun god, accompanying him in his oriental rising. These dead lived lives of joy and fulfillment, eventually becoming prismatic clouds, gems, butterflies, or hummingbirds.

Tlalocan means the "Place of Tlaloc," the god who with his rains creates verdancy on the earth or withholds it. His home is among the mountains shrouded away behind walls of mist. Here is a Garden of Eden enjoyed only by Tlaloc's favorites, those whom he has struck with lightning or whom he has caused to drown, or those who have died of dropsy or running sores and skin diseases. Entry into Tlalocan was thus by invitation only. All good things were enjoyed there; fields and trees fruited without stint, and drought was unknown.

Cincalco was a special example of the above, a paradise and banqueting hall within the mountain.[34] The name means "House of Maize." The lord and master within was Hueymac, a Toltec form of the night sun; there he presided, seated in princely state. One of the entrances to this fairyland was located in the Hill of Chapultepec just outside Tenochtitlan.

Xicco was the interior of a mountain into which only a few persons of legendary power, antique heroes such as Topiltzin of Tula or

Nezahualcoyotl of Tezcoco, would vanish, there to sleep against the time of their Arthurian return.[35] *Xicco* is a locative form and means "the Navel," or innermost point.

Tonacacuauhtitlan, (the "Orchards of the God Tonacateuctli") was a heaven to which went all children whose early deaths had protected their innocence.[36] It was a beautiful land in the midst of which stood a tree with breasts dripping milk into the mouths of the little ones. From this land the souls were sent down into the world after an indeterminate period to take form again in a woman's womb.

The variety shown in these various otherworlds is paralleled among the Aztecs by a variety of cultic arrangements for the disposal of the dead.

LIFE AND DEATH

An understanding of what a society thinks about "the beyond," as I have outlined it in the preceding section, goes far to define what that society also thinks about death. Briefly, the Aztec thought that death was like the payment of tribute imposed upon the defeated. Life was a known impost, a capitation tax that at a set time had to be handed over—death was that act of conveyance. All existence was thus a tributary condition, well understood by the Aztecs who had subdued others and had themselves been several times subdued. The levying of tribute on a beaten enemy was to them the basic style of intertribal and international relationships, and they called upon this understanding to suggest their relationship with the supernaturals. There was no morality involved in this—only the situation of being, as an individual, the weaker and defeated party. Death was the handing over of owed tribute, and the owed tribute was the last of life. Such was the Aztec individual's understanding of his plight. It will be immediately apparent to the reader that not all of the otherworlds we have described support this understanding.

THE USE OF HALLUCINOGENS

For the Aztecs there always remained a mystery. In their social gatherings the warriors oftentimes gave up the Elysian orthodoxy that had been taught to them by the priests, and they announced their feeling of betrayal in moving poetic terms. There are many such *suspirae de profundis* in Aztec literature. Here is one, somewhat freely translated.

> If indeed I keep on weeping,
> Plunged in the despair of not knowing—
> If indeed my heart repels the terrible thought—
> Then perhaps I shall not descend into the Mysterious Land.
> Our hearts here on earth cry out together,
> "Let it be that we never die, O my comrades!"[37]

In such effusions the warrior who was continually told by the priests that his death brings an assurance of joy plainly doubts it. Lamenting together with his companions he confesses his unknightly terror. These gatherings must have been essentially sub rosa rituals. Probably many meshed with the well-known gatherings of Aztec nobles for the purpose of ingesting narcotics and, under their influence, of foreseeing the future as it touched them individually. Predictably the visions that they sought generally concerned the time and manner of their demise.

Behind the Aztec was a very old tradition of the use of hallucinogens.[38] The early Mesoamericans had used the mushroom (*nanacatl*), peyote (*peyotl*), several forms of datura (*tlapatl, mixitl, toloa*), morning glory seeds (*ololiuhqui*), and others. They could be chewed, crushed and then drunk in octli, or, when bitter, mixed with honey. The ingestion of these drugs was for them the exact equivalent of religious possession, for each of the plants was identified as the person or the flesh of a particular deity. The narcosis that the drinker of the potion suffered was thus a vivid rendezvous with divinity, and this drug-induced proximity to the supernaturals was for an individual the single most compelling cult situation in which he could ever find himself truly alone with deity. It was always a harrowing expeience for him.

Needless to say, it was a cult with little structure. Nobles gathered, often before battle, to drink a prepared brew and to sing and dance together. Music, in fact, seems to have been considered necessary to lead one properly into the land of visions. It was only in such sessions as these that the warriors could free themselves of the old dogmas and challenge the destinies that society had imposed upon them. In the poem translated previously, the warrior does not believe that he will join the sun in death, as he has been taught, but will, along with the meanest macehualli, slip down into the gray land of Mictlan. Therefore, his despairing cry, "Let it be that we never die, O my comrades!"

THE DISPOSAL OF THE DEAD

Preliterate peoples have often evolved spectacular ancestor cults, and we may wonder here why the Aztecs did not do so. One might well have thought that their stress on heroic deeds and legitimacy in noble lines should have produced an overriding ancestor worship. The explanation for this must be the extraordinary Aztec concentration on human sacrifice that left little room for a competing emphasis on the progenitors as supernatural benefactors. But the dead were certainly not forgotten, and the variety in the Aztec burial cultus comports with the richness of their speculation on the places and qualities of the otherworlds that I have noted previously.

Two types of disposal predominated among the Aztecs: burial and cremation. The former was the lot of all commoners, of the young,[39] the unmarried, women dying in childbirth, and those selected by Tlaloc. It was the funereal counterpart of an afterlife that would be lived within the earth, either at the place of the sunset, in Mictlan, or in the halls of the mountain king. Cremation, on the contrary, was the visual sign that the soul would ascend to live in the bright heavens, this being generally synonymous with the house of the sun. Rulers on death were cremated as were the great lords of the realm and all warriors who had killed or whose blood had been shed. Only afterward were the bones and ashes collected for interment. It is true that the captured warrior who was sacrificed was eaten in the city of his captors, and his body—or certain parts of it—neither burned nor buried. Nevertheless, in the bundle image or wooden simulacrum made of him by his family in his own city, he *was* cremated and thus ascended into the sky.[40]

Some types of disposal of the dead did not fall into either of the two categories. When a merchant died on the road far from home, his corpse, tightly wrapped, was bound onto one of the carrying racks and then taken up to the summit of the nearest hill.[41] There the wooden frame would be set upright in the ground and left to predators, the elements, and dessication. This was a symbolic display of the merchant's belief that, like a warrior, he too was a minion of the sun god and that after death he went up into the sky to live with him. The merchants, as a class, were far older than the Aztec state—therefore this means of disposal of their dead may have a history as old as that of cremation.

Newborn and very small infants were buried in or close to the family corn bins.[42] We are not informed as to the meaning of this means of disposal, but we can guess that the spirit of blossoming and juvenescence, symbolized by the buried child, was thereby mated to the stored seed. A vigorous and early sprouting of the corn after the next sowing would thus be assured.

In most cases of mature individuals, the body was tightly trussed with knees drawn up to the chest, and then swaddled with a multitude of blankets.[43] Whether for burial or cremation, therefore the dead person was presented in the customary posture of one seated and alert. There was the additional custom of facing the mummy bundle to the north where the ancestors lived and to which place it was supposed that the dead man would be taking his journey.

THE WARRIOR'S OBSEQUIES

Funeral customs were thought to go back to the time of the priest-god Quetzalcoatl who, fleeing from the evil Tezcatlipoca, incinerated himself on the shores of the Gulf of Mexico.[44] Out of that burning he then appeared to men as Ce Acatl, the warrior god of the morning star, thus illustrating the capacity of fire to transfigure the person.

We have seen that the ancestors could be conceived of as the circumpolar stars congregated in the northern sky. They were thus points of fire and were known as *Mimixcoa*, ("Cloud serpents"), after the god Mixcoatl whose myrmidons they were thought to be.[45] This mythology, although celestial, does not comport with the other view of the fallen warrior who, as we have seen, joins the daytime sun in his ascent of the heavens. It is possible that the view of the ancestors as stars in the north is Chichimec in origin, whereas the view of them as retainers of the sun comes from the more urban contexts of Teotihuacan and Tula. Individuals who were interred went as a matter of course to Mictlan, the Place of the Dead. It was the crematory process that translated the ancestors into the sky, and we know that that process was reserved for the magnates and warrior class alone.

In neither case did a true ancestor cult emerge. Four years after the death of adult Aztecs all personalized rites addressed to them ceased[46]; they then became simply one of the dead, and whether they ended in Mictlan, in the circumpolar sky of night, or in the house of the sun depended on their manner of death, status, and deeds when they were alive.

A description of the death and last rites of the Aztec warrior, as they were carried out over a four-year period, is in order here. The reason we choose the rites connected with the warrior is simply that we have information on them, whereas knowledge of the average person's sepulture is lacking.[47] The rites honoring the dead man and making offerings to him were called the *quitonaltia*.

Assuming that an Aztec army commanded the field after battle, the dead belonging to that side would be cremated then and there. This was dictated by the impossibility of carrying the bodies back over difficult trails and sometimes prohibitive distances. A weapon belonging to the fallen warrior would be retrieved for his family, and where possible his topknot, for in that resided his individuality. Those others of their missing comrades who had been captured and dragged off by the enemy for eventual sacrifice were considered to be as good as dead, and their obsequies could be instituted at any time by the families and in the same fashion as if the corpse were available. There was no difference between the dead and the captured—both were the sole property of the god.

Once the army reentered the home city, the bereaved families were notified of their loss by old warriors of the calpulli who handed over to them whatever mementoes of the dead man had been salvaged. The family now selected some fat pine sticks and bound them together in a fascine along with the remaining arrows or darts of the dead man. These were wrapped in a thick mantle to form a mummy bundle and designed to represent the deceased as the god Mixcoatl. This effigy was the *euillotl*,[48] and it could be further adorned with paper attire, a paper banner, and a paper hawk's wings attached to the back. This promulgated the individual as one of the Mimixcoa, those mythological retainers of the warrior god Mixcoatl who were also stars.

There now began the traditional period of eighty days of mourning during which, among other deprivations, the widow was forbidden the luxury of washing. At the end of that period she was expected to scrape off her cheeks the accumulated dirt clotted by tears and deliver it, wrapped in a bit of paper, to the priests. This was accepted as a token of the grieving that society expected of her.

The wake began in the home of the deceased. Friends and relatives came to visit the corpse, or mummy bundle as the case might be, to condole with it on the event of its death and to offer gifts. Where possible a dog was bought and ceremonially shot through the neck. This was Xolotl, the tracking companion of the ancient Chichimec hunter, here to be read as the guide of the dead soul who had to pass through the treacherous ways and waters of Mictlan to come to his final rest.[49]

Warriors and men of importance all through their lives had worshipped a particular god, one whom they favored and to whom they had entrusted their fortune. At the moment of death, they might be given that god's insignia, face paint, or hairstyle to wear instead of the Mixcoatl mask. How this was supposed to affect the chances of the deceased in the afterlife we do not know.

Once completed, the effigy was taken either to the calpulli temple or to the *tlacochcalli* (both a temple and an armory), and there at midnight it was burned. The nocturnal aspect of this cremation seems to relate the dead man to Mixcoatl who was the god of the dawn, for just as the morning star rose in splendid solitude to introduce Tonatiuh, so did the dead warrior become a star acting as harbinger and escort of the sun.

If there had been many casualties and losses on the field, a mass cremation at home would be arranged. At the end of the four-day wake held by the families of each of the dead men, all the effigies would be assembled in the open area facing the Temple of Huitzilopochtli, and there they would be burned together. The spectacle would be accompanied by dancing and drumming, wailing, and the clapping of hands.

The ashes were then collected in a receptacle or urn. The dead man's two locks of hair, the ones taken at birth and at death, were included as essential relics. For eighty days the urn became the center of a diminishing private cult that included fasting restrictions placed upon the families and visits from the relatives. At the end of the period the family underwent a purification that was designed to finally free them of the contagion of death. Formal farewells were addressed to the dead man, and he was finally dismissed. The ashes in the container were buried on Mount Yohualichan,[50] near Culhuacan, or inserted into the masonry of appropriate edifices in the temenos.[51] Some might be taken to Teotihuacan, the legendary birthplace of the sun, for interment in the ruined but still holy pyramid there.[52]

The soul that had been thus set loose would take four years in all to complete its journey or its time in the otherlife. In that period, visits were annually made by the survivors to the burial site with offerings of food and drink. The dead man's presence was symbolized at these rituals by a small wooden image that was burned each time. After the fourth year all rites ceased, for the dead man had now merged homogeneously into the crowd of ancestors, vaporizing into the ancestral swarm.

As we have seen, two of the months of the Aztec year, the ninth and tenth, were classed as feasts of the ancestral dead. It is no coincidence that Xiuhteuctli, the god of fire and of the family, was centrally honored in those two months as well as in the month at the end of the year, Izcalli. It is probable that the bereaved family united their fourth-year farewell to the dead man with one of these public festivals wherein priests officiated. This would have been logical considering the centrality of cremation in the four years of private observances as well as in the cult of the state.

A ROYAL FUNERAL

The Aztecs were aware of their mortality and did not often attempt to deny it. In the case of a great person or charismatic ruler, however, they would assert that at death he "became a god" (*oteot*).[53] The baroque and eerie rites with which they disposed of him clearly display this desire to deify—a characteristic of mankind that is one of the relentless forces within him and which leads to the formulation of many of his cults.

It may be incorrect to say that the Aztecs, who knew in themselves that all men, including the great ones, were brothers in death, nevertheless saw their rulers transfigured into gods. Knowing the power and spareness of their Mictlan mythology, one can doubt it. The belief, if it existed explicitly, that a dead tlatoani did indeed become a god, can only have pointed to a god without any jurisdiction whatsoever and therefore one powerless to affect nature, society, or the individual. In a speech addressing Tezcatlipoca and referring to the newly dead ruler, the officiating priest said,

> You have thrust him under your feet. Already he has been taken away. He has gone by the road we all take and to the house in which we all must dwell, a house of eternal shadows, in which there is no window, nor is there any light. Already he is in a sleep from which none can wake him.[54]

This is in direct contradiction to the apotheosis theory wherein the dead ruler moved into the afterlife as a god, and we are probably correct therefore in viewing the Aztec royal obsequies as necessarily vague, a compromise ritual in fact that backed away from stripping the dead man of everything and yet did not place him in the heavens. We will note this dilemma as it is expressed in the funeral cult of Axayacatl, fifth ruler of Tenochtitlan, to which we now turn.[55]

Axayacatl had been a driving leader of his people and a spectacular warrior. He died in fact from a wound received in a particularly desperate affray in the Matlatzinca territory. His passing therefore might be expected to have moved the ritualists to have elevated him to a heavenly status, to have seen to it that his deification became normative for future rulers. This did not happen. Rather, he was treated more as an ixiptla, a representative, of the god—an intermediate and temporary expedient at best.

The death of a tlatoani was announced by an outcry of the royal women as they slapped their palms over their mouths, shrieking and ululating. For days afterward this chilling and demented sound kept breaking forth from the palace, providing the leitmotiv for all the rites that followed. As they keened, the women kept falling to the ground and rising, to fall again in their grief and fear.

At his expiration, the dead ruler was washed and then dressed successively in the robes and regalia of four of the great deities, Huitzilopochtli, Tlaloc, Yohuallahuan (a form of Xipe), and lastly Quetzalcoatl.[56] In other words, the corpse impersonated those deities one at a time for each of the four days of the obsequies. The choice of gods is informative. First was the patron god and supreme warrior of the imperial city whose ixiptla the ruler had been all along. Second was the god who had kept the living tlatoani and his people alive. Third was the sun whose rejuvenation had meaning for the deceased.

And lastly was the god of priests, of culture, and of wisdom, a god whose eventual return was fervently prophesied and believed in everywhere. This combination of qualities signaled leadership, life, rejuvenation, and reappearance. Certainly, cult could not more clearly delineate immortality, the summa of human desires; yet this is the only place in the obsequies where that hope was so patently enunciated.

After the corpse was washed, a piece of precious jade was placed in its mouth to be an enduring and incorruptible heart. The tlatoani's scalp lock (in which was contained the memory of his soul and the destiny dates associated with it) was cut off and placed in a container later to hold the ashes.[57] Runners had been sent out in all directions to carry the dreadful news and to summon all the allies, the governors, and vassals to their last meeting with the *huey tlatoani*. These magnates immediately took to the roads, walking swiftly, carried in fast litters, or propelled over the lake waters in urgent canoes. Even lords of enemy cities were invited, for protocol was a thing apart from hostility—these entered and left the city at night lest their armed attendants stir up trouble. All of the magnates bore rich gifts, their last to the dead man.

The dead ruler was laid out in state, but for purposes of being greeted and receiving gifts he had been duplicated as a mummy bundle wrapped in as many as twenty rich mantles. Masks of the four great gods were also placed successively on this simulacrum, whereas paper wings fanned out behind him. Lesser nobles grouped around the bundle endlessly sang the *miccacuicatl* (the "dirge for the dead"). The body itself, laid out on new mats, was segregated during these four days owing to its advancing decomposition. At some point here, the first and most important human sacrifice in the cult was made. Every tlatoani had a personal chaplain, a priest retained in the palace for the purpose of making offerings to the gods, seeking oracles, explicating penances, and reading the meaning of signs and prodigies. This priest, dressed as an ixiptla of the city god, was now sacrificed, that he might be ready in the otherworld when his lord arrived. The priority of cult in Aztec cult could not have been more graphically acknowledged—the first and most critical thing that the tlatoani took with him into the afterlife was expert assistance in the etiquette of pleasing the gods.

During these first four days, the princes and governors who had been able to come paid their last respects to the dead man. Each one was ushered into the presence and there delivered his *ave atque vale* in formal and florid language. He offered gifts that the dead man would take with him on his journey, domestic slaves, royal insignia and apparel, jewels, rich food, and clouds of incense.

At the end of the four days, during which the deceased was still considered to be ruling, both the body and the bundle effigy were solemnly taken up and carried by the greatest men in the realm in a procession to the sacred hearth of the city. For the occasion, this had been built up into a roaring fire. Priests then initiated the cremation by first asperging the crowds with fir boughs dipped in holy water. This was a ritual washing designed to purify the palace retainers and nobles for the solemn event to follow.

Interpreted as a passage in cult, the event was a mixed metaphor. As we have seen, cremation bespoke the release of a soul to rise into another and more blessed celestial world filled with light and joy, yet now a priest appeared at the pyre dressed as the sepulchral lord of the underworld, Mictlanteuctli. His joints were shown as dissociated eye sockets and devouring jaws; his face was a skull. The ambivalence of the ruler's deathly journey was again apparent, and again it iterated the Aztecs' inability (or reluctance) to attach themselves to one permanent ideology. As the corpse and the bundle effigy were now pushed into the fire, the screams of the palace women rose to a crescendo, seeming to be the voice of agony itself. So was the ruler returned to his father, the fire.

The ixiptla of Mictlanteuctli now began his dance around the pyre.[58] He was accompanied by four priests in black who kept poking up the fire with long poles to hasten the burning, posturing and grimacing to authenticate the action. In this passage the theatrical genius of the Aztecs surely reached new heights.

As this was going on, the sacrificial ritual of accompaniment began. Representative retainers of the dead ruler, buffoons, clowns, hunchbacks, drummers, domestic slaves and concubines, had been selected as an entourage to accompany the deceased. Included in the lot, whose numbers might reach 200 in all,[59] were the slaves who had been brought as gifts by the various rulers and governors round about. These unfortunates, all splendidly dressed, each had baskets packed with jewels and treasures strapped onto their backs. Together they were assembled by the pyre and there exhorted to be diligent in their duties to the dead man and to make sure that the treasures that they bore were not mislaid en route. Appropriate farewells were then made to the doomed ones, and they were destroyed. Among them were always some wives and concubines who voluntarily gave themselves up in an authentic suttee to accompany their lord into the shadows.

The manner in which the members of this retinue were sacrificed was unique to this occasion. They were individually taken over to the *teponaztli*, the deep-toned wooden drum, bent backward over it, and there had their hearts ripped out. The hearts and the blood from the wounds were thrown into the fire where the body of the tlatoani was continuing to burn. The bodies of these retainers were then taken to another pyre where they also were burned. The use of the drum instead of the venerable *techcatl* made the sacrifices personal to the tlatoani, for that drum represented the dances and the gaiety of life in the palace. Those sacrificed would carry on in the afterlife as they had been accustomed to do in the palace, serving the ruler and entertaining him.

None of the preceding comports with any of the previously mentioned Aztec otherworlds, so we must conclude that it represented a special variant of Mictlan not otherwise specified in myth. It was explicit only in the royal cult that is here being described.

After it was all over, such bones as had survived the burning were collected as well as the piece of jade that had represented the dead man's heart. Along with the locks of hair from the tlatoani's head, all these relics were placed in a stone box. The visiting lords were banqueted, thanked, and given gifts on their departure.

There now began the part of the ritual known as the quitonaltia that means literally "they cause warmth [or good luck] for him."[60] This had reference to the fact that the offerings that had been made to him so augmented the tlatoani's surviving essence that he became, by reason of heat, a strengthened soul. The quitonaltia lasted for the eighty days that followed the collection of the ashes. For the remaining members of the family it was a period of fasting. A new but smaller effigy of the deceased was made, adorned and masked, and then placed on top of the reliquary in a special room in the palace.

During those eighty days the image was often regaled and honored. Slaves were sacrificed, ten to fifteen on the fourth day, four or five on the twentieth day, two or three after forty days, one or two on the sixtieth, and then on the last day, in a final burst of blood gifts, some ten victims in all. On this last day, a diminished replay of the cremation of the effigy was carried out, and the stone reliquary containing the ashes, hair, and heart was finally buried.

There was no royal necropolis in any Aztec city so far as is known. Each ruler was buried in slightly different circumstances. Moteuczoma I, for instance, was buried under a patio in his palace, whereas Ahuitzotl's ashes were interred near the cuauhxicalli in the sacred enclosure. The urns or stone boxes of other rulers were inserted into the masonry of the great pyramid, or even under the floor in the cella of Huitzilopochtli. The journey taken by the dead man traditionally lasted four years, so commemorative offerings were made on the annual occasions during that period. After that there was only the memory of him.

The cult of the royal dead naturally contracted or expanded depending on the charisma (or lack of it) of the deceased. One thing, however, is apparent, namely that the cult was not leading the way to any clear religious definition of the afterlife or of divinity. However splendidly the soul made its exit, it still appears to have been Mictlan oriented. Neither Tlalocan nor the sun myths had affected thinking regarding the death of a ruler. So he was not made into a god in any true sense, however fulsome the attention lavished on him in the cult. He continued to be a ruler, that is certain, but he ruled silently in the land of the unfleshed. The Aztecs always paid in full their respects to mortality.

Ultimately cult is untranslatable, for us and all other people. Our reason may attack it, striving to force it into the limited range of our understanding. But it is difficult to do, as this book has shown. Cult is not a language; it is a second, and a separate, form of living.

Appendix A
List of Calendar Festivals

Ordinarily a list of religious festivals would strike one as an exercise in boredom. In the case of the Aztecs, however, we are contemplating a living and ever-changing theater, one of almost Elizabethan exuberance, so we can perhaps count off our list with some interest. Our attention rivets on the splendid trappings and choric gestures of the actors, the sense of suspense as the preliminaries are dragged out, the final supreme concentration in the sacrament at the top of the "jade steps," and the many interludes, either irrelevant, orgiastic, comic, or rhythmic. A fullness of religious commitment and belief appears in most of the actions performed by the Aztecs and convinces us that these festivals were not rote diversions but were lived with a most unusual intensity.

The list here given presents each known festival. In some instances, parts of the festivals have been adverted to in preceding chapters and should be viewed, not as duplications, but as matters needing emphasis. Nor are things always clear. Uncertainty can occur because there was an intermingling of cults as well as ritual experimentation by the Aztecs throughout the year. In this appendix the coverage of a particular festival may be reduced if it is treated at some length in the text. Both passages, text, and appendix should then be read together. We begin with the month supposed by many scholars to have initiated the series.

"THE RAISING OF THE POLES" (CUAHUITLEHUA)[1]

This month, which probably began sometime in early February,[2] honored Tlaloc, the god of rain, and Chalchiuhtlicue, the goddess of lakes and running water. Thus, as might be expected, the year opened on a statement of the agriculturist's needs for the coming year.[3]

The main part of the ceremonies concerned Tlaloc and set a fertility pattern that would continue through the three following months. In these rituals the victims sacrificed were exclusively children. Richly adorned and seated in litters, they were taken far up in the mountains in solemn processions where they were sealed up in caves to die, or else they were ceremonially drowned in a certain section of Lake Tezcoco. Adjunct to these sacrificial rites were excursions that the people made out into the fields to pluck handfuls of green grass or green boughs so as to sympathetically force verdure on the new year. Poles and branches were set up in various places in the city;[4] from the poles fluttered pieces of paper spattered with liquid rubber, symbolizing the presence of the gods and spirits of rain. The children to be sacrificed, who were thought of as small Tlalocs, were alluded to as "human banners."

There are hints that a significant part of the first month was intended to be introductory to the one following. In Cholula, as well as in Tenochtitlan, an *ixiptla* of Nine Wind (Quetzalcoatl), god of the wind and the first priest, led dances of slaves reserved for sacrifice during the second month.[5] At midnight of the first day of that second month, the ixiptla was destroyed and his body eaten by the merchants who had purchased him.

"THE FLAYING OF MEN" (TLACAXIPEHUALIZTLI)

Although this was the second month in the year, it was so important as an initiator of the year that, as we have seen, its rites had already begun in the first month when captives and slaves, who had been specially selected for sacrifice, daily performed ritual dances.[6] The special rites would end only with the closing of the third month. Just as the Tlaloc sacrifices could be spread over a number of the months, so here the cult of the god Xipe spilled over into neighboring months, both before and after.

This cult becomes even more impressive when we realize that in one fashion or another it was observed in almost all of the important cultures in Mesoamerica. Xipe was a nearly universal god, and his great festival here was a Paschal event. We must draw the reader's attention to the fact that here at the year's opening we find that two gods (of rain and sun—Tlaloc and Xipe) both compete to dominate the fertility aspects of the coming year, yet in very different ways. The priests made no attempt to fuse the two cults, and they remained variant readings of the supernatural world.

The god honored in the cult of Xipe—certainly the most remarkable rite in the whole year—was also called "Red Mirror," a reference to the fact that he was the diurnal sun. This feast of his was certainly equinoctial, for it came in the latter part of March and featured among other things a great fire.[7] What confirms the essentially solar character of Xipe's cult, however, is the fact that its central passage duplicates some of the events recounted in the myth of the Fifth Sun; its placement in the calendar at the vernal equinox points also to the same events.

In the myth mentioned, each of the four cardinal directions were, at the beginning of time, possible rising places for the new sun, an event that was tensely awaited by the assembled gods. The sun chose eventually to rise in the east, but he refused to come up above the horizon even in the east until all the gods had been sacrificed and he had feasted upon their hearts and drunk their blood. In this confrontation of the sun god with the pantheon, the champion of the latter was the morning star. It was he who dared to duel the sun, yet even he had to fall defeated. It was Xolotl the evening star who thereupon sacrificed the gods, after which he ran away weeping. The sun finally rose victoriously in the east, made sovereign by the divine offerings.

So ran the myth. In the cult of this month the most valiant of the war captives held by the state, each standing in for the sun, were forced at a tragic disadvantage to fight the most agile of the Eagle and Jaguar orders, devotees of the sun and themselves classed as priests.[8] These duels took place on the large circular stone known as the *temalacatl*. Four other priests, called the "Four Dawns" and painted each the color of one of the four directions, stood by to view the unequal gladiatorial contest. Also present were all the gods in the persons of their priests each wearing the skin of a sacrificed victim. Altogether, they represented the totality of the gods who had been destroyed so that the sun might live. Another priest clad as an indeterminate animal and called the "Gods' Uncle" or "Old Bear" lamented the loss of the victims as if they were his own kin. At the end of the ceremony, when as many as fifty or sixty men may have been sacrificed, the assembled gods and the Eagle and Jaguar knights performed a dance around the sacrificial spot, each carrying by the hair a freshly severed head.

It can be seen that all the major elements of the myth were translated here into cult. Matching the elements of the two is easy. But there is a problem. If the personae and the acts in the cult drama insist on the fact that the sun was triumphant and that it was his opponents who were destroyed, the depictions in the codices reverse this, and show the sacrificial victim, who was tied to the stone and who dies, to be Xipe himself. This ambiguity has been considered.

The preceding cult passage nevertheless forms only the nucleus of what was a much larger presentation—two other things were going on at the same time, one a public presentation of the concept of solar (and, therefore, universal) renewal symbolized by the wearing of skins, the other the private rites observed only by those warriors who had previously made a capture and who for this celebration gave up their captives to be sacrificed. These captors offered to their friends solemn banquets of the flesh of their human offerings, and they finally harnessed the remnants of their power through possession of their hair and bones. These latter rites were private and took place within the homes of the successful warriors.

Beside the gladiatorial sacrifice, where a captive performing on top of the circular stone mentioned before had to fight armed men whose victory was assured beforehand, there was another related type of blood sacrifice that was restricted to this cult. This was called the "Shooting of Men."[9] A victim was tied to a high wooden frame in spread-eagle fashion and there became the target of darts and arrows. It is probable that he represented the morning star, and those who shot at him were therefore partisans of the sun. His blood dripped down on a round and scalloped flagstone representing the earth, which was thereby fertilized.

Either one, or both, of these rites could be performed in the Flaying of Men. They came to Mexico-Tenochtitlan, if we may guess, from different cultures, one (the gladiatorial combat) dramatizing the duel between the sun and his opponent, the other (the death by arrows) concentrating on the fertilizing effect of the death. The former may well have come down to the Aztecs from Teotihuacan through the Toltecs; the latter probably was a later import from the Gulf Coast.[10]

There were four passages in the cult where the wearing of skins occurred.[11] The first featured the wards of the city, each of which sent out an impersonator of its own patron god properly painted and apparaled. These ixiptlas, as we have seen, were then sacrificed. The skins were stripped off the cadavers and donned by men who then became ixiptlas (in a higher degree) of the same gods. They were herded together in four groups and bound together by cords, each group moving among the people and witnessing in one of the four cardinal directions. Then en masse, as the full pantheon of the gods, they went to assist at the duel we have already spoken of between the doomed gladiators and their slayers, the Eagles and the Jaguars. For this passage in the cult, the legs of these gods were bound together for the whole day so that they could move about only as a unit, this symbolizing not only their unanimity in turning their combined sovereignty over to the sun, but as well the wholeness of the supernatural world.

In the second episode of skin-wearing a mock combat was fought between two parties. One group, clad in their human skins, represented the god Xipe, and they were accordingly referred to as Xipeme or Xixipeme. As weapons they carried fertility-producing rattle sticks. The group was led by the high priest of Xipe, here called *Yohuallahuan*. Opposed to them were warriors armed and intoxicated with drink for the occasion.

In the third episode an elitist factor enters. The skin of a particularly highly placed victim, a chief or magnate who had been saved for such a magnificent occasion, was assumed by the Mexican ruler himself in a separate dance.[12] Thus, he identified himself with the god of renewals, Xipe.

In the fourth episode the Xipeme went about for the twenty days of the following month blessing babies, whole households, and receiving gifts from all they met. People switched each other with branches of the zapote, the tree of Xipe, to give themselves vigor. At the end of those twenty days all the skins, dried and rotting by then, were formally placed in an underground crypt in the great temple and sealed away.

"THE LESSER AND THE GREATER VIGILS"
(TOZOZTONTLI, HUEYTOZOZTLI)

Child sacrifices to Tlaloc had not ceased since the beginning of the year, for rain in this critical early growing time was often lacking.[13] The preceding month had stressed the advent of the resurrected sun god. These two months together formed an extended May Day and featured the effect of that fructifying epiphany upon the earth goddess. The Tozoztontli saw the early spring flowers gathered and presented by special priests to the vernal goddess Coatlicue in Xipe's temple.[14] And coincident with the birth of flowers was the appearance of the new corn.[15] The sacred seed corn that had been put down the year before was now brought forth, and in rituals performed in the milpas, Cinteotl, the maize god, was acknowledged as born to the goddess. These were mainly women's rites, however, for women alone could invoke the goddess effectively, crying out "O My Lady, come quickly."[16]

Special banquets marked all the ceremonies, and tiny children of both sexes were encouraged to dance in circles hand in hand. With the new maize sprouts just appearing in the fields at this time, the dance of the little ones was appropriate. An equally important part of the cult in the Greater Vigil was centered around mountains (Tlaloc) and lakes (Chalchiuhtlicue).

For this festival, rulers from most of the Aztec cities in the great Basin solemnly processed to Tlaloc's celebrated shrine on the mountain behind Tezcoco.[17] In the dense forest around this shrine and out on the crags overlooking the splendid view, log cabins and leafy bowers had been thrown up for the repose of each of the rulers and their subchiefs. They had brought with them a young boy, dressed as the rain god, and in the dawn they sacrificed him in front of the stone idol of Tlaloc. His blood was used to asperge the idol, and the images of the lesser mountain gods grouped around it. After that, a regal repast was spread out in front of the god and left there with a guard of armed men to see to it that the food was not pilfered. Unique was the fact that this famous central shrine with its enclosure walls and idols had no resident priesthood. The attached cult had to be activated anew each year by the cities in the plains and lakes below.

Meanwhile a giant fir tree, called "Our Father," had been brought down from the mountain of Culhuacan into the city of Tenochtitlan.[18] With its boughs and foliage undamaged, it was carried by the people in huge forks so that no part of it could be desecrated by contact with the ground. This tree was erected in the plaza facing the main temple with four other lesser trees spaced at the corners of a square around it and tied to it with twisted straw cables. Dancing, masquerades, and general drunkenness (which included children) accompanied this passage of the cult. This was also a time for giving names to the babies born during the previous year, while the new mothers were ritually cleansed of the taint of childbirth. As the month came to an end, the tree was taken down and rafted out into the lake. A fleet of canoes, all covered with rich awnings, accompanied it to a sacred site in the shallows. In the midst of the procession went one canoe carrying a little girl destined for sacrifice and dressed in the habiliments of the mighty goddess of the lake. At the appropriate spot, the tree was forced down into the bottom mud so that it stood upright beside the dead hulks of other trees from previous years. At that spot, along with rich offerings, the child was struck down and then thrown into the lake to drown. The fleet returned to Mexico in utter silence. Thus was water venerated in all of its aspects, whether rain, spring water, or lake water.

The new corn just appearing above the ground might now be expected to grow. The first flowers, the new corn, and children were all seen to be homologues, reinforcing each other.

TOXCATL (MEANING UNCERTAIN)

Running throughout the whole of this month there was a constant censing of the gods, of households, and of all household objects from which we can deduce that the intent of the cult was placatory.[19] The god to be placated was Tezcatlipoca who often brought to men the terrors of pestilence, sterility, drought, and starvation.[20] Placation, penance, and forgiveness were all intermingled in this cult, for the lot of the living was Tezcatlipoca's to dispense.

The festival was set apart by the lavish use of wreaths and necklaces of popcorn worn by all the participants and adorning the god's statue. A great cable of braided strings of popcorn was carried about in the ceremonies and was called *toxcatl*, which was said to signify "drought."[21] This orientation toward anxiety, however, was carefully orchestrated into the theme of the omniscience of the divine, and the god best known for that again was Tezcatlipoca.

The climactic day was allotted to the sacrifice of a carefully selected and trained slave or war captive who was the ixiptla of Tezcatlipoca.[22] What is unique is that this person had been impersonating the god in the city of Mexico for the entire preceding year. The crux of this cult is to be found in the fact that, even as the ixiptla of the last year was being sacrificed, a new one was chosen to enact the same role for the next year. The period of time during which other gods were represented in the living persons of ixiptlas was at the most four Aztec months—in contrast to these, the Toxcatl cult was essentially unending, there being no time of year when the god could not be heard and occasionally seen on his nocturnal rambles. The two associated cities of Tenochtitlan and Tezcoco each had their own ixiptla of Tezcatlipoca walking through their streets and receiving veneration in their plazas in an endless theophany. And when the time of Toxcatl came, the concentration of the god was further intensified by sacrificing only his one ixiptla and no others. The quadrennial celebrations of this cult were, however, marked off by the sacrifice of many attendant victims designed to serve Tezcatlipoca as food in a world beyond.

The Toxcatl was built around two aspects of the god: the one was his youth and sexuality, the other his omniscience and the concomitant power that he had of erasing sin. Corresponding to the first emphasis was his patronage of the various *telpochcalli*s in the cities, which were schools for the unmarried young men of the city wards. The Toxcatl, in fact, was almost like a graduation from these institutions, and therefore was tantamount to entry into adulthood.[23] During this month the nubile girls, dressed as if for their marriages and wearing tiaras and leis of popcorn, danced with the young men, and sang antiphonally with them, very much in the style of a generalized mating dance.[24]

As for the second emphasis, that of the god's omniscience, the Toxcatl provided an opportunity for the individual—as opposed to the whole society—to commune with the supernatural. The signal that the god was present and attentive came when the ixiptla, at any time of day or night during the year, blew several shrill notes on a clay pipe to each of the four directions. This aural signature was understood by all secret sinners as being directed at them, and at the sound they prayed that their derelictions might remain still undiscovered and unpunished. Penitents who felt themselves unable or unwilling to confess, beat themselves with the spiny-edged leaves of the maguey plant, and invoked Tezcatlipoca in his avatar as Night-and-Wind. Others who heard the voice might, on the contrary, pray to the god for that that they most desired, whether fame on the battle-field, riches, success, or many sons.

In the person of his ixiptla, the god was constantly at the center of this cult. Throughout the year the ixiptla was accorded reverence and, always under heavy guard, was escorted on midnight peregrinations about the city, dancing and blowing on his pipe, or strolling at his leisure while grandly smoking cigars and sniffing flowers. In the last month of his life, he was accorded the company of four women who were said to be four of the great goddesses. During his last five days he ostensibly ruled the city, and the real *tlatoani* for that interval retired. Finally, in a spectacular ceremony he was destroyed, being taken for that purpose to the south shore of the lake. His flesh was then served up for the greatest lords to eat.[25]

It is obvious that this cult is unlike any of the others. It was not solely a magical incantation by the group to ward off the god's ire. Rather it was an acknowledgment that, not only could society as a whole confront the divine, but so also could the Aztec individual. It stripped the individual bare and was consequently to him not only the most immediate of the cults but also the most alarming. Every four years, the Toxcatl was celebrated with special splendor; it was then turned into a general remission of sins.[26] It was believed that Tezcatlipoca quadrennially forgave every sin, allowing the individual finally to relax in the knowledge that his secret had been kept and had to all intents and purposes been erased from the record. This is the only one of the Aztec cults that so pointedly involved the individual.

"THE EATING OF SUCCOTASH" (ETZALCUALIZTLI)

An important part of this festival concerned the priests. We can tell this from the fact that the divine patron of the priesthood, Quetzacoatl, and his monstrous twin, Xolotl, were honored with a special dance and with occasional penis mutilations performed by over-zealous priests. This sacerdotal emphasis, however, went along with a continuing Tlaloc cult for the cult took place during the growth of the corn when rain was still needed.[27]

In all the plebeian households there was also observed a parallel celebration of the instruments of the peoples' toil, the digging sticks, tumplines, baskets, and carrying frames that enabled the farmer to work his milpa and carry back the produce.[28] A display of these necessary objects was set up in the home by the family; salutations and speeches were directed to the instruments, apologies made for the hard usage they had suffered, and thanks given for their assistance. Food offerings were also made to them, and they were then washed.

Rain was not stressed here as much as were the waters of the earth, the lakes and mountain springs. All individuals whose livelihoods were concerned with water, such as canoe makers, fishermen, reed gatherers, and fowlers, had special obligations and interests in this cult. Ixiptlas were chosen by them for both Tlaloc (rain) and Chalchiuhtlicue (lake) and they were supposed to act out the roles of husband and wife.[29] In fact, there is a hint that this cult may have included a hierogamy, or sacred copulation. Both ixiptlas were finally destroyed and buried, not eaten as was customary in the other cults. Ixiptlas of the Tlaloque (multiple rain gods) were also sacrificed; their hearts were taken out to Pantitlan in the lake and there thrown into the water.[30]

During this month a special and very desirable dish was prepared in most of the households, the *etzalli*, a kind of succotash; this was not only eaten by families but was given to the priests who, now garbed as the rain gods, went dancing in the streets and begging at every door.

In this month also, the colleges of priests underwent a severe vigil and fast.[31] At the end of their exercises, they imposed punishments upon those of their number believed to have been negligent or awkward in their duties. These penalties were always connected with water, and sometimes ended in drowning. While this was going on, others of the Mexican priesthood went down at midnight to the ice-cold waters of the lake, thrashed about, and waded through the reeds and mud, while squawking and flapping like ducks and other lake fowl. At this high altitude illness and death from exposure must have often resulted.

There were thus two emphases in this month, water and the purification of the priests.

"THE LESSER AND GREATER FEASTS OF THE LORDS" (TECUILHUITONTLI, HUEY TECUILHUITL)

This pair of months involved the worship of the Great Mother and two forms of the young corn, the male, Tlazopilli, and the maiden Xilonen. But laid over this venerable bedrock there was an upper level of the cult that celebrated and confirmed the prerogatives of the ruler and the noble class supporting him. The nexus binding these two together was the concept of abundant food, this being derived from and equated with the order and security given to society by the ruling class. It is a most interesting conjunction.

Most of the Lesser Feast was given up to the nobles and courtiers who went about visiting gardens, smelling flowers, hunting, and reciting heroic poetry.[32] And concomitantly with this there were dances and casual parades of young women. At the same time, there was a serious side to this for during the Lesser Feast, Xochipilli (a form of Tlazopilli) was honored. It is known that he was the patron of the psychotropic plants, such as tobacco, mushrooms, and morning glory, substances that heightened living for the noble class.[33] This was probably the aspect of the corn god that was uppermost at the time.

Additionally, the ixiptla of the goddess of salt (Huixtocihuatl) was sacrificed at dawn at Tlaloc's temple.[34] Salt makers and salt merchants celebrated the day with banquets and heavy drinking. A particularly interesting feature of this month was the ritual ball game played by four gods including the Great Mother and an avatar of the young corn.[35] Some of these activities merged into the events of the following month.

The Greater Feast of the Lords came at a time when the maize in the fields had headed up and sweetened. In the thinking of the Aztecs, this young corn could be manifested in one or the other of two spirits, one male and one female. They were both venerated, though a city might choose to focus on only one of them. The city of Mexico saw the new ears with their hair unbound, so they particularly honored Xilonen the Corn Maiden. But it must be understood that the Corn Maiden was only a thinly disguised avatar of Cihuacoatl, the great Earth Mother, and that this month was hers.[36] The final sacrifice of the Corn Maiden was made in front of the terrible goddess's House of Darkness.

The young woman selected to impersonate Xilonen for some days was kept perpetually drunk to ensure her happiness.[37] She attended feasts in the city and wandered at will through the market, symbolically the place of abundance. At one point, all the midwives of the city escorted her to the summit of Chapultepec, a rock sacred to the rain god. Almost certainly, this was a statement of sacred coupling, there on the hill, of the corn goddess with Tlaloc. The final act of the victim's life was to witness the sacrifice of four males who, while she watched, were hurled into the sacred hearth of the city and then hooked out to have their hearts excised. The young woman herself was then decapitated over the four scorched and open bodies lying piled together, the whole tableau symbolizing the coals of the fire and the reaping and subsequent roasting of the corn over it. Throughout this month also the women danced with their hair unbound. Some of the dances, those performed with torches, were spectacular midnight ballets.

Of almost equal importance were the ancestral cults of the nobles. The God of lineage and legitimacy was Quetzalcoatl, and he was therefore the patron of these rites.[38] It was his ixiptla who was accordingly sacrificed on the last and culminating day of the second of the two months.[39] During all the forty days of these months the various wards of Mexico and the dependent cities around the lake were expected to entertain the nobles with women, banqueting, and entertainment.[40] At these occasions the nobles recounted to each other the deeds, privileges, and titles of their ancestors, while also boasting of their own exploits and breeding.[41] That this was ritualistic, and not merrymaking alone, is proved by the presence of idols representing rulership at these banquets.[42] The ixiptla of Quetzalcoatl was finally sacrificed, not in his own temple, but at the temple of Tezcatlipoca.[43]

"THE LESSER AND GREATER FEASTS OF THE DEAD" (MICCAILHUITONTLI AND HUEYMICCAILHUITL)

The preceding two months had, among other things, honored the nobles and exalted their pedigrees. The two months discussed here carried this emphasis further to include all segments of the people lumped together as the nation or city. Ancestral gods were central. In the first month, the Tenochca element in the Mexican people honored their ancestor god, Huitzilopochtli, with vast floral arrangements and several days of drums and dancing when the great nobles paired with public women in intricate choreographic displays.[44] In the second month, the ancestral god of the Tlatilulca element in the Mexican peple was honored.[45] This latter was the fire god, but here specifically in his Tepaneca form as the god

Otonteuctli—the Tepaneca were that early part of the Mexican people who became the Tlatilulca. The form that this latter god took was a tree that they called *xocotl*.[46]

As the first month opened, the priests of the fire god led the people up into the mountains to select as large a fir tree as possible that, from that point on for forty days, was to hold center stage in the cult.[47] The tree was brought down and deposited at the entrance to the city. It was stripped of its bark and lopped of all its branches, thus representing a fallen and lifeless body. Priests and people worshipped it for twenty days, flagellating themselves, letting blood, dancing, and censing the god as he lay supine at the gates of the city. In the second month, we see it erected in the precinct of the temple of the fire god, who was the universal ancestor. But now the huge pole had been richly adorned to indicate its now living state. Young people, the girls rouged and covered with red feathers, performed bacchanalian dances around it while drunkenness among the elders was encouraged and a general indulgence took place. At the top of the pole a small platform had been affixed and on it was placed a dough image of a bird. Ropes were attached that dangled down to the ground. The object for the assembled young men, all from the noble class, was the capture of the god at the top of the pole, and to this end, at a given signal, they swarmed up. The fortunate one who first laid hands on the image hurled it to the ground where it shattered into bits; the waiting crowd scrambled wildly for pieces of it that they could carry back to their homes. It was in a sense a communion meal, for the people were eating the flesh of the ancestor. The pieces raining down from the sky were tantamount to the entrance of children into the wombs of their mothers, with the resulting increase of the tribe.

Merchants played a key role.[48] They had bought five slaves and prepared them to play the roles of the gods grouped around Yacateuctli, the patron deity of their profession and also a fire god. Yacateuctli was an avatar of Quetzalcoatl who, as we have seen, stood at the head of all the great lineages and thus was an ancestral god in his own right. In the persons of their ixiptlas, he and the other four associated gods were offered directly to Otonteuctli by being cast into the ever-burning hearth, first being carried around the fire as burdens on the backs of the merchants. After each god perished, four or five slaves were killed in an appended sacrificial rite. These were donations by private and wealthy individuals.

Thus these two months joined the cults of two ancestral gods, respectively tree (Otonteuctli) and fire (Yacateuctli and Xiuhteuctli). But though dual in origin and symbolism, the combined effect of the two months was single. In this cult, the people acknowledged their ancestors and announced their oneness with them. At one point as the Greater Feast began, the people of Tenochtitlan ascended to their rooftops at midnight and, addressing themselves to the northern skies, called upon their dead to return for this occasion to their former homes.[49]

At the end of the cult, the great pole was felled and broken up so that the devout might carry relics away with them.

"THE ROAD SWEEPING" (OCHPANIZTLI)

This month was devoted totally to the Great Mother, one of whose common appurtenances was the broom. More than any of the other seventeen, this month was monopolized by female deities. Ixiptlas of three of the greatest goddesses were slain on succeeding days, and their skins worn by priests: Atlantonan, Chicomecoatl, and Toci.[50] Only the rites connected with the last two are known to us in any detail. In these the Aztecs celebrated two aspects of the Great Mother: her bounty and her warlikeness. The former produced a typical harvest home and ritual thanksgiving, the latter produced a war muster and mock battles between parties of women. We may see little in common between these two qualities, but to an agricultural society dominated by a war elite the connection must have seemed obvious.

We are informed that the demonic element so often associated by the Aztecs with women was also celebrated in this cult. Ixiptlas of the fierce Amazonian spirits who were called the "goddesses" were sacrificed and skinned at the Xochicalco.[51] Worn by priests for a while, these skins were finally deposited underground. A composite avatar of all of these, a deity called simply the "Goddess," was also sacrificed.[52]

A central activity, and one that lasted for eight days, was the hand-waving dance of the warriors, unusual in that it was performed only to the beat of drums. The dancers remained in place and marked the rhythms with coordinated movements of the arms. There was no singing. In fact, throughout most of the entire Ochpaniztli festival absolute silence was maintained in spite of the great numbers of people involved.[53]

In the agricultural part of the cult, a young girl was arrayed to look like the corn goddess Chicomecoatl.[54] On her head she wore a quetzal feather to symbolize the green maize plant. After an eight-day fast followed by a thanksgiving banquet and general indulgence, she was decapitated over a pile of corn, chile, beans, and squash. Her body was flayed, and a priest assumed it, along with all of her regalia.

As for the Great Mother's other avatar, Toci, again an ixiptla was selected forty days before the rites about to be described. This woman was not a virgin but a matron. Her death was a masterpiece of horror and symbolism.

Toci is the Aztec version of the great Huaxtec mother Tlazolteotl. Huaxtecs and Mexican Aztecs had fought each other for years before the Conquest, and at some point the latter had secured such a victory over the former as allowed them to make off with their goddess. She was escorted to Tenochtitlan and was installed in the Tlillan, the Mexican Earth Mother's temple where she lived surrounded by the idols of other subjected peoples. But Toci was much too great a deity for such a demeaning imprisonment, and a shrine with an elevated wooden platform in front was also built for her just beyond the city on the south side. This curious shrine was called *Tocititlan* and was important in the cult.[55]

For several days during the festivities, Toci's ixiptla was forced to spin cotton, to parade through the market, and to dance and sing. At night she was stuffed back into her cage. For the finale, a priest carried her on his back faceup, he himself bending far forward. In this position her head was sawed off drenching him in her blood. The body was flayed, and the raw skin donned by another priest. Led by this priest, now acting as a divine war chieftainess, a mock battle was fought through the city out to where the southern causeway entered. Possibly it mimed a ceremonial expulsion of Tlazolteotl from Tenochtitlan. It was taken quite seriously, and serious injuries, even deaths, resulted.

The running battle continued to the shrine of Tocititlan, where the straw image of Toci sat high above the crowd in a thatched shed open on all sides. Sacrificial victims were forced to climb up the open-work scaffold to be met by stunning blows at the top that toppled them to the ground below. The priest wearing Toci's skin, after tasting the blood of the broken bodies, then groaned deeply to imitate the sound of the earthquake, the only voice by which the Great Mother ever spoke. In conclusion, he doffed his skin and placed it on the idol, thus ending that passage in the cult. All of these events symbolized not only the victory of the Mexica over the Huaxtecs, but also the goddess's right to be domiciled at least on the edge of the city.

There followed one more rite in the cult of this goddess.[56] Here the tlatoani presided over a full military review of his warriors. New warriors were now inducted into their majority and certified for war, whereas the older veterans were presented with rich gifts and other recognitions of their services and status. At that juncture certain of the nobles donned the regalia of the great gods of war, fire, and the heavenly bodies, and proceeded to shoot arrows into victims tied spread-eagled on an elevated wooden frame. The blood dripping on the earth replenished the Great Mother. The cult ended as it had begun, with a general sweeping of the streets, symbolizing the expulsion of all ills that had accumulated in the city.

It is apparent that the Ochpaniztli festival signified the end of the harvest and the beginning of the season of war, but its excessively complicated structure, as well as the hiatuses in our knowledge of it, appear to hide other meanings.

"THE LESSER AND THE GREATER FEASTS OF SPANISH MOSS" (PACHTONTLI, HUEYPACHTLI)

Although these two months concentrate on the gods as a pantheon, we are probably justified in seeing them as a significant priestly manipulation of earlier nature rites realigning them to express the concept of divine sovereignty. In the Lesser Feast the sovereign deity is Tezcatlipoca; in the Greater Feast it is Xochiquetzal, but in both cases it is a question of an extremely dramatic ephiphany. All the celebrants wore garlands of Spanish moss in their hair throughout the festivities, though we do not know the reason.

The Lesser Feast was often called the "Arrival of the Gods." It was the common belief that, following the harvest home, all the gods had departed and left the world empty.[57] But humans needed the gods; their absence was insupportable and so people prepared against their return. This month began with the autumn equinox.

For an important vigil that occurred at the end of the month, the priests had prepared an uncooked corn cake in the temple.[58] Periodically during the designated night, this was inspected until the telltale sign was discovered, a footprint impressed in the doughy mass. Trumpets were thereupon blown to summon the people who rushed from their beds, no matter how dark or inclement the night, to welcome their gods. The first god to come was Tezcatlipoca the Youth. Others followed, and on the third day the last of them came, the oldest and the slowest of the gods, the fire gods Xiuhteuctli and his avatar Yacateuctli. In honor of these antiquarian gods a special holocaust was performed. Captives were thrown into the ever-burning fire while youths dressed as monsters pranced around. The drinking of *octli* by the celebrants during this time was said to be the washing of the various deities' feet in token of the long journey they had taken back. The Lesser Feast ended with the townsmen, arrayed in feathers of all colors, performing the serpent dance.

One agricultural passage found in this month had nothing to do with the worship of all the gods.[59] This rite followed the previous harvest home and sanctified the putting down of the dried and shelled seed corn into storage spaces under the ground. Two young girls, selected traditionally from a certain family, were chosen to represent this seed corn. The nobles, arrayed in exotic costumes, danced around these two girls while priests moved through the crowds scattering maize kernels of the four directional colors; these seeds were fought over by people who scrambled to add some few of them to their own stores underground against the next season, thus sanctifying the bins. For the entire day, while this was going on, a priest held aloft the knife with which he would later slay the girls. They were finally sacrificed with their legs crossed to specify their virginity and, by extension, the seed corn's pristine and consecrated quality. The girls were not eaten but were buried in a special pit in one of the Tlaloc shrines —thus the seed corn was put down in the earth to sleep until the next year's sowing.

The ritual core of the Greater Feast centered around the goddess Xochiquetzal. She summarized in her person the entire pantheon of gods[60] who were here cast as spirits of the land seen under the forms of the great mountains.[61] In this part of the cult, all of the great gods, in the persons of their ixiptlas, were sacrificed at Tlaloc's shrine and carefully rolled, rather than tumbled, down the temple steps. Many gods of specific localities or mountains, who were worshipped with Dionysiac excesses and thereby classed among the Four Hundred Rabbits, were at this time taken in the persons of their ixiptlas to a conglomerate shrine, the Tochinco, and there sacrificed together. The concentration on mountains allowed an alternative name for this month, namely the "Festival of Mountains."

The more imposing mountains were of course Popocateptl and Iztaccihuatl, but every year the rites were moved to a different peak so that no god would feel slighted. Fires were lit, however, on all the mountains.

While these public rites were going on, the people in their homes were carrying on private rites of great antiquity. Squat images made of dough were moulded, adorned, and given the names of specific mountains. Among these images were placed miniature trees from whose branches hung the Spanish moss that gave its name to the festivals. Also scattered among the images of the mountains were curled roots or twisted boughs plastered over with dough and purporting to be dragons. These were the "small winds," testy gods who swarmed out of caves in the mountains to bring diseases to men. At a set time in the family festivities, all of the dough idols were slain with women's weaving sticks and dismembered. The pieces were later dried in the sun and eaten in small amounts throughout the year, thus maintaining a perpetual communion between the family and those gods.

The state, however, provided a more theatrical staging of the coming together of all the gods. It occurred on the last day of the month and was in the form of a farewell to flowers, for this was now the end of October.[62] Xochiquetzal, the Great Mother in her avatar as the goddess of love, presided over a truly aphrodisiac scene. Her part was played by a priest wearing the skin of a girl sacrificed to the goddess. Ensconced in a bower of flowers as the goddess, he greeted all of the gods and courteously seated them around him. Priests clad as animals of various sorts gamboled about the goddess. Boys wearing plumage sat in artificial trees and were shot at with harmless blowguns by the festive nobles. Young people were introduced to drink and sex, though the extent of these rites is unknown. They celebrated by draping themselves with Spanish moss, the plant possibly symbolizing what our mistletoe does, namely condoned license. All of the events centering around the goddess were in dance form, and the overall effect must have been that of a suite of elaborate ballets. Friar Durán said that it was the most solemn dance in the land.

The previously discussed two months had welcomed the gods back and offered them brilliant spectacles. With the spirits of the land content, all was well. Grimmer business could now be attended to.

"FLYING ARROW" (QUECHOLLI)

This curious month (whose name is uncertainly translated here)[63] was dedicated to contention, wrath, and the cult of war.[64] In the rites, however, war appears under the guise of hunting, a collateral kind of activity. Throughout the rites an angry atmosphere was consciously cultivated.

The month was divided into two equal parts, each of ten days. The first part celebrated Mixcoatl as the god of arrows and darts; the central event of this was a ceremonial battue. The second part was a series of sacrificial rites illustrative of the Mixcoatl cycle of myths. In the first part, Mixcoatl was the focal deity; his consort Itzpapalotl dominated the second part. Taken as a whole, the Quecholli stems from a preagricultural stage of Chichimec life and points to an old and thoroughgoing religion.

In the first half, Mixcoatl was commemorated as an ancestral warrior and archetypal hunter.[65] Offerings were made to the dead who were here thought of, not as inhabitants of the underworld, but as followers of Mixcoatl (i.e., the mimixcoa) and therefore as star folk. Food, token arrows, and torches were placed on graves, the torches symbolizing the night of stars in which the dead were embedded as points of fire.

The centerpiece of the festival however was the reenactment of a Paleolithic battue. For five days, the hunters abstained from sexual activity, fasted, drew blood, and made arrows that were to be blessed by the god of the city. A procession then exited from Mixcoatl's shrine in Tenochtitlan to the foot of Mount Zacatepec where the drive of game was to begin. Each Aztec city of course focused on its own

preferred mountain. At the summit, a rustic shrine had been erected
for Mixcoatl, and toward this point all the game was driven. The most
daring of the hunters entered the corral of beaters and wrestled the
wild game to the ground instead of dispatching them with arrows—
such capture was of course taken from the time-honored custom of
the Aztec battlefield. All of the animals were then killed sacrificially
in front of the god. There followed a boisterous return of the successful hunters to the city. The ruler welcomed them and conferred
honors and titles on the successful ones.

The second half of the Quecholli festival was suggested by the
tale of the descent of the demonic goddess Itzpapalotl ("Obsidian
Butterfly") from the heavens.[66] While taking part in this cult, the
nobles were considered to be, and were called, Mimixcoa—the ancestral dead who were the stars. At some point in the proceedings, victims representing the Huitznahua (a designation similar in reference
to the Mimixcoa) were sacrificed in the temple of Coatlan.[67] There
was, however, a more specific sacrificial event that was the killing of
two men and two women, representing respectively the two avatars of
Mixcoatl (Xiuhnel and Mimich in the myth), and two deer women
who came down from the skies and were forms of Itzpapalotl. In the
city of Huexotzinco the four, slung on poles as if they were deer, were
carried up the temple steps to be sacrificed. In the cult in Tlaxcala, a
female ixiptla who took the part of Mixcoatl's consort had her head
smashed against a stone that had been given the name of the cactus
upon which in myth the demonic goddess had settled before her own
death.[68]

Only the following month can vie with this one for its close ex-
plication of a specific myth. The point to be stressed is that the myths
in both months are explicitly celestial.

"THE ERECTION OF BANNERS" (PANQUETZALIZTLI)

In one sense this is a replay of the preceding month, but whereas
that one looked back to a very old Chichimec past and a Chichimec
god who was shared equally by all the Aztecs, the Erection of Banners
was a cult wherein each of the Aztec cities honored its own patron
god, and because all these cities were of recent Aztec foundation, the
rites were also recent and patriotic. The commonality of this Aztec
month allowed it also to be known as the "Feast of All" (*Coail-*

huitl).[69] In Tenochtitlan, it was the celebration by the people of their city god, namely Huitzilopochtli, whereas, for example, in Chalco it was that city's god, Tezcatlipoca, who was honored.[70]

In Tenochtitlan, small banners were erected everywhere.[71] They were placed in fruit trees, in cactus, and in maguey. Every house was decorated with at least one of these banners. Larger banners were sited at spots made memorable by some deed of Huitzilopochtli.

In Tenochtitlan, the cult was built around the myth of the gigantomachy.[72] As we know from that myth, Huitzilopochtli was born without a father out of the Earth Mother who resided in Mount Coatepec.[73] She had previously given birth to gods and titans who are referred to as the Four Hundred Huitznahua, otherwise the stars. Under the leadership of the goddess Coyolxauhqui (the moon), these titans formed a plan to destroy their mother who had shamed them by her furtive pregnancy. Huitzilopochtli sprang from his mother's womb fully armed as the conspirators approached; he subdued them, sacrificed them, and then ate them. His victory was completed when he finally decapitated Coyolxauhqui. Behind the Mexican myth is the story of the conflict between the sun (Huitzilopochtli), the moon (Coyolxauhqui), and the stars (the Huitznahua).

In the cult the mythic events were enacted in front of the central temple that thus became Mount Coatepec, the mountain of the Earth Mother. It began with dances in which great numbers of Mexicans participated, singing the praises of the god. In fact, warriors and public women holding hands danced in long lines during every one of the twenty days. The many intended victims were also much in evidence, being forced into various ritual postures for several days preceding their deaths. There was of course an ixiptla of Huitzilopochtli himself who was to become the sacrificial centerpiece.

Four representations of Huitzilopochtli were used in the ceremonies. One was a dough image destined to be ritually killed by the high priest and then served out to all in bits and pieces—a communion meal. A second dough image was made of the god Tlacahuepan, an avatar of Huitzilopochtli and said to be his brother. The third was another avatar, Chonchayotl, whose part was played by a living ixiptla. The fourth was a bundle image called *Paynal*, the "Racer." Carried by a priest, this image was brought down from the temple (i.e., the mountain Coatepetl) and passed along at great speed on a roughly twenty-mile circuit. This coursing stopped first at the Ball Court of the Gods near the main temple where ixiptlas of four gods who ruled the game were brutally killed and then dragged about the court thus smearing the area with their blood. The running then went over the northwestern causeway to Nonohualco where Paynal's brother god, Cuahuitlicac, had a shrine, then to the mainland, down the lakeside, and finally back into the city over the southern causeway. Devotees raced along behind the god and stopped with him for the various human sacrifices customary along the way. The route repeated the path of the early Mexica carrying their god with them through the many vicissitudes of their history to the culminating foundation of the city.

While the Running of Paynal was taking place, the mythic battle of Mount Coatepec was being reenacted in the area of Huitzilopochtli's temple. The intended sacrificial victims who had been provided by the merchants were identified as the party of the god and fought with small flint-tipped bird arrows. Opposing them were war captives representing the Four Hundred Huitznahua who were aided by Mexican warriors designated by the ruler and armed with wooden clubs. Drums pounded to accentuate the clamor of the fray. The Huitznahua in single file, crouching and weaving in full battle array, were led by a priest impersonating Coyolxauhqui. The crucial moment came when Cuahuitlicac, that one of the Huitznahua who defected, broke away and raced up the mountainside (i.e., the temple steps) to inform his brother Huitzilopochtli of the approaching danger. If a Huitznahua partisan was captured in this mock battle, he was instantly sacrificed by being bent backwards over one of the great drums and by having his heart torn out. Death and severe injuries were not uncommon. The battle was halted by the flight of the Huitznahua when Paynal returned, to be placed again in his shrine.

At this point, as related in the myth, the god seized the initiative by hurling the Fire Serpent down from the mountaintop. This was a supernatural weapon, which had been provided to Huitzilopochtli by a priest representing the friendly god Tochancalqui, and was represented in the cult by a large paper dragon manipulated by priests, red feathers representing its flaming tongue. At the foot of the steps there was a stone receptacle in which slips of paper had been placed, each one representing the person of one of the intended victims who were now lined up under guard awaiting their end. To symbolize the destruction of the evil Huitznahua by Huitzilopochtli's weapon, the priests now set fire to the scraps of paper and cast the dragon down on top of them. All flared up and were destroyed. The defeated leader, Coyolxauhqui, was present as a decapitated head in stone placed at the summit of the great pyramid. The dismembered pieces of her body, which in the myth had been hurled down the mountain, had been incised in deep relief in a circular stone at the foot of the balustrade.[74] Thus hurling his fiery rays into their ranks, the sun in his rising triumphed over the stars and the moon. He pursued the enemy down the temple steps, four times chased them around the base of the Coatepetl and, finally catching them on the south side, there ritually slaughtered them at their own shrine, the Huitznahuac.

In the persons of their high priests, all the gods of the Aztec pantheon now came to Coatepec to congratulate the god on his victory and to offer him submission. Dough cakes in the form of hands and bones, four hundred of them, were scattered about at the feet of the image of Huitzilopochtli that had been placed in a bower of flowers and green boughs in front of the shrine. The assembled gods danced about the dough image and the bones, thereby consecrating them.

Only then did the slaughter of the victims begin, which part of the cult obviously mimed the victory banquet of the god. Besides these unfortunates, a special group of victims representing the Four Hundred Huitznahua were slain at the shrine dedicated to them.

At day's end, favorite cuts of meat from the large number of corpses formed the central dishes at many banquets, while a special brew of octli was consumed. So ended Mexico's celebration of its mascot god.

An appended rite, which actually took place on the third day of the succeeding month, featured another mock battle between priests (led by a demonic and berserker ixiptla of Huitzilopochtli known as *Chonchayotl*) and young novice warriors. The latter attempted to defend the palace, the priests their own quarters. Though a mere incident in a larger cult, this is of interest, marking as it does a natural hostility between priest and warrior.

The activities of the cult were wound up on the following day with the ritual scattering of ashes, an act that was designed to force the ghosts of the slaves sacrificed in the holocaust to descend into the underworld, thus removing their vaporous presences from among men.

"FALLING WATERS" (ATEMOZTLI)[75]

Because so much of the city's effort was devoted to war in this month, there was a relative cessation of ritual. Tlaloc was the god honored because in this month (November) one might expect thunderstorms. Prayers for rain were offered, and the people in family groups again moulded small images of the various mountains, entertained them, and then killed and ate them. These images (*tepicme*) represented the dwarf rain gods so commonly believed in throughout Mesoamerica. In sets of four, slave children were also sacrificed.

TITITL (MEANING UNCLEAR—PERHAPS "THE WRINKLED ONE")[76]

This was a celebration of the great Earth Goddess in her avatar as Leading Old Woman, Ilamateuctli.[77] Her ixiptla, contrary to the rule, was supposed to be sad and give tokens of distress. Dressed all in white, she was made to dance in the morning, while after midday all the gods, in the persons of their priests and also dancing, escorted her up the pyramid steps to be slain.[78] The victim was decapitated and the goddess's priest led a dancing line of gods around the temple top swinging the just-severed head in his hand. For this occasion he wore a hideous two-faced mask, one of the faces looking backward. At some point there was a mock battle between the women of the city, who were pelted with soft missiles by boys or young men. A model grain bin belonging to the goddess was also burnt on the cuauhxicalli by the gods who raced up the temple steps to destroy it, a flower being the prize for the winning of the race.[79] This is to us a curious and confused cult, and we do not really have the key to it.[80] Certainly in some sense it celebrated death, for we know that an ixiptla of Mictlanteuctli was destroyed in this month.[81] But the stress is definitely on the totality of the gods, here presented as being under the presidency of the goddess.

Some, at least, of the Izcalli rites honoring the family dead were initiated in this month and therefore rightly belong here.[82] Images of pinewood were fashioned of those members of the family who had died within the previous four years. But beside these specific references to death in the family, there was also a larger cult statement, for after appropriate midnight ceremonies, an ixiptla of the Lord of the Underworld was escorted to the *tlalxicco* and sacrificed there by the high priest of Cihuacoatl, the underworld god's consort.[83] Thus the year ended on a general salute to death.

"SHOOT, SCION" (IZCALLI)

This month initiated the year and stressed new life. In its quadrennial form it has already been discussed at length in the first chapter and need only be noted here. The annual festival lacked the human sacrifices and some of the ritual aforementioned.

Here we might note that this festival and the preceding one together form a large cult conglomerate dedicated to Cihuacoatl in her two kennings, death and new beginnings. One of our best sources tells us that Izcalli was the first festival that the gods created.

Appendix B
List of Movable Festivals

*(Festivals 3, 8, and 12 are omitted here because they
are considered together in chapter 5)*

The first festival celebrated the sun god known as "Four Movement" (*Tonatiuh*). This feast belonged exclusively to the lodge of Eagle and Jaguar knights, though the people as a whole were also supposed to support the cult by offerings of their blood.[1] It was known from a prophecy anciently left behind by Quetzalcoatl that when the sun failed in his mission and the world ended, it would be on a day Four-Movement. Thus, on this day it was fitting that the sun's chosen people, the knights, should send to their celestial patron an ambassador bearing their petitions and gifts.[2] This ambassador was a war captive carrying a bundle of gifts on his back. He ascended up to the *cuauhxicalli*, proclaimed his message in front of the idol, and there died. Young warriors in training sat in rows piercing their arms and pushing reeds through the incisions. A vast display and banquet of the lords followed, the commoners being excluded.

The second feast celebrated the god Seven Flower, who appears to have been another avatar of the sun but who was here the patron of artists and painters of books. Coincidentally, the goddess Xochiquetzal, patroness of the weaving of beautiful fabrics, was honored by women who specialized in these.

The fourth feast honored the god Two Rabbit (Izquitecatl). This was the festival of all those connected with the growing and harvesting of the maguey plant and the brewing of *octli* from it. The divine plant was honored with singing and dancing.

The fifth festival celebrated the god One Flower who appears to have been an avatar of one of the gods of spring flowers and the new corn. It was mainly a fiesta for the nobles.[3] The ruler announced beforehand how many of the thirteen days of that tonalpohualli week would be allotted to dancing and display.[4] When the celebration was about to begin, two poles entwined with flowers were set up in front of the palace door, and until they were dismantled the ruler continued to dispense gifts and honors to the dancers, singers, and people of the palace.

The sixth festival was dedicated to the god One Reed (Quetzalcoatl).[5] All of the ceremonies took place in the priestly quarters called the *calmecac* within which presided an image of the god. This day was honored exclusively by the nobles, for Quetzalcoatl was not only the god of lineages who protected their legitimacy, but was also One Reed (Ce Acatl), a god of war and therefore of special interest to the privileged class.

The seventh festival belonged to One Death, an avatar of the omniscient Tezcatlipoca and the author of sudden reversals.[6] On this day, slaves were treated cautiously and with kindness. Their wooden collars, presuming that they wore them, were removed. Slaves represented living examples of the god's power to overturn any man's fortune and cast him down.

The ninth festival was dedicated to Four Wind, an avatar of Quetzalcoatl seen under the guise of one of the rain gods.[7] Because this was the day when—as myth had it—hurricanes had destroyed the people of the second aeon, it was peculiarly unlucky and was therefore suitable for the destruction of malefactors.[8] The day was reserved for the merchants, who had an intimate connection with the god Quetzalcoatl, and they honored him by exposing their accumulated wealth in the courtyard of their ward temple.[9] To further celebrate wealth that night, they gave banquets in their homes boasting of their lucrative journeys and mercantile skills while at the same time demeaning those of their peers. This was a celebration of hoarded wealth and mercantile daring.

The tenth movable feast belonged to the god Two Reed, that avatar of Tezcatlipoca who presided over feasting.[10] For this feast, every household of affluence had purchased a pair of idols in the market, one of Tezcatlipoca, the other of Two Reed (Omacatl), and these they venerated at their banquets. When the day came round again in the tonalpohualli the old idols were given to less well-provided households and replaced with new ones. In one of the ball courts of the city that was dedicated to Tezcatlipoca, a series of ixiptlas, here called the *Omacame*, were sacrificed. Like the preceding cult, this one also celebrated wealth but wealth as it was translated into good living.

The eleventh feast celebrated Mexico's patron god Huitzilopochtli in his avatar as One Knife.[11] This involved bringing out the idol's raiment and regalia and displaying them to the rays of the sun.

The thirteenth celebrated One Dog, a form of the fire god.[12] The cult was public, with burnt sacrifices and the installation of a new image of the god, but it was also observed privately with all the great lords and merchants offering feasts in their homes, with the hearth as the center of the rites. On this day it was also customary to hold elections where needed and to designate governors and ambassadors. This opened a four-day celebration with dances, gift giving, and the assignment of honors. At the end it was customary to announce what wars had been decided on.

The fourteenth feast, and the last one, celebrated One Water, a figuration of the goddess of lakes and standing waters, Chalchiuhtlicue.[13] This was basically confined to people whose livelihood was connected with water: canoeists, fishers, reed gatherers, and the like.

Notes

CHAPTER 1. AZTEC CULT AND RITUAL RENEWALS

1. See my discussion of the four basic religious emphases in Aztec religion, Brundage 1982, Introduction.

2. Heyden 1981, pp. 1–6; Heyden 1976, p. 17f.; HMAI, Supplement I, pp. 231–235.

3. Fire was also Father Four Reed, Serna 1953, pp. 203, 249, 367. There are obviously two traditions here, for fire was also One Dog, Caso 1967, pp. 194, 196.

4. Sahagún 1950–1969, 4:111.

5. Hernández 1946, p. 137. This initial offering was called *tlatlazaliztli*, Sahagún 1956, 1:243. In all cases sacrifices to the fire preceded those of all other gods, Serna 1953, p. 65.

6. Las Casas 1966, p. 160.

7. The Tzonmolco was the only legitimate source of purified new fire in the state, excluding of course Mount Huixachtli, Sahagún 1950–1969, 2:190.

8. The *tlexictli* (Torquemada 1969, 2:264) may well have been sited in the temple area belonging to Mictlanteuctli and known as Tlalxicco, "the Navel of the Earth," Torquemada 1969, 2:148. The latter place was where the fire god resided, Sahagún 1950–1969, 6:19. Both localities were attached to the Tlillan. The tlexictli is depicted in *Codex Borbonicus* 1974, plate 34.

9. Sahagún 1950–1969, 2:218.

10. For the four directional avatars of Xiuhteuctli, each differently colored, Sahagún 1950–1969, 2:190.

11. For references to Xiuhteuctli, Brundage 1979, pp. 22–25, and *passim*; *Codex Telleriano-Remensis* 1964, plate 12; Sahagún 1950–1969, 2:168.

12. See note 3.

13. Torquemada 1969, 1:39, p. 147; Ixtlilxochitl 1965a, p. 46. The statement that the god of the Chichimecs was Mixcoatl (Sahagún 1950–1969, 6:34; Sahagún 1956, 2:81) must then be taken to mean that although the sun was central in their religion, they worshipped other gods. See for instance the list of fifteen in *Anales de Cuauhtitlan* 1945, p. 6.

14. Matos 1979, p. 212; see note 3 above.

15. For two slightly contrasting translations, see León-Portilla 1958, p. 73; Sahagún 1950–1969, 2:216f.

16. Durán 1967, 1:108f.

17. Sahagún 1950–1969, 1:131; Sahagún 1956, 1:58f.; Beyer 1965, p. 273; Seler 1963, 2:76.

18. Serna 1953, pp. 167, 294. Piltzinteuctli is identified by Klein (1967, pp. 93–103) as the face on the Sun Stone. See also Sahagún 1958a, pp. 151, 153, 167f.; Olmos 1965, p. 27.

19. Also spelled Xippilli, Sahagún 1950–1969, 2:48. In one understanding, he is the spirit of the spring and green fields, as well as being an aspect of the rising sun, Alvarado Tezozomoc 1944, pp. 95, 211, 407, 410f.

20. *Histoyre du Méchique*, 1905, p. 33.

21. Durán 1967, 1:192–194; Clavijero 1958, 2:279f.

22. Durán 1967, 1–193.

23. Sahagún 1950–1969, 8:55f.

24. Durán 1967, 1:194.

25. Durán 1967, 1:195.

26. Sahagún 1950–1969, 8:45; Sahagún 1956, 2:313.

27. Sahagún 1950–1969, 2:208.

28. Mendieta 1945, 1:153f.; Serna 1953, p. 175.

29. Gómara 1964, p. 147.

30. Sahagún 1950–1969, 2:93.

31. On the two types of drum, Clavijero 1958, 2:278; Motolinía 1967, p. 244; Sahagún 1950–1969, 2:104; Durán 1967, 1:189.

32. Sahagún 1950–1969, 6:74f.

33. Our fullest source for the dance is Durán 1967, chapter 21. But see also Motolinía 1967, pp. 339–343.

34. On the ring dances, Gómara 1964, p. 147f.

35. Muñoz Camargo 1966, p. 135.

36. Motolinía 1967, p. 341; Hernández 1946, p. 94. Clavijero (1958, 2:280) gives the more convincing figure of 2,000.

37. Gómara 1964, p. 147f.

38. For the great variety of dances see Clavijero 1958, 2:279f.; Hernández 1946, 94ff.; Sahagún 1950–1969, 4:25f., 8:45. The professional singer/dancers knew at least three basic styles, those of Huexotzinco, Anahuac, and the Huaxtecs, Sahagún 1950–1969, 8:45, 9:40f.

39. Sahagún 1950–1969, 2:109f., 141.

40. Sahagún 1950–1969, 2:123.

41. Durán 1967, 1:189f.; Sahagún 1950–1969, 8:43, 45.

42. Sahagún 1950–1969, 4:25f.

43. Sahagún 1950–1969, 2:88.

44. Sahagún 1950–1969, 2:208. For the serpent dance and the popcorn dance, Sahagún 1950–1969, 2:75, 143.

45. The calendar and the almanac can best be approached through Caso 1967, *Los Calendarios Prehispánicos*, a series of important articles brought together under one cover.

46. Such a person was referred to as a *nentlacatl*, meaning a nonperson, Sahagún 1950–1969, 2:158; 1956, 1:22f.

47. The Mexica set the beginning of history (i.e., their calendar) with the year One Knife, the date of their departure from Aztlan. The day One Knife was the birthday of their god Huitzilopochtli.

48. Sahagún 1950–1969, 4:25; Durán 1967, 1:233.

49. These are listed in Sahagún 1950–1969, book 4.

50. Sahagún 1950–1969, 2:35–39; Serna 1953, p. 172f.

51. Sahagún 1950–1969, 2:41.

52. Fire was the first thing created by the gods, preceding even the sun, Olmos 1965, p. 25. The fire festival was instituted in the second year after the sky was lifted up, Olmos 1965, p. 33.

53. Clavijero 1958, 2:160; Torquemada 1969, 2:285; Sahagún 1950–1969, 2:162.

54. *Codex Telleriano-Remensis* 1964, 1:12. From *pilquiza*, "to become young again, to be rejuvenated," Símeon 1956, p. 342. Garibay gives the order of events in this cult as (1) eating the specially designated tamales; (2) throwing into the fire the small game caught by boys; (3) kindling new fire; (4) libations to the fire, and drunkenness of the elders; (5) sacrifice of *ixiptlas*, (6) dance of the nobles; and (7) piercing of the children's ears, Garibay 1958, p. 91. My own sequence of events varies somewhat from this.

55. Sahagún 1950–1969, 2:159, 161f., 168.

56. Serna 1953, p. 132f., 194; Sahagún 1950–1969, 2:190. One source says the ruler acted as high priest at the making of the new fire, Torquemada 1969, 2:153.

57. Sahagún 1950–1969, 1:12, 2:160; Hernández 1946, p. 162.

58. Serna 1953, p. 76f.; Sahagún 1950, 2:167.

59. Torquemada 1969, 2:285.

60. Sahagún 1950–1969, 2:190. The richer merchants were able to purchase slaves and prepare them to die as ixiptlas of the fire god, Sahagún 1950–1969, 2:168f. The ixiptlas represented specifically the god Ixcozauhqui, *Codex Magliabecchiano* 1970, plate 46.

61. See chapter 6.

62. This section on the Izcalli sacrifices is based mainly on Sahagún 1950–1969, 2:162ff., 168f.

63. Sahagún 1950–1969, 1:30, 2:34, 164, 191; Torquemada 1969, 2:153.

64. Sahagún 1950–1969, 1:29.

65. Sahagún 1950–1969, 1:30, 2:165, 4:144.

66. For the part played by small children in the Izcalli, see Sahagún 1950–1969, 1:30, 2:33f., 164ff., 169f., 4:144; Torquemada 1969, 2:286; *Codex Telleriano-Remensis* 1964, 1:12.

67. Sahagún 1950–1969, 2:157.

68. There is a discrepancy in our sources (which Sahagún notes, Sahagún 1950–1969, 2:41) concerning the temporal placement of this cult. Pedro de los Ríos (*Telleriano-Remensis* 1964, plate 7; *Vaticanus Latinus 3738* 1964, plate 22) understands it as being a movable feast (i.e., in the *tonalpohualli*), whereas our other sources place it generally in the month of Tepeilhuitl (i.e., in the calendar). I prefer to believe that the festival was fixed in the calendar but could be moved ahead by fiat to another year when and if necessary. The confusion in our sources could have been caused by the similarity in the names of the following three rituals: *xochilhuitl* in the calendar (Xochiquetzal's annual festival during Tepeilhuitl), *chicome xochitl* (a male god known by his date name alone—Sahagún's second movable feast) in the almanac, and *ce xochitl* (Sahagún's fifth movable feast featuring dance and merriment for the palace folk) also in the almanac. Each of these three festivals featured flowers. It is, of course, possible that the rites of the latter two feasts were incorporated in the Atamalcualiztli. See also note 71 below.

69. The choice of eight years as a unit of time may well be related to the fact (well known to the Maya at least) that five synodic periods of Venus equaled eight vague years in the calendar, Aveni 1980, pp. 186, 261f. Caso believes that the Aztec festival does indeed commemorate the completion of the Venus solar cycle, Caso 1958, p. 39.

70. There are numerous translations of this difficult hymn. I have used the one in Sahagún 1950–1969, 2:238f.

71. *Codex Telleriano-Remensis* 1964, plate 5. This assumes that, by priestly juggling or the interpolation of an extra calendrical year, one could make Seven Reed occur somewhere in Tepeilhuitl or Quecholli.

72. The story of the fornication of Quetzalcoatl with the harlot Xochiquetzal in the former's chambers in Tula is surely a popular rendition of this fertility myth.

73. There are many representations of this well-known plate from the *Codex Madrid*. Perhaps the most accessible is to be found in Sahagún 1956, 1: opposite p. 240.

74. Disguises, masks, and mimicry in this celebration are strongly emphasized in all our sources. I do not know why.

75. Sahagún 1950–1969, 2:177f.

76. This myth is well known. See the many references in Brundage 1979.

77. *Codex Borbonicus* 1974, plate 34. Also Nowatny's commentary accompanying the edition, p. 22. For another analysis of this festival, Saenz 1967, p. 20ff.

78. For the New Fire ceremony at this spot, Brundage 1979, pp. 25ff.

79. Torquemada 1969, 1:210.

80. Aveni 1980, pp. 31–35. The Pleiades were known as *miec* (the bevy or crowd) or *tianquiztli* (the market—implying a crowd).

81. Sahagún 1950–1969, 7:26.

82. There is a good description of the dispersal of the New Fire in Sahagún 1950–1969, 7:29f.

83. Caso 1967, pp. 134–140.

CHAPTER 2. DEFINITIONS AND REDUCTION OF THE DIVINE

1. For examples of personal piety, Sahagún 1956, 1:24 f.

2. Motolinía 1951, p. 106f.

3. Brundage 1979, p. 50.

4. The only Aztec demons I am familiar with who had a fully developed cult were the Cihuateteo, and we must note from their names that they were of the nature of *teotl*. The word for "divine," or "sacred thing" (*Estudios de Cultura Nahuatl* VI, 88; Molina 1944, I, 107) is *teoyo*, which of course suggests plenty of leeway. The *malteotl*, for instance, was nothing more than a fetish, Sahagún, 1950–1969, 2:60.

5. On the mask pool, Brundage 1979, pp. 50–53.

6. Spencer and Jennings 1965, p. 314f.; Underhill 1965, p. 208.

7. *Ixiptla* is actually the noun in its possessive form. The absolute form **ixiptlatl* does not seem to occur in the texts; it is assumed, but not documented, Andrews 1975, p. 446. Siméon does, however, list it.

8. On the demonic, Brundage 1979, p. 62ff. See also note 4. Mictlan-teuctli, who might be classed as partially demonic, could occasionally have an ixiptla, see note 10. So also could Cihuateotl, though whether her plural identities, the Cihuateteo, were represented by ixiptlas is unclear.

9. Durán 1967, 2:467.

10. Sahagún 1950–1969, 2:180f.

11. Brundage 1979, p. 67f. The ixiptla of Tezcatlipoca as Tloque Nahuaque, mentioned by Sahagún (1950–1969, 6:34), is there simply a literary, not a cultic, use of the word.

12. Sahagún 1950–1969, 1:45.

13. Sahagún 1950–1969, 1:68.

14. Sahagún 1950–1969, 2:68; Serna 1953, p. 185.

15. Sahagún 1950–1969, 2:66ff.

16. Pomar 1971, p. 10f. The *calpixqui* kept a reserve of about ten presentable captives who might play Titlacahuan's role. The one chosen for the part received special training; Sahagún 1950–1969, 2:66, 68.

17. Durán 1967, 1:59; Acosta 1962, p. 253.

18. On the ixiptla's perambulations, Durán 1967, 1:59; Sahagún 1950–1969, 2:68–71. Pomar (1971, p. 10f.) gives us the information that the ixiptla wandered about only at night, and we can accept this if we are thinking mainly of the cult in Tezcoco.

19. Sahagún 1950–1969, 2:70.

20. Every fourth celebration of the ixiptla's death in the Toxcatl, however, other victims, called "prisoners taken for his food," were sacrificed, Durán 1967, 1:44.

21. Clavijero 1958, 2:143; Serna 1953, p. 185.

22. See note 20.

23. For the Ochpaniztli festival see appendix A.

24. For this cult, Durán 1967, 1:137–141.

25. Sahagún 1950–1969, 2:120ff. Sahagún does not clearly distinguish Chicomecoatl here from Toci. Logic would seem to assign the Ochpaniztli cult to the former, yet the latter's rites, perhaps because of their exotic quality, do seem to encompass the others. Durán definitely assigns the month to Toci, Durán 1967, book I, chapter 14, and accompanying illustration. *Codex Borbonicus* (plates 29–31) assigns the rites of the month to Chicomecoatl with Toci and her ithyphallic Huaxtecs serving as accessories. We find that the corresponding goddesses involved in the Ochpaniztli festival in *Codex Telleriano-Remensis* (1964, 1:5) are Xochiquetzal and Tlazolteotl, a matching pair.

26. Motolinía 1951, p. 119; 1967, p. 63.

27. Torquemada 1969, 2:151.

28. Motolinía 1967, p. 64; 1951, p. 119.

29. Torquemada 1969, 2:119; Las Casas 1966, p. 86.

30. Sahagún 1950–1969, 2:42; Torquemada 1969, 2:120.

31. Sahagún 1950–1969, 2:43f.

32. The children walled up in caves became afterward indistinguishable from the Tlaloque living blissful lives inside the mountains, Torquemada 1969, 2:151.

33. This rite, held at the Pantitlan in the lake, was a logical accessory to the cult of Tlaloc on the mountainside.

34. An attractive theory—but nothing more than a theory—is the connection these Tlaloque may have with the children prominently displayed in early Olmec art.

35. There is an exhaustive description of the dough image of Huitzilopochtli in Sahagún 1950–1969, 12:51ff. See also Durán 1967, 1:28, 156, 271f.

36. Ponce de León 1965, p. 373; Clavijero 1958, 2:158; Torquemada 1969, 1:73; Sahagún 1950–1969, 3:5f.

37. Sahagún 1950–1969, 1:47ff.

38. Torquemada 1969, 2:64, 279.

39. Sahagún 1950–1969, 2:23; Torquemada 1969, 2:279; Hernández 1946, p. 156; Clavijero 1958, 2:155.

40. Among the Chichimecs of Michoacán it was believed that the gods descended to earth on poles or trees, *Chronicles of Michoacán*, 1970, p. 185. Tree worship was common everywhere in Mesoamerica, Motolinía 1951, p. 107f.; Mendieta 1945, 1:94; Cervantes de Salazar 1914, p. 35.

41. *Tlacateteuhtin*, Sahagún 1950–1969, 2:42.

42. Durán 1967, 1:86–89.

43. For a fuller treatment of Xochiquetzal see Brundage 1979, pp. 159–162.

44. For a summary of the festival, see appendix A.

45. Chapter 1, *The Izcalli Festival*.

46. These meetings of all the gods (with the sole exception of the cosmogonic myths—where however the totality of gods is immediately lost in delegation) are neither described nor hinted at in Aztec myth. I believe that the gods were assembled *in cult* in splendid and showy concourse, as mentioned in the text, mainly for reasons of theatrical éclat.

CHAPTER 3. NODAL POINTS OF MEETING

1. *Anales de Cuauhtitlan*, 1945, p. 30.

2. Sahagún 1950–1969, 2:159.

3. The "little ones" were pervasive and probably very old. Sahagún (1950–1969, 1:47–49) treats them as dough images, but they were made of other materials as well, such as yarn, Torquemada 1969, 2:64. They were common in all homes, both high and low, and at street crossings and fountains, Clavijero 1958, 2:83.

4. Serna 1953, p. 315, 324.

5. The *tlaquimilolli* could be a piece of wood crudely carved to represent a god and wrapped in a bundle, Mendieta 1945, 1:85f.; Torquemada 1969, 2:78. Huitzilopochtli, Itzpapalotl, and Quetzalcoatl could be carried about in this fashion or installed in temples. *Codex Nuttall* (1975, plate 15) and the *Selden Roll* have clear depictions of these.

6. Mendieta 1945, 1:85ff.; Torquemada 1969, 2:78. In the case of Huitzilopochtli, the image called Paynal was probably a tlaquimilolli designed to be carried about with ease.

7. *Anales de Cuauhtitlan*, 1945, p. 51.

8. Alarcón 1953, p. 31; Serna 1953, p. 94.

9. *Handbook of Middle American Indians* 1964–1976, 10:122f., 125; Ixtlilxochitl 1956b, p. 457.

10. *Manuscript Tovar* 1972, p. 95. In Tezcoco Texcatlipoca's black idol was seated, Pomar 1971, p. 10; Durán 1967, 1:37.

11. Alvarado Tezozomoc 1944, p. 366.

12. Las Casas 1966, pp. 55, 90f.; Torquemada 1969, 2:290; Motolinía 1967, p. 77.

13. Sahagún 1950–1969, 2:179.

14. Sahagún 1950–1969, 2:175.

15. Pomar 1971, p. 14.

16. References to small domestic images of the great gods are frequent, particularly those of Huitzilopochtli, Tezcatlipoca, Quetzalcoatl, and Tlazolteotl, Sahagún 1950–1969, 7:25. See also note 3.

17. See chapter 1, *The Atamalcualiztli Festival*.

18. The exact siting of all the places in the *ithualli* mentioned in Sahagún, 1950–1969, 2:175–193 (and further depicted in Sahagún's plan, see Seler, 1960, 2:771) is not possible. Marquina's reconstruction (1960) has been standard but there is room for disagreement on his details. The recent excavations under Matos help greatly in one area.

19. Sahagún (1950–1969, 2:179–193) specifically names certain gods worshipped in the ithualli. At the same time, we hear from other sources of these gods being worshipped in shrines in the calpullis outside. An instance is the merchant's god Yacateuctli worshipped in the calpulli called *Pochtlan* in the city—but his shrine in the ithualli was also called *Pochtlan*. It is probable that in such cases of duplication, the shrine in the calpulli was primary, whereas the ithualli shrine was used for citywide or state purposes.

20. Mendieta 1945, 1:91; Torquemada 1969, 2:140f.; Motolinía 1951, p. 136.

21. Sahagún 1956, 1:242.

22. Sahagún 1956, 1:241.

23. The number of temples in the Mexican ithualli is unclear. Motolinía says that in the typically large Aztec enclosure there were from twelve to fifteen temples, Motolinía 1951, p. 137. Durán (1967, 1:22) says there were four principal temples, each assigned to one of the four directions, whereas altogether there were ten or twelve temples in the enclosure, 1:190. Elsewhere he says eight or nine (1:20) in which number he probably does not include the great central temple. See here Acosta 1962, p. 38.

24. Herrera 1944–1947, 3:236; Gómara 1964, p. 166.

25. Sahagún 1950–1969, 12:55.

26. See note 23.

27. Clavijero (1958, 2:93) says there were five priestly edifices and three houses for male and female acolytes.

28. Weaver 1981, p. 74.

29. The entrances of some temples were in fact designed to represent the open maw of the earth monster, Klein 1976, p. 146ff.

30. For a summary of the myth see Brundage 1979, p. 137ff.

31. Ibid., p. 140f.

32. Durán 1967, 2:49. As a religious building this was classed by Alvarado Tezozomoc as an *ayauhcalli*, a "house of mist."

33. Matos Moctezuma 1981, pp. 19–23.

34. The matching two "Red Temples" (so called by the excavators), symmetrically placed north and south of the main temple, are puzzles, *El Templo Mayor* 1981, pp. 259–267; Matos Moctezuma 1981, pp. 37–41. They face east, thus opposing the orientation of the great temple. One of them produced an offering cache containing musical instruments in stone, *El Templo Mayor* 1981, pp. 265, 267.

35. Ixtlilxochitl 1965a, p. 382. The figure is given as 120 by Durán 1967, 1:19. Bernal Díaz gives 140.

36. In the days of the Spaniards there was a true *techcatl* in front of Tlaloc's shrine (Sahagún 1950–1969, 2:133). Whether this replaced the earlier *chacmool* is not known. See next note.

37. A chacmool was placed before the Tlaloc shrine in the earliest level yet recovered (reign of Huitzilihuitl). Sahagún tells us, however, that by the time of the Conquest this had been replaced by a techcatl, *El Templo Mayor* 1981, p. 138. What this cult change meant we do not know. For the suggestion that the chacmool represents Tlalteuctli, Matos 1979, p. 209.

38. *El Templo Mayor* 1981, pp. 132f., 164f.

39. Pomar 1971, p. 13f.

40. *El Templo Mayor* 1981, p. 81.

41. Ibid., p. 58.

42. García Cook and M. Arana, n.d.; Matos Moctezuma 1981, p. 37.

43. *El Templo Mayor* 1981, p. 58. There is a good possibility that there were two *xiuhcoatl* heads, one for each of the staircases, Marquina 1960, p. 53. Note that there are two contrasting types of "dragons" at the Temple Mayor, the feathered serpent representing Quetzalcoatl, and the nonfeathered serpent for Tlaloc, *El Templo Mayor* 1981, p. 188.

44. Durán 1967, 1:20; 2:333. It is difficult to understand where these "bestiones" were placed. Durán gives the Nahuatl word as *tzitzimites*. It is

of course possible that Durán misinterpreted the nature of the stone banner-men flanking the shrine entrances.

45. *El Templo Mayor* 1981, p. 63. Coatlicue and Cihuacoatl are prac-tically interchangeable; either can figure as Huitzilopochtli's mother.

46. Ibid., pp. 205f., 216–219.

47. In a paper dealing with autosacrifice in the temenos and presented at the Dumbarton Oaks symposium, Cecelia Klein adduced persuasive evidence for siting the Tlacochcalco and the Tlacatecco on the north and south sides of the Templo Mayor, respectively. The former she equates with the edifice uncovered by the excavators and called by them the "House of the Eagles"; the latter, suggestions of which are known to Matos and others, still lies under the modern city. My own sense of the general layout of buildings in the sacred precinct owes much to Klein's crucial identifications.

48. In the aforementioned paper, Klein has also thrown additional light on autosacrificial practices as being an important part of the political fur-niture of the Aztec elite in Tenochtitlan. I am indebted to her for elucidating this nonreligious aspect of royal and noble autosacrifice.

49. The Tlillan (Cihuacoatl) must not be confused with the Coatlan (Coatlicue). These two goddesses are confused in the mythology, but seem-ingly not in cult. Cihuacoatl was the Earth Mother in the nuclear state cult; Coatlicue was the Earth Mother worshipped in the third calendar month, be-ing thought of in connection with the first flowers of spring as well as being a terrifying presence. She had her shrine in the city ward of Coatlan—not to be confused with the shrine of the same name in the ithualli, Sahagún 1950–1969, 2:57.

50. Cortés and his secretary (Gómara 1964, p. 165) present the Tlillan as three flat-roofed buildings. Durán is more detailed, but unclear, Durán 1967, 1:130f., 2:301f. See also Torquemada 1969, 1:235, 2:146f.; Herrera 1944–1947, 3:255f.

51. Durán 1967, 1:130.

52. Durán 1967, 1:127f., 129f.

53. See chapter 1, *The Role of Fire in the Aztec Religion*.

54. Apparently the same as Tecanman, Sahagún 1950–1969, 2:184, 209.

55. Again there is confusion. Sahagún (1950–1969, 2:182) is quite ex-plicit that the Coacalco was a prison for captive gods and therefore belonged to the Tlillan complex. He then calls it an apartment for visiting lords, Sahagún 1950–1969, 8:44. The word is to be thought of as meaning a "gathering place," a communal hall or the like, and thus possibly designates two different buildings, one in the temenos, the other attached to the palace.

56. In Mexico-Tenochtitlan there was a barrio known as Huitznahuac, and we must assume therefore that the temple of that avatar of the sun was

located there, Sahagún 1956, 1:210, 212, 229, 232, 235. The name of the temple is given as Coatlan, Torquemada 1969, 2:155. Attached to the temple was a ball court called *Tezcatlachco*, Torquemada 1969, 2:151. The close connection of Huitzilopochtli with the god Huitznahua (Sahagún 1950–1969, 2:71) would imply, however, that some type of shrine to the Huitznahua existed also in the temenos, see Garibay 1958, p. 42f. The Huitznahuac is once depicted with its facade decorated with white circles (i.e., stars) set in a black background, *Codex Mendocino* 1964, part II, plate 19.

57. Sahagún 1956, 1:237; Torquemada 1969, 2:152; Clavijero 1958, 2:93. A clearly related rite is depicted in *Codex Borgia* 1976 (plates 19, 45) where Tlahuizcalpanteuctli is shown at the foot of a tree (a pillar equivalent) on a *tzompantli*. For the Venus pillar cult, Brundage 1982, pp. 177–180.

58. *Anales de Cuauhtitlan* 1945, p. 11f.; *Codex Cospi* 1968, pp. 9–11; Thompson 1972, pp. 64, 67.

59. Durán 1967, 1:99f., 105f.

60. For a reproduction, *El Templo Mayor* 1981, p. 77. An exact identification of the god in the center may not be possible. Yohualteuctli has been suggested (Klein 1976, pp. 110–113), Tlalteuctli (Navarrette and Heyden 1975), and others. The god's date name however is obvious, Four Movement.

61. Durán 1967, 2:268; Beyer 1965, pp. 257–260.

62. Beyer 1965, pp. 254f., 261–265.

63. Durán 1967, 1:107.

64. On the *cuauhxicalli*, Durán 1967, 1:100, 107; Torquemada 1969, 2:148; Sahagún 1950–1969, 2:181. On the temalacatl, Sahagún 1950–1969, 2:190; Torquemada 1969, 2:154.

65. Sahagún 1950–1969, 2:191.

66. For a résumé, see Brundage 1979, pp. 8–12; 1982, pp. 214–224.

67. Sahagún (1950–1969, 2:179–193) lists six skull racks within the temenos, attaching them to the cults of the following gods: Mixcoatl, Xiuhteuctli, Omacatl, Huitzilopochtli, Xipe, and Yacateuctli. The great skull rack is well described in Durán 1967, 1:23. A more average skull rack is described in Sahagún 1956, 1:233.

68. Alvarado Tezozomoc 1944, p. 333; Gómara 1964, p. 167.

69. Herrera 1944–1947, 3:238.

70. Durán 1967, 1:49.

71. Durán 1967, 1:48. We are told that the Tlacochcalco was one of two temples of Tezcatlipoca, the other being the Huitznahuac, *Codex Magliabecchi* 1970, plate 36. Seler equates these two as shrines of the northern and southern Tezcatlipoca, Seler 1963, 1:215. This would then be the sun at the solstices. But see note 47 that might then give us the interpretation that the Huitznahuac was another name for the Tlacatecco.

72. Sahagún 1956, 2:62.

73. Sahagún 1950–1969, 2:192.

74. "The Place of the Shrilling Sound," the voice of the wind according to Seler 1960, 2:957f. Sahagún implies that Quetzalcoatl was worshipped there in his avatar of Nine Wind.

75. Durán 1967, 1:64f.

76. Aveni 1980, p. 248f.

77. Durán 1967, 1:65f.

78. *Estudios de Cultura Náhuatl*, 6:178ff.

79. Sahagún 1950–1969, 4:29, 7:29; Alvarado Tezozomoc 1944, p. 275f.

80. Beginning with Cortés himself, the Spaniards were interested in these Aztec universities that produced not only the priests but also trained warriors, courtiers, judges, treasurers, and even artisans, Sahagún 1956, 2:317, 3:78f. References to the calmecac are abundant in our Colonial sources.

81. Sahagún 1950–1969, 8:18f.; Clavijero 1958, 3:89.

82. Motolinía 1951, p. 138.

83. Durán 1971, p. 229ff.

84. Clavijero 1958, 2:74f.

85. In general a place where a god was worshipped was *ichal itzacual*, "his waiting place, his covert," that is, "his pyramid," Garibay 1964–1968, 2:5, lxxi; Torquemada 1969, 2:40. More specific was the *momoztli*, a circular stone base used as a shrine in marketplaces, on roadsides, and mountaintops. Boughs and food for the spirits were placed on them. Durán states that the word was taken from *momoztlae*, which means "daily." Thus the shrine was a daily place, Durán 1967, 1:172. *Teolocholli* were simply piles of stones cast by travelers alongside the trail, Serna 1953, pp. 92f., 244. The *ayauhcalli*, "mist house," was a covered shrine by the waterside, used generally in the cult of Tlaloc. The island city of Tenochtitlan had one at each of its four cardinal waterfronts, Sahagún 1950–1969, 2:81. In much the same fashion, four altars were placed around springs at each of their four cardinal points, the whole forming a cross, Motolinía 1967, p. 33.

CHAPTER 4. THE MEDIATORS

1. For a résumé on the Mexican *nahualli*, Brundage 1979, p. 182ff.

2. Sahagún 1950–1969, 4:101.

3. Sahagún 1950–1969, 4:50, 102.

4. Sahagún 1950–1969, 4:42ff.

5. Molina 1944, 2:113. The word comes from *texoxa*, "to bewitch some-

one," specifically "to stare at someone in order to enchant them," Molina 1944, 2:162.

6. For the many synonyms in Nahuatl for "sorcerer" and "possessed one," Molina 1944, 1:53, 70.

7. Sahagún 1950–1969, 10:30.

8. These two titles applied to the same learned priest, Sahagún 1950–1969, 4:142, 6:197f., 10:31; Sahagún 1956, 1:315.

9. Sahagún 1956, 2:185; Clavijero 1958, 2:166.

10. Sahagún 1956, 2:169f., 172, 174.

11. *Codex Magliabecchi* 1970, plate 77.

12. Brundage 1982, p. 97f.

13. The female curer is shown casting the maize kernels as dice in *Codex Magliabecchi* 1970, p. 78.

14. Sahagún 1956, 1:47f.

15. Durán 1967, 1:54.

16. For the role of the suffering priesthood, see especially the rites observed in the Etzalcualiztli festival, Sahagún 1950–1969, 2:78–90. See also Durán 1967, 1:55.

17. Sahagún 1950–1969, 1:75, 6:35; Ponce 1965, p. 375. On the ambiguity in the term *tlamacazqui*, see Garibay 1953, 1:139 footnote.

18. Motolinía 1967, p. 33

19. Pomar 1971, p. 14f.

20. Ixtlilxochitl 1965b, p. 39.

21. For Tlaloc in Teotihuacan, Brundage 1982, pp. 149–158.

22. Brundage 1979, p. 140 (quoting Chimalpahin).

23. Brundage 1982.

24. Sahagún 1950–1969, 6:17, 41, 43–45, 50. The Mexican ruler was also considered quite naturally to be a place holder for Huitzilopochtli, Durán 1967, 2:62; Torquemada 1967, 1:123f.; *Manuscript Tovar* 1972, pp. 30, 32; Hernández 1946, p. 52.

25. Sahagún 1950–1969, 6:63.

26. Sahagún 1950–1969, 6:25.

27. Durán 1967, 2:317; Hernández 1946, p. 47; Las Casas 1966, p. 146.

28. Durán 1967, 2:464.

29. Torquemada 1969, 2:298; Gómara 1964, pp. 210, 213; Durán 1967, 2:188, 213.

30. Hernández 1946, p. 52. See also Pomar 1971, pp. 12, 36.

31. Torquemada 1969, 2:298.

32. Sahagún 1950–1969, 6:52.

33. Acosta 1962, p. 229; *Codex Ramírez* 1944, p. 153.

34. *Codex Ramírez* 1944, p. 83.

35. Sahagún 1956, 1:308. We note that there were also four ages within which priests were classified, boyhood, youth (these were the *tlamacazque* per se), mature men, and elders, Durán 1967, 1:50.

36. Torquemada 1969, 2:222.

37. Durán 1967, 1:48f.

38. Durán 1967, 1:27.

39. Durán 1967, 1:25, 27.

40. Torquemada 1969, 2:184f.

41. The cult of the Tezcatlipoca young people was referred to simply as "the youth," *telpochtiliztli*, after the name of the god's avatar, Telpochtli, Torquemada 1969, 2:220; Clavijero 1958, 2:110. Those who showed aptitude for the priesthood could be moved into the *tlamacazcalli*, Durán 1967, 1:50.

42. León-Portilla 1958, pp. 75–79.

43. On all matters concerning Quetzalcoatl as a priest, Brundage 1982, chapter 3.

44. Durán 1967, 1:65.

45. Durán 1967, 1:14.

46. Torquemada 1969, 2:221.

47. Sahagún 1950–1969, 7:27.

48. Sahagún 1950–1969, 2:197.

49. Clavijero 1958, 2:110.

50. Durán 1967, 1:153.

51. Durán 1967, 1:131.

52. Las Casas 1966, p. 70; Pomar 1971, p. 22.

53. Hernández 1946, p. 22.

54. Sahagún 1950–1969, 2:208; Torquemada 1969, 2:184.

55. Sahagún 1950–1969, 12:53f.

56. Sahagún 1950–1969, 4:78; Sahagún 1956, 1:275f.

57. Sahagún 1950–1969, 2:44, note 17.

58. Sahagún 1950–1969, 2:207.

59. Sahagún 1950–1969, 2:212.

60. Sahagún 1950–1969, 2:83.

61. Sahagún (1950–1969, 2:206–215) lists nineteen *teohuas* of high rank, each attached to a separate god's cult. All of them were under the supervision of the *Mexicatl teohua*, that is, "the one who has the Mexican god," p. 206.

62. The difference—if there is any—between the *teopixqui* and the *teohua* is unclear. Sahagún refers to the teohua of Huitzilopochtli as an "in-

timate" (*privado*) of the god. He is not to be confused with the *quetzalcoatl* or high priest, Sahagún 1956, 1:274.

63. Sahagún 1956, 1:162.

64. *Codex Mendocino* 1964, lxvf. (where they are pictured and referred to as *alfaquí*, who is in Spanish "a Moslem learned man."

65. Sahagún 1950, 8:52f.

66. Durán 1967, 1:30 f.; Torquemada 1969, 2:117.

67. Olmos 1965, p. 79; Torquemada 1969, 2:117, 175; Motolinía 1967, p. 44; Mendieta 1945, 1:108. These priests were called *papahuaque*, from *papahtli*, "tangled or unwashed hair," Durán 1967, 1:50f.; Molina 1944, 1:23.

68. *Anales de Cuauhtitlan* 1945, p. 32.

69. Torquemada 1969, 1:191.

70. Sahagún 1956, 1:248f., 307f.

71. Sahagún 1956, 2:212.

72. Torquemada 1969, 2:147.

73. Sahagún 1950–1969, 3:69; Motolinía 1967, p. 43f.; Pomar 1971, p. 22.

74. Torquemada 1969, 2:177.

75. Ixtlilxochitl 1965b, pp. 178, 218; *Códice de Azcatitlan*, p. 114.

76. In Mexico the office was passed down in the family of Tlacaelel, Motolinía 1967, pp. 123, 125.

77. Torquemada 1969, 2:352. The *cihuacoatl* was in charge of Mexico during the absence of the ruler, Alvarado Tezozomoc 1944, p. 435. For ceremonies he wore the "eagle clothes" of the goddess, Durán 1967, 2:431; Motolinía 1967, p. 129.

78. Pomar 1971, p. 22.

79. León-Portilla 1958, pp. 47, 49, 59; Sahagún 1956, 1:242f.

80. Sahagún 1950–1969, 2:216.

81. Durán 1967, 1:152f.

82. Note 80.

83. Muñoz Camargo 1966, p. 159.

84. León-Portilla 1958, pp. 71, 73.

85. Sahagún 1950–1969, 7:11.

86. Sahagún 1956, 1:306; Sahagún 1950–1969, 8:57, 81; *Codex Ramírez* 1944, p. 147f. These night journeys were essentially a part of the cult of Tezcatlipoca. A priest could undertake a night journey as part of a curing, *Manuscript Tovar* 1972, p. 100f.

87. In the Mixcoatl mythology, the knife was the goddess Itzpapalotl, Sahagún 1950–1969, 6:14; Brundage 1979, p. 171ff. A similar god (Itztapaltotec) was specifically the obsidian knife.

88. For the conch-shell in the cult of Quetzalcoatl, Brundage 1982, pp. 72, 79.

89. Séjourné 1969, p. 214.

90. For a representation, Matos Moctezuma 1981, foto 28.

91. Weaver 1981, pp. 74, 79, 124.

92. For Tezcatlipoca's connection with the mirror, Brundage 1979, p. 81f.

93. Sahagún 1950–1969, 2:85.

94. Sahagún 1950–1969, 2:88.

95. Sahagún 1950–1969, 7:46.

96. Séjourné 1969, p. 278. In late iconography Quetzalcoatl is associated with other staves, see examples in the Mixtec *Codices Nuttall* and *Vindobonensis*. It is probable that the *chicahuaztli* staff is also the sacred tree in Cholula (worshipped by Quetzalcoatl) called the *chicahualizteotl*, Ixtlilxochitl 1965a, p. 23f.

97. This is backed up by *Codex Borbonicus* 1974, plate 24. In this case, the point of the staff would be a *tonalmitl*, "sunbeam," Molina 1944, 1:101.

CHAPTER 5. THE DRAMATIZATION OF
CONFLICT AND HOSTILITY

1. Sahagún 1950–1969, 6:14.

2. Here follows a presentation of Tezcatlipoca tailored for the purpose of this book only. For a fuller consideration, see Brundage 1979, chapter 4; 1982, chapter 6.

3. Sahagún 1950–1969, 1:5.

4. Sahagún 1950–1969, 2:37.

5. The flower war has been treated in general terms in Brundage 1979, pp. 205–208. Here we view it as a part of cult.

6. Most of the poems in Garibay's three volume collection (1964–1968) display this obsessive view of the knights as lovely flowers.

7. Pomar 1971, p. 46.

8. Hernández 1946, p. 66. Battlegrounds designated especially for the flower wars were *yaotlalli*, Clavijero 1958, 2:240.

9. The antagonists arrived to pitch camp at the battlefield on the day preceding, Pomar 1971, p. 47. This time was probably reserved for display and cult performances.

10. Alvarado Tezozomoc 1944, p. 462.

11. Chimalpahin 1965, p. 152.

12. Alvarado Tezozomoc 1944, p. 482.

13. Tlacaelel, the leading Aztec voice on war, proclaimed that valor was even more important to the knight than legitimacy, Durán 1967, 2:237.

14. Brundage 1979, pp. 196–200.

15. Ixtlilxochitl 1965a, p. 257.

16. *Carta de Molina,* in *Colección de Documentos para la Historia de México* 1858, 1:272.

17. Hernández 1946, p. 67.

18. Pomar 1971, p. 38.

19. Ahuitzotl. The occasion was the dedication of the newly enlarged temple of Huitzilopochtli.

20. There are conflicting accounts of the Tlacahuepan incident. Perhaps the most acceptable is in Durán 1967, 2:433–437.

21. Because of the importance of *tlachtli* in Mesoamerican life, I have dealt with it at length in Brundage 1979, pp. 8–12; 1982, pp. 214–224. Here I am expanding my view of it as a cultic reading of cosmic process and have seen it as a divine conflict (among the gods) as opposed to human battle (the flower war).

22. Coe and Diehl 1980, 1:393.

23. The role of Xolotl in the ball game is documented in Brundage 1982, chapter 5.

24. *Codex Borbonicus* 1974, plate 27.

25. Alvarado Tezozomoc 1944, p. 13.

26. See note 23.

27. Corona Núñez 1957, p. 22.

28. Motolinía 1967, p. 337f.

29. Garibay 1958, p. 152f.

30. Sahagún 1950–1969, 2:120.

31. Torquemada 1969, 2:187.

32. Durán 1967, 1:51f.; Clavijero 1958, 2:105.

33. León-Portilla 1958, p. 73.

34. Sahagún 1956, 1:248.

35. *Codex Borgia* 1976, plates 29–46.

36. For the avatars of Quetzalcoatl and their movement one into the other, see Brundage 1982.

37. Sahagún 1950–1969, 6:37.

38. Brundage 1979, p. 62f.

39. Sahagún 1950–1969, 1:6, 2:37, 4:41, 81.

40. Motolinía 1967, pp. 92–95.

41. Sahagún 1950–1969, 4:81.

42. One House is not given by Sahagún as one of the movable feasts, but on that day the demonic goddesses were known to descend, *Codex Telleriano-Remensis* 1964, plate 22. For the other three feasts see Sahagún 1950–1969, 2:36–38.

43. Serna 1953, pp. 177, 179f.

44. Sahagún 1950–1969, 1:19. Specimens of these multiple idols can be seen today in the Aztec hall of the Museo Nacional de Antropologia.

45. Brundage 1979, p. 173f.

CHAPTER 6. SACRIFICE AS A SUBSTITUTE FOR RENEWAL

1. Sahagún 1950–1969, 6:93.

2. Weaver 1981, p. 44.

3. Olmec iconography constantly features a curious infantile being, sometimes held in the laps of the kings. This creature may not be a proto-Tlaloc, but does point to the use of children in cult. Misshapen and dwarfed human beings were still being offered to the Tlalocs in Aztec days; see the projected sacrifice of a hunchback in a Popocatepetl cave, Olmos 1965, p. 26.

4. On the Tlaloque and their mountain homes, Brundage 1979, p. 71f.

5. Children offered to Tlaloc were *teihzoque*, *Codex Magliabecchi* 1970, plate 34 (see also plate 32), from the verb *ihzo*, "to make a blood sacrifice."

6. Torquemada 1969, 2:119; Las Casas 1966, p. 86.

7. Motolinía 1951, p. 119.

8. Matos Moctezuma 1981, p. 37.

9. The Aztecs were certainly the world's most notable headhunters, Motolinía 1951, p. 127; 1967, p. 72; Gómara 1964, p. 167.

10. Sahagún 1950–1969, 2:49, 114.

11. Durán 1967, 2:143; Sahagún 1956, 1:188.

12. See chapter 2, *The Ixiptla.*

13. Serna 1953, p. 188.

14. Mendieta 1945, 1:145f.; Sahagún 1956, 1:112, 146. The captor and his whole family were cleansed of guilt in the matter of this death by penitential deprivations for twenty days thereafter, Sahagún 1950–1969, 2:59.

15. Sahagún 1958a, p. 179f.; *Anales de Cuauhtitlan* 1945, p. 13. It may have been ultimately a rite originating in the north, *Historia Tolteca-Chichimeca* 1976, plate F.28r; Torquemada 1969, 2:291.

16. Durán 1967, 1:140.

17. Hernández 1946, p. 67; Mendieta 1945, 1:144; Motolinía 1967, p. 299.

18. Sahagún 1950–1969, 1:32.

19. Durán 1967, 2:465; Alvarado Tezozomoc 1944, p. 347f.

20. Sahagún 1956, 2:314.

21. Torquemada 1969, 2:536, 541; Clavijero 1958, 2:242.

22. Motolinía 1951, p. 116.

23. A person in either category can be referred to as *teomicqui*, "one who has died for the god," Sahagún 1950–1969, 2:197. The souls of magnates and warriors became clouds and beautiful birds; commoners became vermin, Torquemada 1969, 2:82.

24. Durán 1967, 1:64.

25. Durán 1967, 1:181.

26. Sahagún 1956, 1:226.

27. Sahagún 1950–1969, 2:141–144.

28. Sahagún 1950–1969, 2:88.

29. Sahagún 1950–1969, 2:94. The *pepechhuan* were thought of as companions of the *ixiptla* after his or her death.

30. See appendix B, *First Movable Feast*. To prevent the world ending on the day Four Movement, all the lords fasted the previous four days, *Codex Telleriano-Remensis* 1964, 2:2. For details of the ritual, Durán 1967, 1: chapter 10; Sahagún 1950–1969, 4:6f.

31. Sahagún 1956, 1:143.

32. Durán gives full details of the procedures of sacrifice, 1967 1·23f, 2:172ff.

33. Gómara 1964, p. 87; *Codex Vaticanus Latinus 3738* 1964, plate lxxiv.

34. Olmos 1965, p. 44f.; Sahagún 1950–1969, 2:143.

35. Sahagún 1950–1969, 2:47.

36. Sahagún 1950–1969, 2:94. I am indebted to Dr. Arthur J. O. Anderson for the reference to the sawfish bill used in Huixtocihuatl's cult.

37. Sahagún 1950–1969, 2:48.

38. Motolinía 1951, p. 115. Bodies of "bathed ones" were not sent tumbling down but were carried down the pyramid steps, Motolinía 1967, p. 59. The bathed one, who was always a slave, went after death to Mictlan, unlike the warrior who ascended into the heavens. Thus the distinction was made between a mere mortal and a *cuauhtecatl*, who was a "son of the sun," Alvarado Tezozomoc 1944, p. 216, 253.

39. Alvarado Tezozomoc (1944, p. 333) tells us that in ceremonies where many were killed at a time, the bodies were taken out to a sacred spot in the lake and there dumped. The fact that some headless bodies were taken back to the various *calpullis* for eating meant that the limbs were still attached, Sahagún 1950–1969, 2:24.

40. Sahagún 1950–1969, 2:114.

41. Sahagún 1950–1969, 2:60; Sahagún 1956, 1:149.

42. Only nobles and knights were allowed to eat human flesh, Durán 1967, 2:195.

43. We have two depictions of this event, the first one in *Codex Telleriano-Remensis* 1964, 4:19, the second a dated piece of sculpture commemorating the event, and which is now in the Museo Nacional de Antropología. The event is mentioned by many Colonial sources, attesting to the impression it made. Our most consecutive account and the one we use here for the bulk of the details, is Durán 1967, 2: chapter 43.

44. *Codex Telleriano-Remensis* gives the figure 4,000, and then again 20,000. Chimalpahin (1965, pp. 111, 220f.) gives a figure 10,600, and then again 56,600. Ixtlilxochitl (1965a, p. 273) and the *Anales de Cuauhtitlan* (1945, p. 58) both give 80,400. Torquemada (1969, 1:186) gives a figure 72,344. Clavijero (1958, 1:311) admits to differences, giving 64,060 and 72,344. Veytia (1944, 2:243–246) thinks the number 16,000 is exaggerated. We might opt for a number between 4,000 and 16,000.

45. Veytia 1944, 2:243.

46. *Codex Telleriano-Remensis* 1964, 4:19.

47. Molina 1944, 2:93; Sahagún 1950–1969, 2:48.

48. Mendieta 1945, 1:83. A well-known representation of this god is to be seen in the *Codex Borgia* 1976, plate 32.

49. Motolinía 1951, pp. 114f., 124, 130.

50. Our only reference to this god is in *Codex Telleriano-Remensis* 1964, 2:32. See the corresponding passage in *Codex Vaticanus Latinus 3738* 1964, plate 53. I am indebted to Dr. A. J. O. Anderson for the translation of this god's name.

51. See for an example *El Arte del Templo Mayor* 1980, p. 69.

52. Sahagún 1950–1969, 9:87f. Durán (1967, 1:63f.) gives this as *itzpacalatl*.

53. Sahagún 1956, 1:287f.

54. *Leyenda de los Soles* 1945, p. 140f.

55. Ixtlilxochitl 1965a, p. 75.

56. Ixtlilxochitl 1965a, pp. 73, 75; Chimalpahin 1965, pp. 74, 78.

57. *Anales de Cuauhtitlan*, 1945, p. 23.

CHAPTER 7. THE AZTECS' STATEMENT OF
INDIVIDUALITY THROUGH CULT

1. On the *tonalpouhqui*, Sahagún 1950–1969, 4:1, 142, 152, 6:197, 10:31.

2. Sahagún 1950–1969, 4:30. Children born under a good sign were named immediately, Hernández 1946, p. 170. All other things being equal, however, it was customary to name the child four days after birth, Serna 1953, p. 116; *Codex Mendocino* 1964, p. 118, plate 58. Motolinía says seven days (i.e., the eighth day), Motolinía 1951, p. 111f.; 1967, p. 40. The naming ceremony four days after birth was accompanied by baptism in the family fire, Clavijero 1958, 2:166f.

    3. Sahagún 1950–1969, 4:34.

    4. Veytia 1944, 1:136.

    5. Molina 1944, 1:89.

    6. Sahagún 1950–1969, 2:171.

    7. Sahagún 1950–1969, 4:3, 6:204.

    8. Molina 1944, 1:89. The family name (*nenotzaloni*, 2:69, or *netzatzililoni*, 2:71) may be the same.

    9. Baptism and naming were only remotely connected. For these rites see Sahagún 1950–1969, 4:113, 6:175f., 201.

    10. Molina 1944, 1:89.

    11. Durán 1967, 1:68.

    12. *neyolmelahualiztli*.

    13. *tlapouhqui* means diviner, "one who counts up or reads things." The *tonalpouhqui* was a tlapouhqui who specialized in construing the almanac.

    14. Sahagún 1950–1969, 1:27.

    15. Sahagún 1950–1969, 6:29. These individual confessions, often undertaken because of a serious illness, must not be confused with public confessions by the whole people at certain festivals, such as the feast of Xochiquetzal, Durán 1967, 1:155–157.

    16. For a full account of the confessional rites, Sahagún 1950–1969, 1:24–27; Hernández 1946, p. 55.

    17. Sahagún 1950–1969, 6:34.

    18. Sahagún 1950–1969, 6:32.

    19. See note 15.

    20. *tlamaceuhqui* is thus a meritorious and pious person. The word applies either to priests or laymen, see Sahagún 1950–1969, 8:81.

    21. Muñoz Camargo 1966, p. 157.

    22. Sahagún 1950–1969, 3:7f.; 1956, 1:236.

    23. Sahagún 1950–1969, 6:33.

    24. Durán 1967, 1:55.

    25. Muñoz Camargo 1966, p. 47.

    26. Pomar 1971, p. 22. Depictions of such penitential areas are known from the códices.

27. León-Portilla 1958, pp. 71, 73; Brundage 1979, p. 213f.

28. Brundage 1982, pp. 129–132.

29. Durán 1967, 1:55; Motolinía 1951, p. 125; 1967, p. 69.

30. Mendieta 1945, 1:112f.; Motolinía 1951, pp. 124f., 129ff.

31. Sahagún 1950–1969, 6:31. For other ways of referring to Mictlan, Garibay 1953, 1:19, 195f.; Alvarado Tezozomoc 1944, pp. 244, 264f.

32. Mendieta 1945, 1:90.

33. Sahagún 1950–1969, 7:21. The ancestors who become stellar beings are the Mimixcoa.

34. Brundage 1979, p. 48. The rock of Chapultepec, which was thought of as Cincalco, was also known as *Hueymacco*, "the place of Hueymac," Chimalpahin 1965, p. 69. It was also associated with the bush or tree, *acaxochitl* (*lobelia fulgens*), Sahagún 1950–1969, 11:211.

35. Ixtlilxochitl 1965b, p. 55.

36. Sahagún 1950–1969, 6:115, 1956, 2:143f.; Garibay 1958, p. 142.

37. Translated out of one of the poems in Garibay, 1964–1968. This despairing theme is a constant in this collection.

38. Brundage 1979, p. 184ff.

39. *Codex Vaticanus Latinus 3738* 1964, plate 77.

40. Alvarado Tezozomoc 1944, p. 94f.

41. Sahagún 1956, 3:33; 1950–1969, 9:25. The family at home additionally buried in effigy the merchant who had died abroad, Sahagún 1950–1969, 4:69f.

42. Sahagún 1956, 2:144.

43. The mummy bundle was the *quixococualia*, Alvarado Tezozomoc 1944, pp. 93ff., 233, 255.

44. For details on the warriors' funeral cult, Durán 1967, 2:153–155, 287–290. See also Alvarado Tezozomoc 1944, pp. 232–235.

45. The Mimixcoa are derived from the north and from Chicomoztoc— which equates them with the earliest Aztecs, Sahagún 1950–1969, 2:230, 9:10.

46. Sahagún 1956, 1:295; Motolinía 1967, pp. 31, 246.

47. See note 44.

48. Sahagún 1950–1969, 3:44.

49. For the importance of dogs in Aztec funerary thought, Sahagún 1950–1969, 3:44, 4:20. Around the neck of the warrior's mummy bundle, before it was burned, there was placed a pendant paper dog painted blue. This was the *xoloitzcuintli*, or "page dog," the dead man's guide into the underworld.

50. Alvarado Tezozomoc 1944, pp. 95, 234f.

51. Durán 1967, 2:436; Clavijero 1958, 2:178.

52. Clavijero, ibid. Interment at Teotihuacan had a special effect upon the dead soul.

53. Sahagún 1950–1969, 10:192; Motolinía 1951, p. 106.

54. Sahagún 1950–1969, 6:21.

55. Alvarado Tezozomoc 1944, pp. 238–244. He goes into detail as well on Tizoc's funeral (pp. 264–266) and on Ahuitzotl's, pp. 389–392. The funerary rites for rulers were thoroughly covered by the early Spanish sources; see in addition Torquemada 1969, 2:521ff.; Ixtlilxochitl 1965b, pp. 191–195; Durán 1967, 2:295–300.

56. Durán 1967, 2:298.

57. Torquemada 1969, 2:521.

58. Durán 1967, 2:311f.

59. The number of retainers killed in the suttee was between fifty and sixty, Durán 1967, 2:300. Besides these, twenty male and twenty female slaves were destroyed by shooting them with arrows in the neck, Sahagún 1956, 1:296. Then one must count in the slaves given to the dead ruler by the royal guests at his funeral. My figure of *circa* 200 is based on the preceding.

60. Torquemada 1969, 2:522.

APPENDIX A. LIST OF CALENDAR FESTIVALS

1. The first month has more names than any other month in the calendar, *The Tovar Calendar*, 1951, p. 35.

2. Sahagún 1956, 1:89; Torquemada 1969, 2:250f. March is also given, Cervantes de Salazar 1914, p. 36; Durán 1967, 1:63.

3. The first day of the new year was Tlaloc's festival, Sahagún 1956, 1:89.

4. Durán 1967, 1:292. From this custom of plucking new grass or fresh boughs comes one of the names of the month, *Xiuhtzitzquilo*, which can mean either "Taking the Year in Hand," or "Taking New Grass in Hand." The name is thus a significant pun.

5. Durán 1967, 1:63f.

6. Sahagún 1956, 1:109, 238; Sahagún 1950–1969, 2:187; Durán 1967, 1:63.

7. Durán (1967, 1:102) conceives of this as a sun festival. The fact that it comes in March would imply that it was also equinoctial. For the fire, Alvarado Tezozomoc 1944, p. 224.

8. The gladiatorial sacrifice in this month has become well known, Sahagún 1950–1969, 2:47, 49–54, 8:84f.; Durán 1967, 1:98ff., 2:275; Pomar 1971, p. 17ff.; Alvarado Tezozomoc 1944, pp. 117, 220ff.; *Codex*

Hall 1947, p. 7f. The latter two sources add the arrow sacrifice of the spread-eagled victim. Chapter 6, *Sacrifices in the Cult of Xipe*, goes into the sacrifices of this month in much greater detail.

9. See preceding note. Arrow sacrifice (*tlacacaliliztli*) was widespread. It is recorded for the Chalca, the Huaxtecs, the Cakchiquel, the Tlaxcalans, Mixtec, Chichimecs, and Pawnee. For its interpretation as a phallic rite, Sahagún 1958a, p. 179f. In the autumn cult of the corn goddess, priests arrayed as various of the avatars of the sun and of the dawning light shot arrows at victims tied up on racks, Durán 1967, p. 140.

10. *Anales de Cuauhtitlan* 1945, p. 13.

11. Sahagún 1950–1969, 1:39f., 2:47, 50, 58f., 8:85f., 9:69ff.; Durán 1967, 1:97, 100f.; Torquemada 1969, 2:58, 252f.; Mendieta 1945, 1:110.

12. Motolinía 1951, p. 116; 1967, p. 60.

13. Torquemada 1969, p. 254.

14. In this festival of the Earth Mother, flower gatherers brought her special bouquets, Torquemada 1969, 2:254; Clavijero 1958 2:80, 139. As the month ended and the next began, the Corn Mother blessed the previous year's sacred maize so that the ears could be returned to the bins as talismans, Torquemada 1969, 2:255. This cult featured women drinking and dancing while a young virgin was sacrificed, *Codex Tudela*, plate 14. The bulk of these rites apparently belong in the Greater Vigil.

15. Durán 1967, p. 249.

16. Durán 1971, p. 424f.

17. This rite climaxed the previous three months of child sacrifice, Sahagún 1950–1969, 2:8. The most complete description is in Durán 1967, 1:82–86.

18. The part of the cult concerning the sacred tree and the drowning of the little *ixiptla* of the lake goddess is treated only in Durán 1967, 1:86–90.

19. Another name for the month was "the Censing," Serna 1953, p. 137. Censing of the state gods is shown as characteristic of the month in *Codex Borbonicus* 1974, plate 26. See also Durán 1967, 1:256.

20. Sahagún (1974, p. 32) states that the month celebrated the birth dates of both Tezcatlipoca and Yacateuctli (god of the merchants). Durán 1967, 1:40, 255) saw connections with the Rogation Days. It is also compared to Corpus Christi and Easter, Sahagún 1950–1969, 2:9.

21. Durán 1967, 1:41; Sahagún 1950–1969, 1:37; Torquemada 1969, 2:264; Clavijero 1958, 2:141.

22. This is probably the best known item in all of Aztec religion, having been first popularized in Frazer's *Golden Bough*. Sahagún has the most to say about him, whereas others add details, Sahagún 1950–1969, 1:68, 2:9f., 66–71; Durán 1967, pp. 39f., 44; Serna 1953, p. 184f.; Pomar 1971, pp. 10f., 21; Torquemada 1969, 2:259f.; Clavijero 1958, 2:143.

23. Clavijero 1958, 2:143; Durán 1967, 1:45.

24. Durán 1967, 1:257.

25. Serna 1953, p. 185.

26. Plenary remission of sins occurred at every fourth year celebration of the Toxcatl, Acosta 1962, pp. 232, 271; Herrera 1944–1947, 4:117f.; Durán 1967, 1:38.

27. *Codex Borbonicus* 1974, plate 26. Quetzalcoatl's connection with the festival, however, also rested on his close relationship with Tlaloc, Brundage 1982, pp. 149–158. At some point during the festival priests performed the rite of penis perforation, the *motepullizo* (from *tepulli*, "penis," and *ihzo*, "to bleed, to make a blood sacrifice"), *Codex Magliabecchi* 1970, plate 34.

28. Durán 1967, 1:260.

29. Motolinía 1951, p. 116; 1967, p. 60f.; Sahagún 1950–1969, 1:21f.

30. Sahagún 1950–1969, 2:89. Elsewhere Sahagún has the ixiptla disposed of in a cave, Sahagún 1974, p. 35.

31. Sahagún 1950–1969, 2:11f., 78–90, 7:17f.

32. Ixtlilxochitl 1965b, p. 161; Clavijero 1958, 2:150; Durán 1967, 1:263.

33. Furst 1978, p. 204.

34. Serna 1953, p. 186; Sahagún 1950–1969, 2:13, 91–94.

35. *Codex Borbonicus* 1974, plate 27. See also note 38.

36. Durán 1967, 1:126. The exact day date of Cihuacoatl's festival is here given as the eighteenth of July.

37. Sahagún 1950–1969, 2:103ff.; Durán 1967, 1:126–128.

38. The ball game shown in *Codex Borbonicus* (1974, plate 27) as the Lesser feast ended and the Greater began is of great interest, as Quetzalcoatl is shown siding with the goddess Cihuacoatl, both playing against a twosome, one of whom was Tlazopilli (the young corn), see *Codex Magliabecchi* 1970, plate 35; Cervantes de Salazar 1914, p. 37. Obviously the game was an omen giver on the harvest to be gathered later.

39. Durán 1967, 1:265f.

40. Durán 1967, 1:266f.

41. Torquemada 1969, 1:297f.

42. Durán 1967, 1:265.

43. Durán 1967, 1:265f.

44. Torquemada 1969, 2:271. We see Huitzilopochtli in this month dancing with Cihuacoatl and Atlahua, all bedecked with flowers, *Codex Borbonicus* 1974, plate 28. Huitzilopochtli is an avatar of Tezcatlipoca, which is why two sources state that it is the latter who is honored in this month, *Codex Magliabecchi* 1970, plate 37; Cervantes de Salazar, 1914, p. 37.

45. Durán 1967, 1:271f.; Motolinía 1951, p. 117; 1967, pp. 46, 61.

46. *Xocotl* means "fruit," and an alternative name of the month is *Xocotl Huetzi*, "[The Tree Called] Fruit Falls." The tree was the Tepaneca god Otonteuctli, but there were five other gods headed by Yacateuctli and worshipped by the merchants (Durán 1967, 1:120) who were also in the persons of their ixiptlas sacrificed in this feast. Thus the month can be considered as dedicated to the fire god (Serna 1953, pp. 130, 186) or Yacateuctli, Torquemada 1969, 2:272.

47. On the details of the tree cult, Sahagún 1950–1969, 2:17f., 111f., 116f.; Durán 1967, 1:271f., 119–123; Torquemada 1969, 2:272ff.

48. See note 46.

49. *Codex Telleriano-Remensis* 1964, 1:4.

50. Durán 1967, 1:141.

51. Sahagún 1950–1969, 2:189.

52. Sahagún 1950–1969, 2:189.

53. Sahagún 1950–1969, 2:118; Sahagún 1956, 1:122; Torquemada 1969, 2:275; Serna 1953, pp. 130, 187.

54. For the Chicomecoatl cult, Sahagún 1950–1969, 2:124f.; Durán 1967, 1:137–140. *Codex Borbonicus* gives a version of the Ochpaniztli that seems to subordinate Toci to Chicomecoatl. This contradicts sources like Serna (1953, p. 130) where the month is dedicated to Toci. See *Codex Borbonicus* 1974, plates 29–31.

55. For the Toci cult, Sahagún 1950–1969, 2:19, 118–122, 124–126; Durán 1967, 1:143–149, 275f.; Serna 1953, p. 187.

56. For this set of war rituals and honors, Sahagún 1950–1969, 2:20, 120, 122–125; Durán 1967, 1:234, 236; Torquemada 1969, 2:276; Serna 1953, p. 188.

57. Hernández 1946, p. 155f.; Sahagún 1974, p. 50f.

58. For the ceremony of the recording of the divine footprint, Sahagún 1950–1969, 2:21f., 127–129; Durán 1967, 1:153f.; Torquemada 1969, 2:278; Clavijero 1958, 2:154; Motolinía 1951, pp. 118, 122.

59. The only references to this rite are found in Durán 1967, 1:154f., 280. Durán says the two virgins represented plenty and famine. This is not particularly convincing.

60. For the involvement of the whole pantheon, *Codex Telleriano-Remensis* 1964, 1:7.

61. For the mountain rites in this month, Sahagún 1950–1969, 2:23f., 131ff.; Durán 1967, 1:166ff., 279f.; Serna 1953, p. 189. Torquemada 1969, 2:279f.

62. Durán 1967, 1:151–153, 155, 193. This month also saw a great slaughter of ixiptlas of various gods but its place in the month is uncertain. Most of these gods were the Four Hundred Rabbits, the *octli*-gods, León Portilla 1958, p. 95ff.

63. Durán (1967, 1:281) says that the word means "dart or arrow," which is somewhat uncertainly supported by Sahagún (1974, p. 52f.). Jiménez Moreno believes that it means "flamingo," whereas Andrews (1975, pp. 403, 465) translates it tentatively as "macaw," taking the word literally as "rubber neck." Torquemada says it is a red and blue bird, 1969, 2:280. Durán's statement seems the more reasonable. Added to that is Torquemada's remark (1969, 2:280) that the name *Mixcoatl* (the god of the festival) symbolizes the flight of darts or arrows through the sky.

64. Torquemada 1969, 2:299; Motolinía 1967, p. 47.

65. For the arrow making and the hunt, Sahagún 1950–1969, 2:25f., 134–37, 181, 185f.; Durán 1967, 1:74ff., 281f.; Herrera 1944–47, 4:119; Acosta 1962, p. 233; Serna 1953, p. 189.

66. In myth the god Camaxtli (i.e., Mixcoatl) is connected with a demonic goddess who fell from the sky in the shape of a two-headed deer, Olmos 1965, p. 37. Carrying her on his back he was able to win battles. This goddess was Itzpapalotl, *Anales de Cuauhtitlan* 1945, p. 37. In commemoration of these events the god created the festival of Quecholli wherein were lighted many fires. Quecholli (*Codex Telleriano-Remensis* 1964, 1:8) was the month when the gods and demons fell out of the sky to spread war and terror.

67. Sahagún 1950–1969, 2:191.

68. Durán 1967, 1:76.

69. Durán 1967, 1:33, 279; Serna 1953, p. 190. The term is also applied to the Tlacaxipehualiztli, Torquemada 1969, 2:296.

70. *Codex Vaticanus Latinus 3738* 1964, plate 69.

71. *Codex Telleriano-Remensis* 1964, 1:9; Durán 1967, 1:284f.

72. The Panquetzaliztli festival is splendidly covered in two major sources, Sahagún 1950–1969, 1:3, 2:27f., 141–50, 175f., 183, 186, 200, 210, 9:63–67; Sahagún 1974, pp. 55–58; Durán 1967, 1:29–36, 283–285. Additional details are added in Motolinía 1951, pp. 97, 114, 125; 1967, pp. 47, 57f.; Serna 1953, p. 190; Torquemada 1969, 2:72, 281f.; Mendieta 1945, 1:109, 112.

73. The birthday festival was called the "Feast of Bread," Olmos 1965, p. 69.

74. García Cook and M. Arana, n.d.

75. Sahagún 1950–1969, 2:29f., 151–154; Durán 1967, 1:287f.; Serna 1953, p. 191f.

76. Andrews (1975, p. 403) translates Titil as "severe weather" with a question mark. Inasmuch as the month fills up the first half of January, his translation is descriptively correct. Caso (1967, p. 133) accepts Troncoso's translation as "wrinkled or creased one" and refers it to the old goddess representing the ear of corn wrapped in its shell of wrinkled leaves. Durán says it means "to stretch," 1967, p. 289. I am not able to make a judgment.

77. Sahagún 1950–1969, 2:31f., 155–158; Durán 1967, 1:289f. She is identified as Ilamateuctli in Torquemada 1969, 2:284f.; Hernández 1946, p. 161.

78. *Codex Borbonicus* (1974, plate 36) has the goddess appear dressed as Cihuacoatl, whereas *Codex Magliabecchi* (1970, p. 45) specifically states that the goddess is Cihuacoatl.

79. López Austin 1967, p. 55.

80. Yacateuctli's ixiptla was also sacrificed in this month, Sahagún 1956, 1:238. See also Clavijero 1958, 2:81; Torquemada 1969, 2:153.

81. Sahagún 1950–1969, 2:180f.

82. *Codex Magliabecchi* 1970, p. 72.

83. Clavijero 1958, 2:75; Sahagún 1956, 1:233. See note 81.

APPENDIX B. LIST OF MOVABLE FESTIVALS

1. Sahagún 1950–1969, 4:6. The day Four Movement was day four in Quetzalcoatl's paquet of 13 tonalli days beginning with One Jaguar, *Codex Telleriano-Remensis* 1964, 2:2.

2. Sahagún 1950–1969, 2:216f. Durán (1967, 1:105–109) gives a remarkable description of the rites. We are informed (Torquemada 1969, 2:148) that both sun *and* moon were sacrificed at the Great Cuauhxicalli (both male) in some festival. This may have been the occasion.

3. In this complicated festival, human sacrifices were offered at three temples, Tetlanman (fire), Chicomecoatl (corn), and Macuilmalinalli (unknown), Sahagún 1950–1969, 2:184, 189. Cakes baked in the shape of the constellation of the Little Bear were eaten, Sahagún 1950–1969, 7:13, 66; Brundage 1982, p. 85.

4. Sahagún 1950–1969, 4:25ff.

5. A date associated with Quetzalcoatl, either as his birth date, death, or departure into the east. For its complexity see in index under "Dates, One-Reed," in Brundage 1982, p. 339. In Cholula there was a four-day fast leading up to the date, *Codex Vaticanus Latinus 3738* 1964, plates 21, 23.

6. Sahagún 1950–1969, 2:37, 4:33ff.

7. *Codex Telleriano-Remensis* 1964, 2:12.

8. *Leyenda de los Soles* 1945, p. 119.

9. Sahagún 1950–1969, 2:37f., 4:45–48.

10. Sahagún 1950–1969, 1:14, 2:184f.; Serna 1953, p. 178.

11. Sahagún 1950–1969, 2:38, 4:77f.

12. Sahagún 1950–1969, 4:87; Serna 1953, p. 180.

13. Sahagún 1950–1969, 2:39.

Bibliography

Acosta, José de
  1962   *Historia natural y moral de las Indias.* Ed. Edmundo
            O'Gorman. 2nd ed. rev. Mexico City: Fondo de Cultura
            Económico.
Alarcón, Hernando Ruiz de
  1953   *Tratado de las supersticiones y costumbres gentílicas que
            hoy viven entre los indios naturales de esta Nueva España.*
            In *Tratado de las idolatrias . . . de las razas aborígenes de
            Mexico.* (2nd ed.) Mexico City: Ediciones Fuente Cultural.
Alvarado Tezozomoc, Hernando
  1944   *Crónica mexicana.* Mexico City: Editorial Leyenda.
  1949   *Crónica mexicáyotl.* Trans. Adrián León. Mexico City: Im-
            prenta Universitaria.
Anales de Cuauhtitlan
  1945   In *Códice Chimalpopoca.* Mexico City: Imprenta Universi-
            taria.
Andrews, J. Richard
  1975   *Introduction to Classical Nahuatl.* 2 vols. Austin: Univer-
            sity of Texas Press.
El Arte del Templo Mayor
  1980   Mexico City: Instituto Nacional de Bellas Artes, Instituto
            Nacional de Antropología e Historia (INAH), and Secre-
            taría de Educación Pública.
Aveni, Anthony F.
  1980   *Skywatchers of Ancient Mexico.* Austin: University of Texas
            Press.
Beyer, Hermann
  1965   *Mito y simbología del México antiguo.* Mexico City:
            Sociedad Alemana Mexicanista.
  1969   *Cien años de arqueología mexicana.* Mexico City: Sociedad
            Aleman Mexicanista.

Brundage, Burr C.
1979   *The Fifth Sun*. Austin: University of Texas Press.
1982   *The Phoenix of the Western World: Quetzalcoatl and the
            Sky Religion*. Norman: University of Oklahoma Press.

Las Casas, Bartolomé de
1966   *Los Indios de México y Nueva España: Antología*. Ed. Ed-
            mundo O'Gorman. Mexico City: Editorial Porrúa.

Caso, Alfonso
1958   *The Aztecs: People of the Sun*. Norman: University of Ok-
            lahoma Press.
1967   *Los calendarios prehispánicos*. Mexico City: Universidad
            Nacional Autónoma de México (UNAM).

Cervantes de Salazar, Francisco
1914   *Crónica de la Nueva España*. Madrid: Hispanic Society of
            America.

Chimalpahin Cuauhtlehuanitzin, Francisco de San Antón Muñon
1965   *Relaciones originales de Chalco Amaquemecan*. Trans.
            Silvia Rendon. Mexico City: Fondo de Cultura Económico.

The Chronicles of Michoacan
1970   Trans. Eugene R. Craine and Reginald C. Reindorp. Nor-
            man: University of Oklahoma Press.

Clavijero, Francisco Javier
1958   *Historia antigua de México*. 4 vols. Mexico City: Editorial
            Porrúa.

Codex Borbonicus
1974   Graz, Austria: Akademische Druck- u. Verlagsanstalt.

Codex Borgia
1976   Graz, Austria: Akademische Druck- u. Verlagsanstalt.

Codex Cospi
1968   Graz, Austria: Akademische Druck- u. Verlagsanstalt.

Codex Hall: An Ancient Mexican Hieroglyphic Picture Manuscript
1947   Analyzed by Charles E. Dibble. Monographs of the School
            of American Research, no. 11. Albuquerque: University of
            New Mexico Press.

Codex Magliabecchi
1970   Graz, Austria: Akademische Druck- u. Verlagsanstalt.

Codex Mendocino
1964   In Vol. I of *Antigüedades de México, basadas en la reco-
            pilación de Lord Kingsborough*. 4 vols. Mexico City: Secre-
            taría de Hacienda y Crédito Público.

Codex Nuttall: A Picture Manuscript from Ancient Mexico
1975   Introduction by Arthur G. Miller. New York: Dover Publi-
            cations.

Codex Ramírez
1944   Mexico City: Editorial Leyenda.
Codex Telleriano-Remensis
1964   In Vol. I of *Antigüedades de Mexico, basadas en la recopilación de Lord Kingsborough*. 4 vols. Mexico City: Secretaría de Hacienda y Crédito Público.
Codex Vaticanus Latinus 3738 (Codex Ríos)
1964   In Vol. III of *Antigüedades de Mexico, basadas en la recopilación de Lord Kingsborough*. 4 vols. Mexico City: Secretaría de Hacienda y Crédito Público.
Códice de Azcatitlan
1949   In *Journal de la Société des Americainistes de Paris*. Vol. 38. Paris.
Coe, Michael D., and Diehl, Richard A.
1980   *In the Land of the Olmec*. 2 vols. Austin: University of Texas Press.
Colección de Documentos para la Historia de México
1858–66   Ed. J. García Icazbalceta, 2 vols. Mexico City: J. M. Andrade.
Corona Núñez, José
1957   *Mitología tarasca*. Mexico City: Fondo de Cultura Económico.
Durán, Diego
1967   *Historia de los indios de Nueva España e islas de la tierra firme*. 2 vols. Ed. Angel María Garibay K. Mexico City: Editorial Porrúa.
1971   *Book of the Gods and Rites and the Ancient Calendar*. Trans. Fernando Horcasitas and Doris Heyden. Norman: University of Oklahoma Press.
Estudios de Cultura Náhuatl
1959–   Vols. 1 through 13 have appeared. Mexico City: UNAM.
Furst, Jill
1978   *Codex Vindobonensis Mexicanus I: A Commentary*. Institute for Mesoamerican Studies Publication no. 4. Albany: State University of New York at Albany.
García Cook, Angel, and M. Arana A., Raul
n.d.   *Rescate arqueológico del monolito Coyolxauhqui: informe preliminar*. Mexico City: INAH.
Garibay K., Angel María
1953   *Historia de la literatura Náhuatl*. 2 vols. Mexico City: Editorial Porrúa.
1958   *Veinte himnos sacros de los Nahuas*. Mexico City: UNAM.
1964–1968   *Poesía Náhuatl*. 3 vols. Mexico City: UNAM.
Gómara, Francisco López de
1964   *Cortés: The Life of the Conqueror by his Secretary*. Trans.

Lesley Byrd Simpson. Berkeley: University of California Press.

HMAI (*Handbook of the Middle American Indians*)
1964–   16 vols. plus one Supplement have been published so far. Austin: University of Texas Press.

Hernández, Francisco
1946   *Antigüedades de la Nueva España.* Mexico City: Editorial Robredo.

Herrera, Antonio de
1944–1947   *Historia general de los hechos de los castellanos en las islas y tierra firme de el Mar Océano.* 10 vols. Asunción, Paraguay: Editorial Guaranía.

Heyden, Doris
1976   "Los ritos de paso en las cuevas." *Boletín*, Vol. II, No. 19, INAH.
1981   "Caves, Gods, and Myths: World-View and Planning in Teotihuacan." In *Northamerican Sites and World-View.* Ed. Elizabeth Benson. Washington, D.C.: Dumbarton Oaks, Harvard University.

Historia Tolteca-Chichimeca
1976   Trans. Paul Kirchhoff et. al. Mexico City: INAH.

Histoyre du Méchique
1905   Ed. Edouard de Jonghe. *Journal de la Société des Americainistes de Paris.* n.s., Vol. 2, No. 1.

Ixtlilxochitl, Fernando de Alva
1965a   *Historia de la nación chichimeca.* Vol. 2 of *Obras históricas.* Ed. Alfredo Chavero. Reprint. Mexico City: Editorial Nacional.
1965b   *Relaciones.* Vol. 1 of *Obras históricas.* Ed. Alfredo Chavero. Reprint. Mexico City: Editorial Nacional.

Klein, Cecelia
1976   *The Face of the Earth: Frontality in Two-Dimensional Mesoamerican Art.* New York: Garland Publishing Co.

León-Portilla, Miguel
1958   *Ritos, sacerdotes, y atavíos de los dioses.* Mexico City: UNAM.

Leyenda de los Soles
1945   In *Codex Chimalpopoca.* Trans. Primo Feliciano Velázquez. Mexico City: UNAM.

López Austin, Alfredo
1967   *Juegos rituales aztecas.* Mexico City: UNAM.

Manuscript Tovar
1972   Ed. Jacques Lafaye. Graz, Austria: Akademische Druck- u. Verlagsanstalt.

Marquina, Ignacio
  1960   *El Templo Mayor de Mexico*. Mexico City: INAH.
Matos Moctezuma, Eduardo
  1979   *Trabajos arqueológicos*. Mexico City: INAH.
  1981   *Una visita al Templo Mayor*. Mexico City: INAH.
Mendieta, Gerónimo de
  1945   *Historia eclesiástica indiana*. 4 vols. Mexico City: Editorial
            Chávez Hayhoe.
Molina, Alonso de
  1944   *Vocabulario en la lengua castellana y mexicana*. Reprint.
            Madrid: Ediciones Cultura Hispánica.
Motolinía, Toribio
  1951   *Motolinía's History of the Indians of New Spain*. Trans.
            Francis Borgia Steck. Washington, D.C.: Academy of
            American Franciscan History.
  1967   *Memoriales*. Facsimile of the Pimentel edition of 1903. Ed.
            E. Avina Levy. Guadalajara.
  1971   *Carta de Motolinía*. In *Colleción de documentos para la
            historia de México*. 2 vols. Kraus Reprint. Nendeln, Liech-
            tenstein: Kraus-Thomson Organization Limited.
Muñoz Camargo, Diego
  1966   *Historia de Tlaxcala*. Facsimile Edition. Ed. E. Avina Levy.
            Guadalajara.
Navarrete, Carlos, and Heyden, Doris
  1975   "La Cara central de la Piedra del Sol: una *hipótesis*,"
            Estudios de Cultura nahuatl, Vol. 9. Mexico City: UNAM.
Olmos, Andrés de
  1965   *Historia de los mexicanos por sus pinturas*. In *Teoganía e
            historia de los mexicanos: tres opúsculos del siglo XVI*. Ed.
            Angel María Garibay K. Mexico City: Editorial Porrúa.
Pomar, Juan Bautista
  1971   *Relación de Tezcoco*. In *Nuevo colección de documentos
            para la historia de México*. Ed. Joaquín García Izcazbalceta.
            Kraus Reprint. Nendeln, Liechtenstein: Kraus-Thomson
            Organization Limited.
Ponce de León, Pedro
  1965   *Tratado de los dioses y ritos de la gentilidad*. In *Teogonía e
            historia de los mexicanos: Tres opúsculos de siglo XVI*. Ed.
            Angel María Garibay K. Mexico City: Editorial Porrúa.
Saenz, César
  1967   *El Fuego Nuevo*. Mexico City: UNAM.
Sahagún, Bernardino de
  1948   "Relación breve de las fiestas de los dioses." In *Tlalocan*,
            Vol. II, No 4.

1950–1969 *General History of the Things of New Spain (Florentine Codex).* Trans. Arthur J. O. Anderson and Charles E. Dibble. 12 vols. (2d ed., rev., vol. 1, 1970; vol. 2, 1981; vol. 3, 1978; vol. 12, 1975). Santa Fe and Salt Lake City: School of American Research and University of Utah Press.

1956 *Historia general de las cosas de Nueva España.* Ed. Angel María Garibay K. Mexico City: Editorial Porrúa.

1958a *Veinte himnos sacros de los nahuas.* Trans. Angel María Garibay K. Mexico City: UNAM.

1958b *Ritos, sacerdotes, y atavíos de los dioses.* Trans. Miguel León-Portilla. Mexico City: UNAM.

1974 *Primeros memoriales.* Translated by Wigberto Jiménez Moreno. Mexico City: Consejo de Historia, INAH.

Séjourné, Laurette

1969 *Teotihuacan, Métropole de l'Amerique.* Paris: Francois Maspero.

Selden Roll (Codex Selden)

1955 Ed. Cottie A. Burland. Berlin: Verlag Gerb. Mann.

Seler, Eduard

1960 *Gesammelte Abhandlungen.* 5 vols. and index vol. Graz, Austria: Akademische Druck- u. Verlagsanstalt.

Serna, Jacinto de la

1953 *Manual de ministros de indios para la conocimiento de sus idolatrias.* In *Tratado de las idolatrias, supersticiones, dioses, ritos. . . . * Ed. Francisco del Paso y Troncoso. 2d ed. 2 vols. Mexico City: Ediciones Fuente Cultural.

Siméon, Remi

1956 *Dictionnaire de la langue nahuatl ou mexicaine.* Graz, Austria: Akademische Druck- u. Verlagsanstalt.

Spencer, Robert F., Jennings, Jesse D., et al.

1965 *The Native Americans.* New York: Harper & Row.

El Templo Mayor

1981 by José López Portillo, Miguel León-Portilla, Eduardo Matos, and Dominique Verut. Mexico City: Bancomer.

Thompson, J. Eric S.

1972 *A Commentary on the Dresden Codex.* Philadelphia: American Philosophical Society.

Torquemada, Juan de

1969 *Monarquía indiana.* 3 vols. Mexico City: Editorial Leyenda.

The Tovar Calendar

1951 Commentary by George Kubler and Charles Gibson. *Memoirs of the Connecticut Academy of Arts and Sciences,* Vol. XI. Yale University Press.

Underhill, Ruth M.

1965 *Red Man's Religion.* Chicago: University of Chicago Press.

Veytia, Mariano
1944   *Historia antigua de México*. 2 vols. Mexico City: Editorial
            Leyenda.
Weaver, Muriel
1981   *The Aztecs, Mayas, and their Predecessors*. 2d ed. New
            York: Academic Press.

Index